W9-BGW-557

FOLLOW THE
SMART MONEY

UNUSUAL OPTION ACTIVITY:
#1 WAY WE CHOOSE OUR TRADES

JON & PETE NAJARIAN

Follow the Smart Money

Unusual Option Activity: #1 Way We Choose Our Trades

Market Rebellion, LLC.

8201 Peters Road, Suite 1000

Plantation, FL 33324

1-866-982-4862

support@marketrebellion.com

Printed in the United States of America

First Edition

ISBN: 978-1-7329113-2-1

ACKNOWLEDGMENTS

Pete and I would like to acknowledge with gratitude our mother, Mignette Najarian and our father Dr. John S. Najarian for their love, support and guidance. Similarly, we'd like to thank our wives, Brigid McGrath and Pete's wife Lisa Najarian for their insights, stability and enthusiastic support of our entrepreneurial spirits. We also love and appreciate our children, Alexis, Kole, Tristen and Finola Najarian and how they love us unconditionally and keep us centered.

This book could have not been completed without the help of our business partners and colleagues at Market Rebellion™, Ron Ianieri, Bill Johnson, Dirk Mueller-Ingrand, Chris Tsiolis, Mike Yamamoto, Laura Peters, and Andrew Coffey, who with their tireless efforts keep our subscription and educational businesses operating at such a high level. Thanks guys.

We'd like to thank the host of CNBC's *Halftime Report*™, Scott Wapner, and our producer Jason Gewirtz for allowing us highlight how the derivatives markets are, in many cases, the tail that wags the dog. They understood like few others that there's a difference between volumes and unusual volumes and we appreciate their support and that of our network CNBC.

Lastly, we must acknowledge the many mentors throughout our lives in sports, Coach Richard Robinson, Coach Levain Carter, Coach Dennis Raarup, Coach Lou Holtz, Coach Jerry Burns, and Coach Tom Osborne, that provided the discipline that is so critical for all aspects of our business lives.

Jon & Pete Najarian

TABLE OF CONTENTS

PREFACE   1

MEET JON AND PETE NAJARIAN   3

CH 1 IT'S NOT REALLY A RANDOM WALK   13

CH 2 THE INSIDE SCOOP ON INSIDE INFORMATION   37

CH 3 THE HUNT FOR UNUSUAL OPTION ACTIVITY   51

CH 4 THE RIGHT F.R.A.M.E. OF MIND   67

CH 5 LONG CALLS & PUTS   87

CH 6 THE GREEKS   127

CH 7 PROFIT & LOSS DIAGRAMS   163

CH 8 SKEWS, TILTS, & DANGEROUS SMILES   177

CH 9 THE STOCK REPLACEMENT STRATEGY   191

CH 10 THE VERSATILE VERTICAL SPREAD   221

CH 11 THE STOCK REPLACEMENT COVERED CALL   251

CH 12 TRADER TALES OF THE "UNUSUAL" KIND   263

SOURCES   283

In Memory of Ron Ianieri

In March 2019, our partner, friend, and colleague
Ron Ianieri, who was the Co-Founder and Lead Educator at
Market Rebellion™, passed away suddenly and unexpectedly.
He was an extraordinary force in options education and
continually fought for the individual investor by providing
quality education and guidance for our members.

Throughout his career, Ron developed renowned options
education content, authored the book Option Theory and
Trading, and was considered one of the industry's leading
educators and mentors. We want to recognize the immense
contributions Ron's educational leadership brought
to the development of this book and to the
Market Rebellion™ community.

On behalf of myself, Dirk and Pete: "Ron, you will
be missed brother."

– Jon Najarian

PREFACE

When I was asked to write the preface for Jon and Pete Najarian's book *Follow the Smart Money*, I was not only honored, but flattered. After all, Jon and Pete are the pioneers in finding unusual option activity and determining if it's meaningful activity that could be the result of inside information that has leaked into the market. While it's illegal to trade on inside information, it's not illegal to use publicly available information – option activity – as a way to follow those who know – the *smart money*.

Besides telling the story of Jon and Pete Najarian and how they discovered and developed unusual option activity, *Follow the Smart Money* shows how to use their revolutionary techniques to identify potentially strong trading opportunities and increase your chances for making larger profits in the stock market.

It gives insights into the algorithm they used when they first developed it – and how they've modified it over the years – to find potential trades. From there, the book shows how they analyze and interpret the data to increase their chances for success and eliminate the majority of false signals. You'll also learn how to pick and execute the proper strategy to use along with the correct construction of that strategy. Finally, the book shows how to manage your positions up through the exit strategy.

For you, the investor, learning how to find great trading opportunities – following the *smart money* – should be exciting enough. Since the first days of trading, back when dinosaurs walked the trading floors, there were basically only two ways to find trading opportunities – fundamental analysis and technical analysis. You either read income statements and sales projections or you simply read stock charts. There are no guarantees because ultimately, these two ways of finding trading opportunities are subjective and rely more on personal interpretation. Further, these techniques are known to everyone, so all of that information gets readily absorbed into prices.

But when you *follow the smart money*, you're following the information potentially known only to insiders and market participants with access to a massive amount of resources. One of the nice things about using unusual option activity to find opportunities is that you may truly identify an order from someone in the know. Jon and Pete will show you how to find and identify "that guy."

Finding winning trades that have the potential for quick returns obviously has an advantage over a trade that starts off as a loser and needs to be managed and massaged over time. Jon and Pete share decades of experience and how they've made a career by profiting from unusual option activity. Just think about how important and valuable it will be to you! This is why you should not only want to read this book but why you *need* to read this book. I am honored to write the preface. Jon and Pete are thrilled to share their amazing journey with you. You can continue to follow your current strategies − or you can *follow the smart money*.

Ron Ianieri

MEET JON AND PETE NAJARIAN

JON "DR. J" NAJARIAN

When I finished college, I wanted to take my football dream to the next level – I wanted to play linebacker in the NFL. It was a big dream, but I'm always up for challenging myself. I never got drafted, but was later contacted by four NFL teams, so I was allowed to sign with any of them. I thought my best chance was in Chicago, as the Bears had a few older linebackers, so maybe I could earn a permanent spot. I had never been to Chicago, other than an occasional connecting flight at O'Hare Airport.

I only played four pre-season games with the 1981 Bears before getting cut and replaced by Mike Singletary, who was later inducted into the Hall of Fame in 1998. While the team may have had some older linebackers, they also had some extreme talent. In the short time I was there, I fell in love with Chicago, but unless another player was seriously injured, I was probably going to be sidelined for the season. I wanted to stay but didn't know what to do. My agent had helped several pro athletes get positions on the prestigious trading floors of Chicago's financial district. He said they liked hiring professional athletes because of their disciplined drive and commitment to excellence – perfect qualities for making money in markets.

Sounded interesting, but finance? I went to college to get a degree in architectural design. I could design a trading floor but wasn't sure I could work on one. The first three months were dreadful. I didn't know what was happening on the trading floor. I understood when someone bought or sold shares of stock – that was easy. But the options is where things got technical. How much should an option move? Volatility? I didn't know a thing about it. But I did have a great time at night on Rush Street, which made for more miserable days at work.

I was a clerk and had to get to work each day at 6am to print trading sheets, which were computer printouts of theoretical option values for the guys I was working for. How much should an option's price move if the stock price moves one dollar? What would the new delta be? I didn't even know what a delta was.

To make things more confusing, most stocks only traded call options. It's hard to imagine now, but back then, only 20% of stocks had put options, which meant traders had to create the puts "artificially," or synthetically, by using short shares of stock and long calls.

Fortunately, my clearing firm had licensed about 60 different training videos that clerks could borrow. They were always loaned out, so I had to get to work even earlier and watch them before my trading day began. I learned calls and puts, verticals, diagonals, calendars, butterflies and condors. Then they got more advanced with ratio spreads. On one of the tapes, there they were – delta, gamma, vega, and theta. It took months of repetition to learn it. If I didn't have tapes, it may have taken years. I still didn't understand it, but at least I stopped hating going to work every day.

As I learned the business, I eventually gained the confidence to commit my own capital of about $15,000 I received playing for the Bears. I bought a little seat at the Midwest Options Exchange for about $10,000. On those seats, you could only trade 16 stocks. If you wanted to trade all stocks, you had to buy a big seat, but it also came with a big price tag – about $150,000. The first few months I barely broke even, but then started making about $2,000 a month, then $5,000, and eventually $20,000. I banked some profits and eventually rented out my little seat and bought a big seat at the Chicago Board Options Exchange (CBOE), and traded in the IBM pit. I was now making more than I could have made playing for the Chicago Bears.

The CBOE was created by the Chicago Board of Trade (CBOT), or commonly known as the Board of Trade, which traded only commodity futures. Like most markets, it went through cycles. If a drought developed and crops were turning to dust, trading was frenzied. If weather was normal, it was nearly empty, and many of the traders would take off at 10am to go golfing. To avoid these dull markets, when stock trading began to heat up in the 1970s, the Board of Trade created the CBOE. Because of the affiliation, CBOT traders had the right to trade at the CBOE for no charge. There were close to 2,000 CBOT seats and only 931 CBOE seats, so when seats were tight, we'd go apply to become a member of the CBOT. That way, we could trade on both exchanges.

The first part of the application was easy. Just a lot of paperwork and a background check. The final stage was where things got rough. Each applicant had to do a face-to-face interview before the membership committee, which was renowned for not approving people. Your goal was to become a member of the Board of Trade. Their goal was to make a mockery of your application and send you on your way. Before you could get the interview, though, you had to find two existing members to vouch for you and say you'd make a good board member. Most of the time, the clearing firm would find them for you since most applicants didn't know anyone.

I met with a couple of recommended traders, who said they'd sign for me. "Fair warning," they said, "the committee is insistent on professional appearance. You'll need to show up with a full suit, pressed button-down shirt, tie pulled all the way up to the top button, and polished shoes. And be sure to have no holes in your resume. Every minute of the past 10 years must be accounted for. Don't embarrass us. If you don't pass, it will be your worst nightmare, and we will not sign for you again."

If an interview at the CBOE was like lunch at the country club, the CBOT was a dinner invitation to Buckingham

Palace. The rules were so different, and they wanted to make sure I understood. If I didn't pass, it was a bad reflection on them, and I'd have to pay another $2,000 to try again in a month. Part of the reason for the tough interview was that the Board of Trade had rigid rules, so part of the selection process was to see if candidates could follow instructions.

A few days later, I was anxiously waiting in the big Star Chamber outside the interview room with other applicants. The guy who went before me showed up in his CBOE trading jacket and tennis shoes, which was, let's say, not fitting to appear before the queen. We could hear the yelling going on inside the interview room. "So… you want to be a member of the Board of Trade? We tell you to show up professionally dressed, and this is what you call business attire? If we tell you to buy $5 million in wheat or $50 million in bonds, how can we trust you to do it? You can't even follow simple steps!"

The agonizing grilling went on for another 10 minutes. They chewed him up and spit him out like ticker tape. After it was done, he still had to thank them, and moseyed out with his tail between his legs. I was next.

"Mr. Najarian?"

"Yes, sir."

"It says on your resume you played football for the Bears in 1981 – is that true?"

"Yes sir, that is true. I played football for the Bears."

"Did you ever tackle Walter Payton?"

"Yes sir, I did."

"Congratulations, you're a member of the Board of Trade."

That was it! Just two questions, and I walked out as a new member. While I didn't know anyone at the Board of Trade, I did know Walter Payton, so my short stint with the Bears may have been just long enough to launch a different career. It's not always about what you know. Sometimes, it's who you know.

In 1989, I ventured out on my own to create a trading firm and had to come up with a business name. I researched Greek and Roman mythology and found that Mercury was the god of commerce, markets, and protector of traders. No need to look further.

Pete joined me in late 1992, and we noticed that when big firms came in with big orders, they were on the right side of the trade an awful lot of times. We'd compare tickets from a few days before and concluded they must have known something. We hired some programmers to create a search algorithm, or algo, for unusual option activity, which we called *Heat Seeker*™, that would tip us off if anyone was placing unusual trades. This was especially important as we were making markets in 60 stocks on the CBOE, PCX, AMEX and Philadelphia exchanges. Our *Heat Seeker*™ algo was the edge we needed, and we continued running Mercury Trading for 15 years before selling to Citadel, one of the largest hedge funds, in 2004.

During my Mercury years, I made a friend, Bob Sirott, who was an anchor on FOX 32 in Chicago, and asked me to speak with him about being the "stock guy" on his morning talk show. I passed his test and the next thing I knew I was indeed "The Money Man" on FOX from 1994 until 2005. Then I began doing both FOX News and CNBC. They were quite competitive, and eventually I had to choose one over the other. My friend Dylan Ratigan was to host *Fast Money*™, which would become one of the biggest shows in finance, so I chose CNBC where I've been a member of the family since 2008.

Pete and I later developed optionMONSTER™ which was a provider of market intelligence, commentary, and trading strategies, mostly based on unusual option activity. We then formed the brokerage firm tradeMONSTER™, and in 2014 brought in General Atlantic Partners, a private equity firm, to help us finance acquisitions and grow the business. We acquired OptionsHouse™ and two years later, the merged firm was sold to E*TRADE™ for $750 million!

Most recently, in 2017, we launched Investitute™ (now Market Rebellion™) to help individual traders master the markets by creating professional-level option training, and also sharing our unusual option activity that made us successful. Anyone can learn it with the right mentors.

It's not always what you know. Sometimes, it's who you know.

PETE "PIT BOSS" NAJARIAN

Trading floors have a reputation of being disorganized, but my experience shows that is an extreme understatement. They're chaotic madness wrapped in pandemonium. Fortunately, I thrive in chaos, and it's helped me become a successful option trader.

For me, the educational process started a long time ago, and not from the place you'd expect. It wasn't from the trading floor. It wasn't from professional football. It was from home. I grew up with three older brothers who had two speeds – fast and faster. They made it a daily point to put me into situations where I had to think even faster. We lost a few windows and lamps, but it was a small price to pay for an early education in thinking fast.

If that wasn't enough, my mom and dad were overachievers. My dad attended the University of California, Berkeley, on a football scholarship and graduated within a couple of years – all while playing football. He even made it to the Rose Bowl in 1949. He later turned down an offer to play for the Chicago Bears so he could attend medical school at the University of California at

San Francisco. After graduation, he became one of the early pioneers in a new field of medicine – kidney transplants.

My mom was a nurse, and after she graduated from college in Minnesota, she wanted to travel the world. She started by taking a job in a surgical lab in San Francisco where she met my dad. It was the end of her world trip, but the beginning of our family.

We were fortunate to have such great parents. It's one of those things that most people don't realize while growing up, but when you see the tragedies that strike so many families, we were truly lucky. My dad accepted a job offer at the University of Minnesota, so we went to a big high school in Minneapolis. It was a great eye-opener to how diverse the world can be.

By now, I had a true appreciation for what my dad had accomplished, as he was busy flying to medical conferences all over the world to present thousands of doctors with the latest innovations surrounding kidney transplants. One of the most remarkable memories I have is that, on several occasions, he flew to Paris for a conference, and rather than hanging out for a few days, he'd stay for three hours, then turn around and fly home – just to make it to my high school football games. I thought it was impossible, but it taught me to be disciplined, make decisions, and be calculated – it's a process. He always said, "no excuses." That was the motto for our family.

The discipline my dad had was difficult to understand sometimes. If anyone can be that sharp and that good in football and medicine, it's something to aspire to. What I learned from him, and his examples, shaped my future.

In 1983, I played linebacker for the University of Minnesota, and these lessons were re-lived. I arrived at a failing team with one win against 10 losses – dead last in the Big Ten standings. The following year, we were fortunate enough to play under Coach Lou Holtz who's mostly remembered by his respected career at Notre Dame, which included a 12-0 season in 1998, a Fiesta Bowl victory, and the national champion title. What many people don't know, however, is that before he coached at Notre Dame, he spent two years – 1983 and 1984 – at the University of Minnesota. He was hard-core about making sure people were doing the right thing in the classroom as well as on the football field.

Coach Holtz had an amazing ability to inspire players. He played linebacker for Kent State University, but you'd never know it by looking at him. When once asked to describe himself, he said, "I stand 5 feet 10, weigh 152 pounds, wear glasses, speak with a lisp, and have a physique that appears like I've been afflicted with beriberi or scurvy most of my life."

Rather than motivating the team with other sports figures, he brought in people from the business community. It stuck with us. Not everyone's born on third base just waiting to make the run. We learned that many people have worked hard to get where they are. When he left to coach Notre Dame, we beat Clemson in the 1985 Independence Bowl, a big feat considering Clemson beat Nebraska three years earlier in the 1982 Orange Bowl and were National Champions the year before.

Not only was Coach Holtz inspirational, he was known for thinking fast and delivering well-timed responses in a pinch. During his first year coaching the Arkansas Razorbacks in 1977, his team was invited to play in the Orange Bowl as a 24-point underdog against the Oklahoma Schooners. It was a true David and Goliath story, and his team pulled off an unbelievable 31-6 victory. Fans celebrated by bombarding the field with oranges. Holtz watched and said, "Thank God we didn't get invited to the Gator Bowl."

He left quite an impression on the student athletes – and the coaching world as well. He was the only college football coach to take six programs to bowl games and the only coach to take four different programs into the top 20 rankings.

This background created a solid foundation in my early years that taught me many things are possible if you have discipline. Discipline comes in many forms, from focusing on what needs to be done, or pushing away from the things you'd rather be doing, to be sure you can do your best. After graduating college, I went on to play professional football for the Tampa Bay Buccaneers and Minnesota Vikings.

After the NFL, I played in the World League after being the number one draft choice of the Sacramento Surge. I played two years in the World League, winning the World Bowl in 1992 as we beat the Orlando Thunder. After leaving professional football, I wasn't sure what I wanted to do. But my experiences told me I could accomplish it once I decided.

During this time, my brother Jon was trading options at the CBOE. The trading floors can get rough and aggressive as all traders compete for space and attention. Prices move quickly, so traders must move faster. It was all about speed, aggression, and fast thinking – much like the NFL. At the time, many of the exchanges were hiring ex-football players, pro wrestlers, or anyone who could muscle their way – or intimidate their way – into the crowd. Jon thought I'd do well, so he invited me to trade options. And no, I didn't start on third base. But he was my mentor.

I started at the bottom as a runner, then a clerk, then finally, years later, a trader. Once I was comfortable with the markets, Jon asked me to join him in business as the risk manager at our firm, Mercury Trading, where I was the specialist in Micron Technology. If there's one thing I've learned, there's no place where more discipline is required than the stock market.

In 2007, I started as a commentator on CNBC. Many of the hosts weren't excited about adding another option trader to the mix. It just didn't seem like an active market. When I started trading in 1992, an average of 800,000 option contracts were traded per day. By 2007, it was 11 million contracts per day, and nobody wanted to discuss the VIX (The CBOE Volatility Index) on television. I would actually get into heated arguments about why we should discuss the volatility of the markets, as it can be a great indicator as to broad market direction. And now, for 2018, we're on pace for 20 million option contracts per day,[1] and guess what we talk about every day on our Unusual Activity segment during the *Halftime Report*™ or on *Fast Money*™?* That's right, the VIX, as it's become one of the most active of any derivatives contracts.

It's been an amazing journey, and I never would have succeeded in the option markets without Jon and Coach Holtz as mentors. I had no knowledge, no experience, and no financial background. But there is one thing I did have.

No excuses.

*The Halftime Report and Fast Money are the property of CNBC, LLC, A Division of NBC Universal.

1

Ch. IT'S NOT REALLY A RANDOM WALK

When I first walked into the Chicago Board Options Exchange (CBOE), I was mesmerized by the thousands of computers mounted across the ceiling of the 40,000-square-foot trading floor. Connected to these screens were what appeared to be miles of pipes, which looked more like the I-90 Chicago Expressway than a trading floor. My mentor said, "Jon, the computers generate so much heat that the architects designed them to distribute the heat from the computers – enough to heat the trading floors during the ruthless Chicago winters."

Each screen had columns of numbers, which were the quotes for every stock and option contract, flickering back and forth from green to red. My mentor said, "Stare at those screens for just a moment. They tell the story of why it's important to keep your positions hedged. You never know when they may turn red."

He explained to me that stock prices follow an unpredictable pattern – an idea academics call a random walk. It's as if a drunk man is trying walk to the front door of his home. He won't walk a straight line, but instead, meander in an unpredictable zig-zag manner. It was all new to me, but it made a lot of sense.

That was in 1981.

But after more than three decades of trading, I have a different view. I've learned that stock prices are moved by more than just random events. When you see the greed, corruption, and manipulation that occurs, it's not *really* a random walk. History has shown that as long as we have financial markets, we'll have those who try to influence prices.

"President Obama signed a bill preventing members of Congress from profiting from insider trading. Didn't you think that was already illegal?"

– Jay Leno, 2012[2]

Fraud and unscrupulous people didn't just spring up in the 21st century. Over 2,300 years ago, a Greek merchant named Hegestratos bought an early form of an insurance policy known as a bottomry, or bottomage. It was an arrangement where the ship's master borrows money upon the bottom or keel of it, so as to forfeit the ship itself to the creditor if the money plus interest isn't paid upon the ship's safe return.

While insuring cargo might have helped investors feel comfortable about financing a delivery of goods, Hegestratos had no plans to buy and deliver corn. Instead, he plotted to sink his empty boat, keep the loan, and sell the corn in another port. As fate would have it, his plan didn't work out, and he drowned trying to escape his crew and passengers when they caught him in the act. It was the first recorded case of financial fraud, but it wouldn't be the last.

Flash forward 2,000 years and American colonies were issuing bonds to help finance the fledgling nation. These bonds fluctuated up and down with the fortunes of the colonies that issued them. As always, there was more money to be gained by those that had more information about a particular positive or negative event that hadn't been widely circulated. Long before he became the talk of Broadway in the brilliant Lin Manuel Miranda's *Hamilton*, then–Treasury Secretary Alexander Hamilton had calculated that he could reduce volatility and thus borrowing rates if he restructured the debt by replacing individual colony debt with bonds from the new central government. Immediately, large bond investors sought out people who had access to the Treasury to find out which bond issues Hamilton was going to replace.

One such investor, William Duer, was a member of President George Washington's inner circle and Assistant Secretary of the Treasury. Thus, Duer was ideally placed to profit from insider information he could glean from his role with the Treasury and its pending actions.

Duer would tip off his friends and trade in his own portfolio before leaking select info to the public that he knew would drive up prices. Post release of that information he would simply sell for a tidy profit. Mr. Duer eventually left his post but kept his inside contacts - sounds familiar, right? He continued to invest his own money, as well as that of other investors, doubtlessly including those that provided him with the inside info on debt issues. Investors from all over the world were buying bonds and stocks of U.S. banks, overwhelming the market, and creating that speculative bubble that history has shown can only end in tears.

But Mr. Duer's greed blinded him to this, and he borrowed heavily to leverage his bets. That inevitable bursting of the speculative bubble left Duer and his conspirators with huge debt – and nearly worthless holdings. Hamilton had to step in, providing that governmental backstop that Hank Paulson provided during our financial crash of 2008. But back then we had debtor's prisons, and that's exactly where Mr. Duer ended up until he died in 1799.

The list of sordid stories has continued to grow – and always will. The world was in disbelief when Nick Leeson single-handedly broke Barings Bank, Bernie Ebbers plundered WorldCom's stock with false financial reporting, and Kenneth Lay embezzled funds by falsifying Enron's accounting statements leading to one of the world's largest bankruptcies in history. And of course, Bernie Madoff's devious Ponzi scheme robbed investors of billions of dollars.[3] Wall Street manipulations, however, don't just take the form of jaw-dropping headlines. They can be subtle, but just as devious.

SHHHH! HERE'S THE REAL NUMBER

You don't need to be a long-time investor to realize there's often a big disconnect between earnings releases and the crowd's reaction. How many times have you held a stock through earnings, hear that it's beaten the estimates – then watch it fall on the opening bell? How could investors be so dumb as to sell when the company is beating its numbers?

Ratings analysts are people who work for big corporations, some of them brokerage firms, while others offer only investment research. You'll hear firms like JP Morgan Chase, Goldman Sachs, Morgan Stanley, Citigroup, Credit Suisse, UBS, Nomura, and Zacks announcing their findings to the public. They may announce they raised their outlook on Microsoft, lowered the price target on Tesla, or initiated coverage of Facebook with a buy rating. Analysts provide a benefit to investors by researching a stock or industry's value by creating sophisticated financial models that account for everything you can imagine including company sales, costs, taxes, interest rates, product demand, competition, and other factors that are likely to affect a stock's price. They have entire teams of CPAs, MBAs, CFAs, and other concoctions of alphabet soup, who are hired to figure out the best estimate of a company's value. By passing this information along to investors, it creates a more informed investor pool, which benefits everyone. At least, that's the theory. Wall Street, however, has figured out a way to make it more lucrative by cutting retail investors out.

Analysts release their estimates on a company's value by publishing lengthy reports. While no estimate is perfect, they're a whole lot better than any single person could produce. A problem arises, however, as new information reaches the market - whether factual, speculative, or a complete rumor. For example, on August 7, 2018, Elon Musk sent a tweet[4] saying he was considering taking Tesla (TSLA) private at a cost of $420 per share, which would make it the largest buyback in history – by a long shot. The stock price shot up over 10% – and Elon, who owns roughly 20% of TSLA shares, instantly became $1.4 billion richer.[5] Well, that'll have an impact on the company's value and get the attention of the regulators.[6] Elon Musk and Tesla settled for $40 million with the Securities and Exchange Commission (SEC) on September 29, 2018.[7]

Analysts update their financial models as new information arrives into the market, but they don't publish new reports, as they're time consuming and costly. However, when large clients or institutions, who sometimes have an equal number of CPAs, MBAs, or CFAs working for them, phone the analysts, they give these top clients the updated numbers, not the ones published to everyone else. These unpublished numbers are called the *whisper numbers*, and it's these numbers the company's earnings must beat before the institutions begin buying. Critics say the problem is that they'll know the numbers – you won't.[8] When a stock releases great earnings and it's not responding like you'd expect, it's a possibility it simply didn't beat the whisper number, so while you were holding, institutions were selling. Trying to predict how investors will react to earnings is nearly impossible because different groups are acting under different expectations. Wall Street, however, makes it even more difficult to focus on results, as the earnings numbers themselves are a little fuzzy.

THE EARNINGS RELEASE GAME

Regulations require that companies release quarterly reports, or 10-Q filings, which are detailed summaries of the company's earnings and financial conditions for the most recent quarter. It's the most important day for any publicly traded company, as it's the day investors get to see the financial report card. Depending on the information, investors can greatly reward – or punish – the stock in seconds. If you look at any stock chart and see large gaps, whether up or down, it's almost certainly due to an earnings report – and probably from beating or missing the whisper numbers.

In January 2018, FactSet reported that 81% of companies had beaten Wall Street estimates, putting it on track for a record pace of earnings surprises since 2008.[9] A trend has developed where companies are not just beating analysts' expectations, they're shattering them. On July 26, 2018, Amazon (AMZN) released earnings of $5.07 per share, but analysts had expected $2.50 per share – doubling the expectations. Shortly after on August 9, Booking Holdings (BKNG), formerly Priceline.com, reported earnings of $20.67 per share versus a consensus of $17.34 – beat by $3.33. How can analysts who are tied so tightly to the companies be so far off on the estimates?

Two researchers, Professors Paul A. Griffin of the University of California at Davis and David H. Lont of University of Otago in New Zealand, found that the number of S&P 500 companies that have beaten estimates by five to 15 cents have doubled over the past 17 years.[10] Some claim it's due to the tremendous growth of the U.S. economy, but the researchers say it defies belief to think that the growth has been so strong that companies have taken analysts and investors increasingly by surprise every quarter with better-than-expected earnings for nearly two decades.

How can companies beat by such large margins? Well, their earnings game has become two-fold. Analysts are biasing numbers downward, but Wall Street biases them upward. Twenty years ago, it was a big deal to see a company beat estimates by a penny or two. Not anymore. Investors are demanding better performances if they're to continue pushing stock price higher. Wall Street gladly delivers – but how?

Companies are increasingly moving away from Generally Accepted Accounting Principles (GAAP), which is the Gold Standard for accountants so investors can make fair comparisons. When standards are lowered, numbers are raised. The researchers said roughly 90% of S&P 500 companies use at least one non-standard GAAP measure in their earnings reports.

While the researchers' study included more than 4,700 companies, the effect was most pronounced in the S&P 500 firms where earnings surprises (ES) increased over 25% in 2016 from only 12.2% in 2000. Further, the number of companies that met or exceeded expectations by one cent fell 15%, and those who beat by one or two cents fell by 5%.

It's a disturbing trend, say the researchers, *"...because given their focus on strong corporate governance practices and accounting controls, one might predict that S&P 500 firms as a group should be the least likely to reflect an increasing trend in positive Street earnings surprises driven by a growing gap in Street earnings and Street expectations. Apparently, S&P 500 firms are driven by a stronger need to generate positive earnings surprises than are other firms."* [10]

The researchers said if it points to earnings manipulation, it's because of a growing acceptance of non-standard measures. Interestingly, they also said that one of the explanations for that many earnings surprises could be, *"...that analysts increasingly bias their Street expectations downwards to generate a more positive market response for their clients – that is, they engage in strategic pessimism. This reason has merit if the reporting firms reward analysts with more business or more access to firm information as a result of helping firms create a positive ES."* [11] It shouldn't surprise anyone that earnings numbers are not only manipulated by the companies, but also by the analysts who make their livings making the companies look great.

FACEBOOK IPO DISASTER: BE SURE TO CLICK "LIKE"

On May 18, 2012, Facebook (FB) had one of the most highly anticipated IPOs, or Initial Public Offerings, in history. It was the largest IPO in technology and one of the largest among Internet stocks. Shares were priced at $38, which gave it a valuation near $100 billion – a number that many analysts repeatedly warned was highly overvalued. Interestingly, nearly every retail investor received phone calls from brokers letting them in on this historic event. Normally, those calls are reserved for the firm's biggest and most profitable clients. This time, however, it seemed that everyone was offered shares. Shares opened for trading at $45, but by the end of the day, closed at $38.22, just 22 cents higher than those purchased on the primary market.

As far as hot IPOs go, it was considered a disaster.[12] Nearly all stocks see their price "pop" on the opening bell but continue to climb from there, and there are sound economic reasons for it.

Most of the time, shares must be underpriced to give the IPO investors the incentive to buy. It's part of the expected return for instantly laying a bunch of money on the company's lap in a matter of days. Even lesser-known companies get higher valuations on day one. On October 12, 2012, Workday (WDAY) had its price set at $28 for the IPO but popped to $48.05 – a 72% jump – on the opening trade and closed even higher at $48.60.[13]

Facebook was different.

Granted, there were some technology "glitches" reported by Nasdaq that didn't help matters.[14] Some traders weren't getting orders filled that otherwise appeared like they should. Others reported receiving prices much higher than they thought based on the quotes at the time of the trade. The exchange did issue an apology admitting there were delays due to a "technical error," but that's about all investors got. Anyone who bought shares watched them fall to about $20 by August 2012:

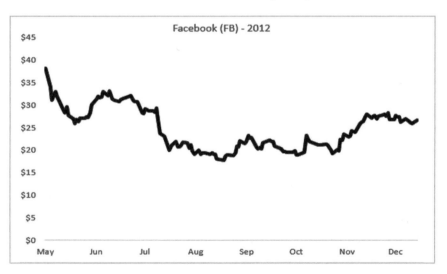

The big issue, however, wasn't the exchange glitches. It was the IPO itself. On May 21, 2012, only days after the disaster opening, Reuters posted a report that alleged lead underwriter

Morgan Stanley received privileged information that wasn't shared with others.[15] The Reuters article also was alleging that Morgan Stanley, along with Goldman Sachs, JP Morgan, and Bank of America, simultaneously reduced their earnings outlooks to nearly identical levels just prior to the IPO.[16]

On May 23, 2012, some shareholders launched a class action lawsuit against Facebook alleging that the company shared forecast revisions with the underwriters ahead of the IPO, and that the underwriters then subsequently lowered their estimates for 2012, *"..which revisions were material information which was not shared with all Facebook investors, but rather, was selectively disclosed by defendants to certain preferred investors."* [17]

The lawsuit also alleged that Facebook told analysts to *"materially lower their revenue forecasts for 2012."*[18] In other words, the analysts were right, and the IPO price was overvalued. What's the rational thing to do when prices are too high? If you said "sell," that's exactly how Facebook and the underwriters answered.

Facebook announced on May 16 – two days before the IPO – that it planned to sell an additional 25% of the authorized shares to raise an additional $3 billion, which increased the IPO share count from 337.4 million to 421.2 million.[19] That wasn't all.

The underwriters had a "Greenshoe" clause, also called an overallotment clause, in the contract that allowed them to oversell by another 15%. In other words, the underwriters had the right to sell short these shares – and they did. With this clause, the number of shares increased from 421 million to 484 million. However, the clause also said the underwriters may buy the shares back for the $38 IPO price.[20] In essence, it's a free $38 call option. What's the reason for a Greenshoe clause?

Underwriters use them to support prices if an IPO isn't well received. If prices fall in the first few days, those who bought the IPO shares take losses, and the underwriter who charged a small

fortune to take the company public simply looks bad. So just in
case prices fall, many contracts include a Greenshoe clause.[21]

If the IPO is a success and the share price rises, the underwriters
exercise the option and buy the short shares back at $38 and
cover their short position. No harm done. But if it's a flop,
they'll buy shares in the open market to cover their short
positions – and earn a big fat profit in the process. These
purchases are called *stabilizing bids* because they support the
falling share prices. Greenshoe clauses are a form of insurance,
so if prices fall in the first few days, there will at least be
some buying pressure coming in at the IPO price. The term
"Greenshoe" came from Green Shoe Manufacturing Company,
now called Stride Rite, which was the first company to use the
clause in a 1919 underwriting agreement.

While these clauses sound like they help investors, the reality
is that any price drops are caused by the IPO purchasers
immediately flipping shares for a quick profit. It's a risk they
take, so they should bear the cost. The SEC, however, sees the
practice as promoting market stability:

*"Although stabilization is a price-influencing activity intended to induce
others to purchase the offered security, when appropriately regulated it is an
effective mechanism for fostering an orderly distribution of securities and
promotes the interests of shareholders, underwriters, and issuers."* [22]

Stabilizing bids, however, are simply a way of transferring risk
from the IPO buyers to a relatively naïve segment of the investor
population. Few investors know that stabilizing bids are often used,
so when stock prices are only allowed to artificially fall so far, it
gives the secondary market the illusion that it's a level of support.
Uninformed investors get the impression that the price probably
isn't going to fall below that, but they have no idea it's artificially
supported. Who would have guessed that so much goes on behind
the scenes of an IPO? In the case of Facebook, you can't help but
think these additional sales were done because everyone – including

Facebook – wanted a profitable piece of the highly overvalued shares. Of course, if a company's stock isn't performing well, there's always the upgrade and downgrade game.

UPGRADE AND DOWNGRADE: A WAY TO GET PAID

On May 6, 2008, with oil prices pushing $122 per barrel, a prominent investment bank's energy equity team upgraded oil with a price target of $141 for the second half of the year and reiterated their prediction for a "super spike" ranging from $150 to $200 within two years. It was an open invitation for investors to jump on board for the next big wave of profits. But oil only climbed $18 higher to $140 – and then instantly did a U-turn. Later that same year, on December 12, with oil at $46 per barrel, the same team predicted it would fall to an average price of $45 per barrel for 2009. It quickly climbed to nearly $92:

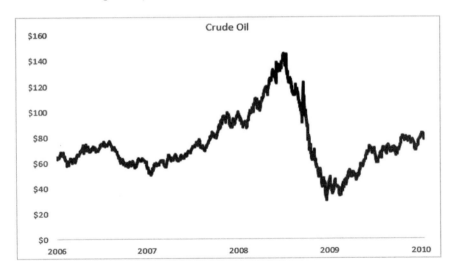

Keeping in mind that the goal is to buy low and sell high, how could an investment bank have a long history of an uncanny ability to upgrade oil at market tops and downgrade it near market bottoms? Is it a coincidence? In 2008, we were in the middle of the 2007-2009 bear market, the S&P 500 lost 50% of its value, and we were seeing record single-day drops. On September 29, the Dow lost 778 points, making it the worst point-drop since Black Monday in 1987. Investors were worried about the banking system from Wall Street's overwhelming exposure to bad mortgage debts. This bank received billions from the U.S. Department of the Treasury as part of the Troubled Asset Relief Program (TARP). Would falling oil prices drive it under?

Oil markets are easier to move than stock prices. Stock prices are based upon *future* earnings, and that's a hard thing to predict. Oil is different. Its price is determined by what must clear the market today, and that's a much easier thing to predict. Roger Diwan from the consulting firm PFC Energy noted that financial players are in a unique position, as they don't need to own ships and tanks; they can just bid up prices on the New York Mercantile Exchange, where they can buy on margin. *"The paper market is infinite, and you don't have to pay for storage."* [23]

We couldn't agree more, and that's what makes it a perfect commodity to influence – provided you have the power to move prices. But would any of the large market participants actually try to move prices? If you must ask, you haven't been following the markets long enough.

BIG BANKS MANIPULATE KEY INTEREST RATE

The London Interbank Offered Rate, or LIBOR, is considered the most important interest rate in the world, as it impacts trillions of dollars' worth of worldwide loans, including mortgages.

In 2018, Citibank reached a settlement with 42 states to pay a $100 million fine for manipulating the key rate.[24] According to the settlement Citi made millions of dollars by fixing the rate, which was discovered through a series of text messages and emails as they misrepresented what they were paying for loans in 2008 and 2009.[25] The regulators also said Citi made millions of dollars in "unjust gains" through government and non-profit firms by fixing the rate.[26] New York Attorney General Barbara Underwood said, *"Our office has zero tolerance for fraudulent or manipulative conduct that undermines our financial markets. Financial institutions have a basic responsibility to play by the rules – and we will continue to hold those accountable who don't."* [27]

Citi wasn't alone. There were a number of banks which were implicated. For example, Barclays reached a $453 million settlement over rate fixing in 2012,[28] and UBS agreed to pay a jaw-dropping $1.5 billion fine for fraud and bribery linked to LIBOR manipulation to regulators in the United States, United Kingdom, and Switzerland.[29] Another bank was Deutsche Bank, which agreed to pay $240 million to settle private U.S. antitrust litigation accusing it of conspiring with other banks to manipulate the LIBOR benchmark interest rate.[30]

Some have speculated that these fraudulent manipulations contributed to the 2008 mortgage crisis by artificially driving up home-loan rates. Whether rates were driven up or down, you can be sure profits were driven higher.

THE FINANCIAL WATCHDOG PROTECTS THE BROKERS

Investors can borrow money to buy shares of stock by using a margin account, which just requires an additional document to be signed, and a minimum of $2,000 equity. One of the ideas behind margin trading is that it allows investors quick access to cash in falling markets, which would add some price stability for the days when the bears are loose.

If you have a margin account, you only need to pay for half

the amount of the trade, and the broker automatically loans you the balance. The margin account acts like a line of credit established with the broker. For instance, you could buy 100 shares of a $100 stock, or $10,000 worth of stock by only using $5,000 worth of cash. At this point, your account equity is 50%, which is found by $5,000 worth of cash divided by $10,000 worth of stock. Most brokers require that your account equity stay above 30%. If it falls below, you'll be required to deposit more money – or sell shares – to make up the difference, which is called a maintenance call, or *margin call*. For instance, if the stock's price falls to $70, you've lost $3,000 worth of equity. Your equity percentage is now $2,000/$7,000, or about 29%, and you must bring your percentage back up above 30%.

However, let's say you have 10 different stocks in a margin account, all doing well, except for one. It plummets after a bad earnings report, which sends your account equity below 30%. In most cases, the broker requires that you meet the margin call by close of business that day, but the broker may immediately begin closing any positions – even without notifying you – to bring your account equity back to the required level. Here's where the bias against traders begins.

You'd think the broker would close the position that's creating the margin call. If nine stocks are up and doing well, it seems that the broker should first close the one that's causing the trouble. The Financial Industry Regulatory Authority (FINRA) does not require this. The broker may close any positions that are creating the most risk for it – not you. FINRA's reason is that traders borrow individually, but brokers loan collectively.[31] It sounds profound, but what does it mean?

It means that while individual investors may hold a troubled stock, the broker isn't required to close it from their accounts. Instead, the broker may choose positions which are creating the biggest risks to the firm. Where's the logic in that? If the broker agreed to the loan when the stock was looking good, the broker should share in the losses when things are bad. Being able to choose which stocks to close based on the risk to the broker is the equivalent to someone being behind on a car loan, but the bank being allowed to choose among repossessing the car, boat, or home depending on which loans are creating the biggest risk to the bank. If a car dealer makes a bad loan, the car dealer takes the losses. If a bank makes bad mortgages, the banks take the losses. But if a broker makes bad loans, the customer now bears the risk. This practice wouldn't work in any other industry.

THE SECRET SOCIETY OF THE SOES BANDITS

In 1984, the Small-Order Execution System, or SOES, was created by Nasdaq to automatically execute orders of "...500 shares or less received from public customers...".[32] As a result of the crash of 1987, Nasdaq implemented it as a mandatory order execution system for all small orders as a result of the lack of market liquidity.

After all, it doesn't make sense to have market makers monitoring a stock that may have little to no volume for the entire day. Still, if an investor places an order, the exchange needs a way to execute the trade, and the SOES system was the answer. It was a computerized trading platform that would either sell shares on the asking price or buy them at the quoted bid, most of the time limiting the order to 1,000 shares or less.[33] For instance, say ABC stock is thinly traded and the exchange posts a bid of $20 and asking price of $21. If you place an order to buy up to 1,000 shares "at market," you'd instantly buy shares at the quoted $21 price. If your order was to sell, you'd receive the $20 bid. It gave retail investors a preference in the trading queue, as it was mandatory for market makers to fill orders at the quoted prices. Market makers, on the other hand, usually traded larger lots, and normally had to walk orders out to the trading floor, haggle with prices, return with trades, which were then relayed back to the broker and finally to the client. The process took time.

The SOES system, however, created a loophole because it automatically routed investor orders to the dealers with the highest bids or lowest offers. Because SOES systems weren't closely monitored, traders could buy or sell shares at favorable prices before the SOES systems were updated. For example, traders might wait for an uptrend to develop, buy on the SOES system, and immediately lay off the trade on another exchange at a more current higher price. It was a way of stealing from the exchanges, and these traders were dubbed the SOES Bandits.[34] As a result, many market makers were caught off guard, and wound up losing money by buying high and selling low.

Sheldon Maschler and Harvey Houtkin were two of the original SOES Bandits.[35] Sheldon founded Datek Securities in 1970, but in 1989, hired two software programmers, Jeff Citron and Josh Levine, who created *Watcher*, which was one of the first programs to provide real-time quotes for Nasdaq stocks through SOES. In 1996, *Watcher* was used as the foundation for Datek Online, and the growth was explosive, employing 500 traders in its first year, many fresh graduates from Ivy-league schools, making $750,000 per year. By 1999, it was the fourth largest Internet broker. Later, Citron and Levine created a similar platform called *Island*,[36] which captured 15% of the Nasdaq's volume by 1998. From 1995 to early 1998, Datek Securities executed about 12 million SOES trades, over 30% of all SOES trades. Not surprisingly, it was purchased by Nasdaq in 2005.

Harvey Houtkin, another early SOES Bandit, created All-Tech in 1998 along with another platform called *Attain*,[37] which was sold to Knight Trading in 2005 and renamed Direct Edge. Knight sold it to Goldman Sachs and Citadel Investments and the ISE. It merged with BATS Trading to become the third largest stock market in the U.S. behind the NYSE and Nasdaq.

The problem with many of these computerized trading systems back then, or Exchange Traded Networks (ETN), is that some of them allegedly engaged in various forms of price manipulation including spoofing, layering, and quote stuffing. The details aren't important, but they all involve forms of creating fake orders to get other computers to alter prices. Rather than using SOES for its intended purpose of executing trades on behalf of retail investors, these early bandits engaged in fraudulent schemes to make proprietary trades. In 2003, the SEC charged Sheldon Maschler and Jeffrey Citron, among others, with participating in an extensive scheme to defraud investors from 1993 to 2001.[38] The defendants agreed to pay over $70 million and disgorgement to settle the charges. Sheldon Maschler was ordered to pay over $29 million and Citron over $22 million, representing the largest penalties the SEC has ever obtained from individuals.[39]

The bigger problem, however, is that these platforms that allow flash orders have been granted exchange status. While it appears that it's a benefit for investors to have other competitors, these platforms are there to gain access to the proprietary market data of the NYSE, Nasdaq, and BATS. Sometimes it isn't just about bending the rules, tilting the playing field, or slanting the news. Sometimes it could be outright fraud.

BAYOU HEDGE FUND SCANDAL

In 1996, Sam Israel founded the Bayou Hedge Fund Group by raising $300 million, which he swindled for personal use. Investors were given bogus reports, saying the fund would grow to $7.1 billion in 10 years, representing a healthy 37% annual return every year.[40] Considering Madoff's steady 10% raised a few eyebrows, you'd think investors would have known better about believing 37%. Just two years later, in 1998, the fund's poor performance led Bayou to create a dummy accounting firm, which they hired to send fake statements to investors. When the fraud was finally exposed, Israel tried to fake his own death to avoid prison. His abandoned truck was found on Bear Mountain Bridge in 2008 with the cryptic message "Suicide is Painless" scribbled in dust on the hood. Debra Ryan, Israel's girlfriend was suspected of helping him escape, and the two were featured on *America's Most Wanted*. Israel was finally captured, convicted, and required to serve 20 years in prison – plus pay a $200 million fine.[41] But cons don't go down easily. He failed to report to prison as ordered on June 9, 2008 and only turned himself in 24 days later on July 2.[42]

BUNGLE IN THE JUNGLE

In late 1993, geologist Michael de Guzman ordered rock samples from a remote site in the jungles of Indonesia on behalf of Bre-X Minerals, a Canadian mining company. Independent auditors assessed the deposits as the richest gold deposit ever discovered, with some reports showing the potential for 200 million troy ounces valued at nearly $7 billion. The stock went from valuations below one cent to CAD $40 in late 1995.[43]

With his newfound wealth, de Guzman used the money to expand the company with sophisticated excavation equipment. Investors knew that with every piece of equipment, every new core sample estimate, and every new Wall Street article, the stock was bound to be worth far more – and they continued to buy. What they didn't know, however, is that the entire operation was a fraud. There wasn't a single ounce of gold on the site. Instead, de Guzman used an age-old mining scam called "salting" where miners would sprinkle gold near sites, much like you'd sprinkle salt on food. What made his scam so ingenious is that he didn't just salt the surface of potential sites. Instead, he ground up the core samples and sprinkled hand-filed shavings from his wedding band into the mix. He was careful with the proportions, not too little to not have value, and not too much to raise suspicion. It fooled everyone, including seasoned independent auditors, geologists, and scientists.

His wedding ring, however, would only carry the scam so far. To keep the scam going, more gold was needed to salt the samples, so he eventually contacted a few local gold panners and bought more than $61,000 worth of gold over a two-year period.

The con was on, and perhaps would still be going today had it not been for the corrupt Indonesian government when President Suharto wanted a piece of the action. In 1996, he revoked Bre-X's mining license and opened the property for bidding by other companies. Eventually Bre-X was forced to share the site with Freeport – conveniently along with Suharto's daughter. Freeport-McMoRan would own 55% of the site while Bre-X would have rights to the remaining 45%. In a single day, the stock dropped from roughly $50 to $37, losing one billion dollars in market capitalization.

Cons never give up, and de Guzman countered by increasing the estimated amount of gold reserves after releasing new drilling results. Previously, he stated the company was sitting on 57 million ounces in reserve but increased to over 70 million ounces, which offset the drop in the stock's price. The stock, once again, began a steep rise.

In 1996, Bre-X was listed on the Nasdaq, and in December, Lehman Brothers alerted investors with a "strong buy" recommendation based on the "gold discovery of the century." The stock shot up like a rocket, eventually trading for a split-adjusted high of CAD $286.50 in May 1996.

In 1997, de Guzman was invited to speak at Bre-X's annual

shareholder meeting in Toronto. In the meantime, Freeport-
McMoRan was eagerly drilling just a few feet away from de
Guzman's site but found no gold. Not a single flake. Upon hearing
the news, Bre-X shares were halted for trading on March 25.

Freeport-McMoRan demanded de Guzman get back to Indonesia
to explain his results. After returning to Indonesia, he took off in a
helicopter piloted by an Indonesian military man. After reaching
an altitude of about 500 feet over some of the thickest rainforests
in the country, the pilot claimed to have looked in the back seat –
and de Guzman had jumped to his death. Bre-X's stock opened
for trading on May 6 at four cents, down 97%. With zero answers
and zero gold, the stock was delisted in May 1997, leaving many
investors penniless, some committing suicide, and wiping out
billions from Canadian pension plans.

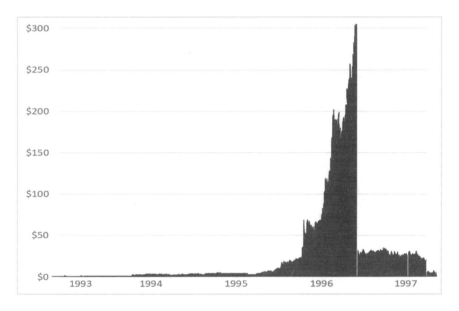

It was the end of Bre-X, but the beginning of a new conspiracy.
To this day, rumors continue to swirl: Was it a suicide, murder,
or just another perfectly planned deception? Even though
a body was discovered, the government declared it "too
gruesome" for the family to see, and only one geologist who

knew de Guzman verified the remains. No DNA or other testing was ever done, and the body was cremated. To add to the conspiracy, a suicide note was supposedly left behind – with his wife's name Teresa misspelled. No criminal charges have ever been brought against anyone, and despite the many civil suits, not one investor has ever been compensated. Michael de Guzman, however, had sold shares totaling over $100 million. The story of de Guzman is such a grand deception that few frauds will ever match it. The Matthew McConaughey movie *Gold* was released in 2016, and several documentaries have been produced on this scandal.

THE MINDSET OF THE THREE-COMMA CLUB

To understand why so many Ivy Leaguers are attracted to Wall Street, you need look no further than the level of compensation the best traders and managers can earn. This is why the biggest traders and best corporate honchos regularly make Forbes' list of billionaires – the three-comma club. Inside this elite club is a level of wealth unmatched anywhere else, but it's all created for one reason – get the stock price higher.

Jack Welch was the highly-acclaimed CEO at General Electric (GE) from 1981 to 2001. During his tenure, he received millions of dollars per year, a Manhattan apartment valued at $80,000 per month, court-side seats to the New York Knicks and U.S. Open, box seats at Red Sox and Yankees games, seating at Wimbledon, country club fees, security services, and all restaurant bills were comped, whether for business or not. If that wasn't enough, when he retired, he received severance pay of $417 million – the highest ever paid to any U.S. executive at that time.[44] To his credit, GE shares did rise 4,000% during his tenure.

In 2017, Broadcom's (AVGO) Hock Tan was the highest-paid CEO, earning $103.2 million – more than 2,000 times the pay of the average U.S. worker.[45]   However, as part of that pay, Tan received bonus shares worth over $98 million, but won't be fully vested until 2021, and the final number of shares he'll receive will depend on Broadcom's value at that time. If Broadcom shares perform better than 90% of the S&P 500 companies, he'll receive shares worth nearly $180 million. But if the company ends up on the bottom 25% of the S&P 500, he'll get no shares. Broadcom did perform well in 2017, with the company increasing nearly 47% versus 22% for the S&P 500 index. But he still has four years to go. Strong incentives are always in place to get share prices higher.

The problem is that these incentives aren't balanced with equal risks. CEOs also receive generous severance packages – regardless of the cause. The result is that CEOs can't lose, so they have the incentive to take unwarranted risks to move the stock price higher. If they fail, they win, but investors lose.

In 2015, United Airlines'(UAL) CEO Jeff Smisek stepped down after the company was accused of trading favors with Port Authority official David Samson. United was trying to get public funding for improvements to its Newark Liberty Airport, where it is the largest carrier. During a Manhattan dinner meeting, Samson said he wished the airline would restore one of its twice-weekly, money-losing flights between Newark and Columbia, S.C., known as the "Chairman's Flight," since he owned a weekend home near the Columbia airport. In other words, United was willing to charge shareholders for the costs so a public official could get more convenient flights. If average employees were found guilty of such egregious acts, they'd be fired immediately. How did it work out for Smisek, a Wall Street insider?

He walked away from United Airlines with $36.8 million in severance and benefits.[46] But there was more, and it was these extravagant perks that rubbed investors' nerves raw. He received free first-class flights for himself plus a companion, free airport parking, and will drive a company car – all for life.[47] He won't even pay the taxes on the free flights, as United agreed to pay those too.

In 2016, when Wells Fargo's (WFC) CEO John Stumpf lost his job over the company's credit card scandal, the Golden Parachute netted him $133 million.[48] In return, investors got a statement from the new CEO Tim Sloan, *"We apologize to everyone who was harmed by unacceptable sales practices that occurred in our retail bank."*[49]

To succeed on Wall Street, financial knowledge doesn't win the game. Sales do. If a company can spin a great story, deliver smooth pitches, and convince clients to buy its products, it'll survive and grow. Wall Street has evolved into a sales machine of promised profits because that's what people want to hear. The salespeople are usually not financial experts, but those who are masters at getting you to do one thing – buy. As Warren Buffett observed, *"Wall Street is the only place that people ride to in a Rolls Royce to get advice from those who take the subway."* The harsh reality is that Wall Street doesn't survive by making money for you. It survives by making money from you.

> *"Wall Street is the only place that people ride to in a Rolls Royce to get advice from those who take the subway."*
>
> – Warren Buffett

Pete and I have learned through the years just how far Wall Street will go to become a lethal opportunity employer. Someone is always trying to alter perceptions, play on emotions, and hype up the opportunity to get you to take the losing side of the trade. It's the way most of them pay for their subway ticket. It's not really a random walk. It's based on talk: Do whatever it takes to get the stock prices higher.

Comedian Robin Williams summed it up best, *"Carpe per diem – seize the check!"*

Ch. 2 THE INSIDE SCOOP ON INSIDE INFORMATION

Swindles, cons, and frauds take many forms on Wall Street. Some are simple. Others, complex. But when these deals go down, insider trading heats up. It's the favorite food of unscrupulous insiders, as it appears to be the surest way to quick money. Few people understand just how big – and easy – the money is. But with good inside information, it's not hard to leverage $10,000 into millions – until you get caught.

All other forms of fraud involve at least some degree of speculation. Madoff's scam didn't guarantee profits. Shorting IPO shares of Facebook didn't guarantee profits. Even manipulating interest rates didn't guarantee profits. Trading on inside information most always does. When you know the answer, it's easy to bet big. You wouldn't be afraid to go "all-in" at the poker table if you're holding a royal flush, and that's why unscrupulous insiders may bet big when they have inside information.

While insider trading is illegal, it's not illegal to hold nonpublic information in confidence or to use publicly available information. Pete and I have a made a career of hunting for the insiders by looking for unusual option activity. It's not the least bit illegal to trade on that information, as it's available to everyone. It's no different than an accountant poring through 10-Q forms to look for undervalued stocks. Just because some people choose not to use it – or are unable to interpret it – isn't the issue. The issue is whether *access* to the information is available to everyone.

Over the past few years, you've probably read many stories about people getting busted, both civilly and criminally, for trading on inside information. Even though it's illegal, it occurs often.

In 2001, Martha Stewart sold $230,000 worth of ImClone (IMCL) shares just one day before the FDA announced it wasn't going to approve one of its drugs.[50] Stewart ultimately went to jail for lying about her trading to the FBI.

In 2009, Raj Rajaratnam, founder of hedge fund Galleon Group, was arrested for earning over $60 million from insider trading activity. He was convicted in 2011 and sentenced to 11 years in prison.[51]

In 2014, S.A.C. Capital Advisors'[52] fund manager Mathew Martoma was sentenced to nine years in prison for masterminding the most lucrative insider trading case in history.[53] According to the SEC he obtained clinical trial information from a doctor working on Alzheimer's drugs for Wyeth and Japanese drugmaker Elan and used it to profit $275 million.[54]

In 2012 and 2013, related to that same case, billionaire Steven A. Cohen's S.A.C. Capital Advisors and a wholly owned subsidiary, CR Intrinsic Investors, paid a total of $1.8 billion to settle allegations of insider trading, without admitting guilt,[55] and his firm also paid $135 million to settle with Elan shareholders.[56]

In May 2018, hedge fund Visium Asset Management was charged with insider trading for two generic drug approvals by the FDA. The fund received inside tips from a hired consultant – who just happened to be a former employee of the FDA.[57] The fund agreed to pay more than $10 million to settle allegations.[58]

During that same month, two partners of the Deerfield Management hedge fund along with two others were found guilty of insider trading and sentenced to three years in prison. Prosecutors said they were tipped off about upcoming decisions from Centers for Medicare and Medicaid Services (CMS) on how much the government would be reimbursing health care companies. The scheme allegedly netted $3.9 million in profits and $193,000 in consulting fees. Deerfield agreed to settle the claims for $4.6 million.[59]

More recently, in August 2018, congressman Chris Collins was charged with tipping his son about Innate Immunotherapeutics' (INNMF) poor results from a multiple sclerosis drug.[60] His son sold his shares before they fell 92% in a single day.[61] Prosecutors said it was the first insider-trading case against a sitting congressman.

Later that same month, NFL linebacker Mychal Kendricks was charged with insider trading.[62] He was tipped by a bank analyst about upcoming bank mergers, bought call options[63] on the target companies, and earned a combined profit of $1.2 million. Kendricks paid his tipper cash, provided Philadelphia Eagles game tickets, and provided invitations to nightclubs and music video taping sessions. In public statements, Kendricks said he knew his conduct was wrong and was prepared "to accept the consequences."[64] After prosecutors announced the charges, the Cleveland Browns released him from the team. Kendricks has pled guilty and faces prison time.

These stories highlight that it's not just insiders who possess inside information. It begins with insiders, but word leaks and may travel quickly, and that generates unusual option activity. If insider trading is illegal, the regulators have sophisticated tools to detect the illegal trading and connect the dots between the tippers and the illegal traders, and the trading potentially carries stiff penalties, why do so many people do it? To appreciate why the hunt for unusual option activity can be so profitable, you must understand what insider trading is – and why it's so difficult to prove.

WHAT IS INSIDE INFORMATION?

Inside information is material, non-public information about a security, i.e., any non-public fact that, once released, would likely have a significant effect on the price of some financial asset, such as stocks or bonds. In the movie *Wall Street*, Bud Fox learned from his dad that Bluestar Airlines would be cleared by the FAA for the 1984 crash. When he passed that information to Gordon Gekko, it was inside information. When Mr. Gekko bought the shares, it was a trade based on inside information. That's illegal.

Company insiders are any officers, directors, and owners of more than 10% of the shares. However, anyone in *possession* of inside information is also considered an insider – including a business whose shares are publicly traded. This explains why you'll see many corporations who buy other companies often own fewer than 10%. For instance, Warren Buffett of Berkshire Hathaway owns about 9.8% of Wells Fargo so as not to become an insider of that bank.

> **COMPANY INSIDERS ARE ANY OFFICERS, DIRECTORS, AND OWNERS OF MORE THAN 10% OF THE SHARES.**

Any insider is prohibited from trading on inside information. The main reason courts have ruled that it's illegal is that it jeopardizes the fairness and integrity of the market. If investors knew that insider information was being used to make easy money, it gives the impression that it's a rigged game.

The SEC defines insider trading as follows: *"Illegal insider trading refers generally to buying or selling a security, in breach of a fiduciary duty or other relationship of trust and confidence, on the basis of material, nonpublic information about the security. Insider trading violations may also include "tipping" such information, securities trading by the person "tipped," and securities trading by those who misappropriate such information."* [65]

No investor wants to invest hard-earned money so that insiders can get easy profits. It would erode investor confidence, they'd stop buying shares, and we'd lose the very benefit that financial markets are supposed to provide.

The penalties are stiff. The maximum prison sentence is now 25 years[66] with a maximum fine of $5 million for individuals, and $25 million for businesses whose securities are publicly traded. Further, individuals may be forced to disgorge up to three times the amount of profits gained or losses avoided.[67]

However, whether and how to protect inside information is a complex subject and often the topic of heated discussions among economists. Some say it should be allowed, as the markets are always better off having stock prices reflect all information – whether inside or not. For any economic policy, it's considered advantageous if the benefits outweigh the costs. Let's say someone who is just a few years from retirement made a large purchase of stock for $100 per share in an IRA. One week later, the shares plummet 30% on negative news, and he's now suffered great financial harm, perhaps unable to retire or maintain his home or other assets. However, if insiders were allowed to trade on that information, it would have been reflected in the share price, and the investor would have purchased shares at $70, not $100. By having the information released into the market sooner, he would have avoided great harm. Remember, there are two sides to every trade – a buyer and the seller – and that means there are two sides to every story. So, some people make the argument, if millions of investors could be saved from billions of dollars' worth of harm, but at the "expense" of a few insiders making some easy money, is it necessarily a bad policy?

The other side of the story is that, if legal, it would make investing riskier. Traders would be suspicious of someone offering shares for sale and won't be willing to pay as much. The result is that buyers end up paying more than they should while sellers receive less. We bring this up because it's the primary reason that insider trading laws are so tricky. Regulators want to encourage the free flow of information, but with limitations. Where are the lines?

Anytime you have a large body of law and cases loaded with technical definitions and driven by complex fact patterns, it's easy to hide. Just because information comes from someone on the inside, doesn't necessarily mean it's inside information. To qualify, it must be *material, non-public* information, where "material" means the information would likely have a significant impact on the stock's price – up or down – upon the news being released. The law defines "significant" as any information a reasonable investor would likely use as part of the decision to buy or sell.

If a CEO tells you that his company will be hiring hundreds of employees over the next three years, it isn't material information. While it may represent good news about the company, it's not material inside information because buying shares of stock the next day isn't going to ensure any kind of quick profit. Instead, the law says the information must be of a "precise nature," which means the news must "reasonably be expected to come into existence," or "an event which has occurred or reasonably be expected to occur." Sounding pretty technical, right?

If the CEO tells you on the QT that his company is about to be acquired, or that it's going to greatly beat – or seriously miss – earnings estimates next week, or that its credit rating is going to be downgraded by Standard & Poor's, that's a different story. That's of a *precise nature*, and a reasonable investor would assume that information, once released, will immediately affect the stock's price. Insiders can be sued by the regulators or arrested for trading, or even leaking, such information not yet released to the public.

The courts have ruled that the only reason to disclose inside information is if another party is entitled to know because of a fiduciary relationship. A relationship of trust exists between insiders and the shareholders of the corporation, and the only time the information should be shared is out of need and not to take advantage of the uninformed stockholders. Still, insiders do it all the time, and the reason is that it's so difficult to prove.

TRADING IT VERSUS PROVING IT

Defining insider trading is difficult enough. Proving it can be very difficult. Like many causes of action for a court case, there are certain elements that must be proven. This section covers some of the key elements concerning insider trading rules, but is not meant to be a complete list. We want to show the complexity of proving insider trading. For more in-depth details, please visit www.sec.gov.

First, prosecutors must show that a trade took place. It's not illegal to be in possession of inside information. In fact, many journalists, attorneys, and corporate secretaries come into contact with material, nonpublic information all the time. That's not a crime. Interestingly, if you're in possession of inside information but avoid a trade, such as not selling existing shares because of good information or by not buying shares because of negative information, it's not grounds for illegal insider trading. The law says it's not okay to make money, or avoid losing money, based on inside information. To prosecute, a trade must be made.

Second, prosecutors must prove that you placed a trade based on material, nonpublic information. The trader or the tipper must know – or should have known – the information was valuable. If you receive a tip that a reasonable person would consider market-moving information, the courts assume you have a fiduciary duty to the corporation – just like an insider. If an insider breaches his fiduciary duty by leaking information, you're now considered an insider and have a legal obligation to not let it leak further. In other words, not only are insiders prohibited from trading on inside information, but they also may not disclose that information to outsiders for the same improper purpose of exploiting the information for their personal gains.

If the CEO of Kool Gizmos tells you it's being acquired by another company, it's illegal for you to trade on that information. However, if the CEO suggests buying shares because his company is working on a faster microchip, there's nothing to suggest the information was a hot tip. Prosecutors must prove you were prompted to buy, and you knew the suggestion was based on material, nonpublic information. Just because you spoke to the CEO and bought shares prior to an acquisition doesn't necessarily mean anything illegal occurred. The reliability of the source is important too. If you're sitting on a park bench and a stranger says, "My friend's dad heard that Kool Gizmos is getting acquired," it's not inside information. No reasonable person would expect that to be useful information in their decision to trade. Knowing the source – and quality – of the information is a tough burden for prosecutors to prove.

Just because you knowingly place a trade based on inside information, doesn't mean it's automatically insider trading. It depends on how the information was obtained. Let's say you overhead the CEO talking to another of his executives about the acquisition. He's not breaching any fiduciary duties since he was speaking with another insider. However, in the eyes of the law, you don't become an insider just because you *overheard* inside information. Moral issues aside, there's nothing illegal about trading on that information. You're not breaching any fiduciary duties since you're not an employee or insider, nor are you a family member of any employee. You simply overheard information. Because there's no fiduciary breach, there's no insider trading. However, it gets even more technical – and stranger.

Third, and probably most difficult to prove, courts have ruled that to be prosecuted, a person trading on inside information must know that the tipper will profit directly or indirectly from the information. This is also why overhearing a conversation doesn't count, as the insider has no means of benefitting. If the CEO says he'll disclose valuable information if you'll agree to split the profits with him, that's clearly illegal. But what if there's no connection, and they can't prove the insider would benefit from sharing the information?

Because of this element of proof, courts have come up with strange and counterintuitive rulings.[68] For instance, if the CEO gives an inside tip to a dentist, it may meet the personal benefit requirement, as it could be reasonably expected to be exchanged for expensive medical visits and may therefore be illegal insider trading. However, if that same CEO gives the same tip to a barber, it may not count toward the personal benefit requirement. However, there are more hurdles for prosecutors to cross.

Just because a stock's price moved up or down – even significantly – it may be difficult to prove it was due to the information being released. Let's say Kool Gizmos was trading for $100 but rises to $103 after the announcement that it received a large government contract. However, on that same day, the overall markets as measured by the S&P 500 index were up 3% based on other broad-based news. Was Kool Gizmos up $3 because of the government contract? Or was it just following the overall market? Perhaps the stock would have been down had the government contract not been announced that day, but that's something that can never be proven. It's not like chemistry class where you can go back and retest under different conditions. Instead, defense attorneys will bring in expert witnesses who will testify that a stock's price is much more driven by the overall market, and the $3 rise in the stock's price had nothing to do with news of the government contract. And all this will be explained to a jury that doesn't know the difference between a stock and an ETF.

Trading on inside information is exceptionally difficult to prove. Even though you may read about a few high-profile cases from time to time, there may be many more that fly under the radar. They're all very fact specific. To the insiders who trade the information, the risks may well be worth the rewards, and that's why they'll do it.

A POSSIBLE ESCAPE HATCH: THE MOSAIC THEORY

At the heart of most insider trading cases lies "materiality." Is the information by itself useful? When all else fails, a defendant may claim the inside information was legally obtained by collecting small bits and pieces of public information, or by non-material, non-public information – a mosaic of information. In other words, putting together a big picture from small publicly available puzzle pieces is perfectly legal.

If a tipper spills some non-public information that's not material, it might be able to be combined with public information that gives the trader an informational advantage. If the CEO of Kool Gizmos says his company's battery is the new standard for electric cars, that may not be material inside information. However, if you hear on CNBC that two major car companies have acquired others for battery technology, you may infer that Kool Gizmos will be in the crosshairs of another one soon. If you buy shares and they happen to spike shortly after that, it's not insider trading, provided you can convince a jury you put the pieces together from publicly available information. Of course, juries may be suspicious of your quick multi-million-dollar windfall based solely on your astute perceptions of public information.

That was billionaire's Raj Rajaratnam's defense. He was the former manager and founder of Galleon Group, a New York-based hedge fund, who was charged with 14 counts of securities fraud and conspiracy. His total profits exceeded $60 million – the largest of any hedge fund insider trading case in U.S. history. His attorneys argued he used a variety of public information to come to the conclusions – the mosaic theory. The jury didn't buy it, and he was sentenced to 11 years in prison plus a civil penalty of over $150 million.

Still, the mosaic theory offers a possible defense for many people who are charged with insider trading, and yes, it helps to not be a high-profile CEO of a multibillion-dollar hedge fund. It's dreadfully difficult to prove insider trading. It does happen, but those cases are usually won because of blatant violations. As long as the rewards are worth the risks, people will continue to trade on inside information.

Let's make it clear, we are not condoning trading on inside information. Instead, we're trying to show why so many people are tempted to do it. The valuable information flows freely through Wall Street, and sometimes it's too tempting for people to pass. Even if high-ranking insiders remain tight-lipped, the pending news is often leaked by a variety of people near – but not in – the inner circle such as executive secretaries who are present at high-profile meetings, attorneys handling the case, company chauffeurs, journalists, or newspapers and magazines laying out articles before the news is released. It has all happened. It seems information is leaked by insiders every single day.

CONGRESS DODGES A BULLET

Information used to get leaked – and traded – through Washington. Prior to 2013, lawmakers found creative ways of writing themselves out of the laws. They said congressional lawmakers have no corporate responsibilities and are therefore exempt from insider trading laws. You can only imagine the daily sessions on Capitol Hill discussing health care laws, Social Security payments, insurance and banking regulations, military contracts, gun laws, and a swarm of other topics that would greatly affect the prices of publicly traded companies, and members of Congress could legally trade on that information. That was a popular source of insider trading, and we could tell, because a lot of it followed whenever there were hearings that made sweeping changes.

In April 2012, President Obama passed the STOCK Act, or Stop Trading on Congressional Knowledge Act, into law.[69] It was designed to eliminate the unfair advantage that Congress had over the markets. It also applies to all employees in the Executive and Judicial branches. The Act requires every member of Congress to publicly file and disclose any financial transactions within 45 days rather than once per year as they used to. However, it's supposed to be filed electronically as a searchable PDF so insider trading or other conflicts would be easier to detect. But one year later in April 2013, President Obama signed a bill making big changes to the law.[70] On the grounds that the online documents posed security concerns, now the financial documents must be posted online, but the details are kept on paper in the Cannon House Office Building. If you want to search someone's records, you must go to Washington and search for a specific name.[71] You can't just browse the records for key words such as stock ticker symbols. You must browse them one by one – and at a cost of 10 cents per page. Effectively, there's no transparency, so there's no effectiveness. It looked like Congress was banned, but the recent changes allowed it to dodge a bullet. Is there evidence?

On Saturday, July 7, 2018, the Trump administration announced it temporarily suspended a program set to pay over $10 billion to insurers for covering high-risk people last year.[72] These risk-adjusted payments are paid into a pool of funds, which are then distributed to those insurance companies that ended up with sicker, costlier patients, just due to luck of the draw. Publicly traded companies with a large Obamacare presence, such as Molina Healthcare (MOH) and Centene Corp. (CNC), could theoretically benefit since they don't have to make those payments any more. Curiously, Molina began a sharp climb beginning on June 28 – nine days before the announcement. During that time, the stock rose from $98.52 to $103.68, or 5.2%. Centene had a similar pattern, rising from $123.78 to $129.30, or 4.5%. Over the same period, the S&P 500 index only rose 2.5%, or about half the amount. Was the additional price increase of these stocks because of the inside information? We'll never know. One thing is certain: Members of Congress knew, and they were virtually free to trade on the information, despite the prohibitions in the STOCK Act. We may not be able to draw up our own search warrants, but we can draw our own conclusions.

The Legal Take

The laws of insider trading are complex, evolving and heavily nuanced. Insider trading is not the subject of a dedicated federal statute. It is instead derived from Rule 10b-5 which at its core prohibits fraud. 17 C.F.R. § 240.10b-5. As a result, the law of insider trading is the product of many district court cases, some circuit court decisions reviewing those district court cases and only a few cases which have reached the United States Supreme Court. The decisions are based on unique fact patterns and are analyzed against common law anti-fraud protections.

The most recent cases involve [agonizing] analysis of whether the tipper must have received a "personal benefit" in order to be fraud culpable for insider trading. When a tippee pays (or provides other taxable benefit) to a tipper, the courts have no difficulty concluding that the parties are culpable.

The more recent cases of Salman v. United States, 137 S. Ct. 420 (2016)[A], and United States v. Martoma, 894 F.3d 64 (2d Cir. 2017)[B], hold parties culpable for insider trading based upon the tipper's "intention to benefit" the tippee, Salman, 137 S. Ct. at 427, and can be established if there is a "meaningfully close personal relationship" between the parties. Id. at 421.

It is noteworthy that the most recent decision in the Second Circuit was a two to one opinion by a panel of three judges with a vigorous dissent (the opinion and dissent occupy 61 pages) which amended a decision rendered [by the same court] a few months prior. The Second Circuit declined to take up the matter en banc. Commentaries have already complained that the Second Circuit's decision creates "great uncertainty in the laws of insider trading."[C]

[A] https://www.supremecourt.gov/opinions/16pdf/15-628_m6ho.pdf
[B] https://law.justia.com/cases/federal/appellate-courts/ca2/14-3599/14-3599-2018-06-25.html
[C] See Colby Hamilton, Second Circuit Denies En Banc Rehearing in Martoma Insider Trading Case, New York Law Journal (August 27, 2018), https://www.law.com/newyorklawjournal/2018/08/27/second-circuit-denies-en-banc-rehearing-in-martoma-insider-trading-case/.

WHERE'S THE SEC?

Publicly traded companies are highly regulated, mostly by the Securities and Exchange Commission (SEC) and the U.S. Department of Justice (DOJ), to help protect investors from fraudulent activities.

"The mission of the U.S. Securities Exchange Commision is to protect investors, maintain fair, orderly, and efficient markets, and facilitate capital formation." [73] In 2018, the SEC's budget was $1.6 billion.

They now have to study and analyze millions of equity and option trades every day. Given the complexity of the markets and the many players participating in it, an untold number of insider trades may be occurring without detection and prosecution. It's an unfortunate part of Wall Street, but you can ride the coattails of the powerful insiders who trade, or leak, inside information – and you can do it legally. By using unusual option activity, you're not trading on inside information. You're using publicly available information to track them. Given that unusual option activity is often not based on insider trading, but still is what we define as *smart money*, the trick is to know where to look, how to interpret the information, and how to set up the option strategies. We'll show you how later in this book.

Valuable information flows through the markets each day, and with today's social media, it only takes one credible person to leak the information, and you can be sure hundreds or thousands will quickly follow. Legal or not, ethical or not, fair or not, like it or not, people will place trades on inside information. No matter what the label, we call them opportunities.

Ch. 3 THE HUNT FOR UNUSUAL OPTION ACTIVITY

When Pete and I were on the trading floors, there would be days when it was fairly quiet – or less chaotic – and we'd have the usual traders pushing and shoving their way to the pits to make the usual five-lot or 10-lot orders. Every once in a while, however, we'd get a flood of brokers coming in to buy options on the same stock, the same strike, and the same short-term expiration.

A few days later, news would be announced that the company was being acquired, the stock would jump 20% on the opening bell, and it became obvious what the flurry of activity was all about. We'd go back and check tickets from those trades and compare the purchase prices with the current market prices and realized it wasn't dumb luck. It was *smart money*.

We began keeping notes every time it happened and found other interesting connections. If these trades were done by smaller firms, a lot of times they didn't pan out, or perhaps with only mild results. But when the big boys came in, firms like Goldman Sachs, Merrill Lynch, Morgan Stanley, Bear Stearns, Lehman Brothers, Prudential, Dean Witter, JP Morgan, Nomura, or Citigroup, we gave it more credibility. They seemed to be right – or smarter – a lot more often.

In those days, however, it was easier, because most of these stocks traded only on one exchange. All of the trading came into one pit. For instance, we were the specialist for Micron Technology, Inc. (MU), so any information that may be floating around on that company had to be traded in our pit. As market makers, we were also allowed to place trades for our own accounts based on the actions we were seeing. It's one of the reasons exchange seats are so expensive. The idea is that, by allowing market makers to trade on that information – even though speculative – it releases it to the markets sooner.

In 1999, the SEC recognized that many exchanges seemed to have a monopoly on certain stocks.[74] For us, Micron Technology (MU) only traded in our pit. Dell Computer (DELL), on the other hand, only traded on the Philadelphia Stock Exchange. When the SEC inquired as to why they're not seeing multiple listings, traders said it was out of fear of the other exchanges listing theirs. In other words, we thought that if we list Dell, the Philly will list IBM, and so on. Well, the SEC said that may sound like a good idea to you, but it sounds like collusion to us. In their view, it was an attempt to keep bid-ask spreads wide, so traders could have wider profit margins. In 2000, the SEC required the exchanges to list each other's options.[75] IBM options, for example, were now traded in San Francisco, New York, Philadelphia, and other exchanges. As a result, we weren't seeing all of the orders, perhaps only 20% to 50%, because many orders were now being filled on other exchanges. What was once an easy thing to track – the *smart money* – suddenly became nearly impossible. That's when Pete and I hired some programmers to build an algo, which we later called *Heat Seeker*™, which would track the order flow at all exchanges. If we saw a big order at Philly, for instance, it would alert us, but that was only part of the information we needed. Knowing that a big order just took place was interesting information, but by itself, it's virtually worthless. We also needed to know if the trade was executed on the bid or offer. If someone's trading on inside information, they'll definitely be buying calls, not selling them, so we needed to know which side of the trade the order was on. With multiple exchanges listing the stock, however, there's no way to tell. So one of the things the program did was to take a snapshot of the moment the trade was recorded and compare it to the bid and offer at that same moment. If it was filled on the offer, it recorded it as a buy, and if on the bid, a sale.

We were the specialists in about 50 stocks, so we later thought, why limit our choices? Let's put the program upstairs where we can tie into all the exchanges and look at all the trades.

Around 1999, as the Internet was coming into force, online brokers flooded the markets, and the exchanges moved toward electronic trading. Bid-ask spreads got so tight that profits nearly disappeared. In 2004, we sold our company, Mercury Trading, to Citadel Enterprise Americas, LLC, but we retained the intellectual property, which meant we still owned *Heat Seeker*™.

At that time, we moved from market makers to market takers. In other words, we weren't required to make markets like we were on the floor. This enabled us to wait for opportunities and find the best trades. We used our proprietary *Heat Seeker*™ program to create subscription services at optionMONSTER™, that later helped us to build the brokerage firm tradeMONSTER™.

Does it pay to hunt for unusual option activity? Absolutely. But remember, not all of unusual option activity comes from people who are in the know.

Sometimes, unusual option activity turns out to be a dud. It could be the result of a legitimate hedging transaction. It may be a fanatical, careless trader acting on nothing more than a hunch. They're part of the financial markets too, so they're expected to show up in the results. We're okay with strikeouts. They're part of the plan when you're going for the big hits. However, when you're following the *smart money*, there's nothing like the exhilaration of an occasional grand slam.

THE BEAR STEARNS COLLAPSE

In 2008, the mood on Wall Street was tense. The mortgage markets were crumbling, which forced major firms like Citigroup and Merrill to write off billions of dollars in toxic subprime mortgages. Like most of the investment banking firms, Bear Stearns Companies, Inc. was in trouble too.

The stock had fallen from about $90 to $65. Despite the fall, on March 11, the company had about $18 billion in cash reserves, which should have been plenty to make good on any near-term obligations – or cover any losses.[76] That was the same day the Federal Reserve announced an expansion of its securities lending program where it would lend $200 billion of Treasury securities to primary dealers for 28 days rather than just over night as in the current program.[77] Bear Stearns wasn't looking too bad. Someone, however, was betting differently.

On that day, someone bought 55,000 put options for $1.7 million.[78] We'll cover put options in detail in Chapter Five, but for now, think of a put option as a bet that the stock's price will fall below a specific dollar level, which is called the strike price.

Option buyers can select from different strikes. The lower the strike price, however, the less likely it is for the put option to pay off. For example, if the stock is trading for $100, the $100 put pays off if the stock price falls below $100. The $95 put will be cheaper to buy, but it only pays off if the stock price falls below $95 – a less likely event. Each lower strike gets a little cheaper to buy, but it comes with a lower probability for a payoff. Options also have an expiration date, so the stock's price must fall below that strike within that time, otherwise there is no payoff. To profit, the stock must not only fall below the strike price, but it must do so by the expiration date.

While Bear Stearns appeared to be financially healthy, someone was betting differently. A large trade like this alone will raise eyebrows – and it certainly did for us – but it's not uncommon to see a big hedge fund or someone take large option positions. What made it so unusual – more like inconceivable – is that these were $30 puts, and there were only 10 days until expiration. That means someone was betting the company's stock would fall from its current $65 price to below $30 in a little over a week, representing a fall faster and harder than ever before – or quite possibly for any stock in history.

Purchasing these puts gave the buyer the right to sell 5.5 million shares of Bear Stearns for the fixed $30 price – no matter how low the stock price may fall. The lower the stock price falls, the greater the value of the put options. At expiration, if the stock's price is above the strike, the option will expire worthless, and the buyer loses the $1.7 million investment. However, if the stock's price is below the strike, the put option will gain value. If the stock falls to $29, the $30 put is worth the one-dollar difference, or a total of $5.5 million for all the contracts. If the stock falls to $25 at expiration, the $30 put is worth the $5 difference, or $27.5 million for the entire investment. The very most this put option could be worth is $30 – the strike price – assuming the stock price falls to zero.

Having a stock price fall from $65 to below $30 in a week is a long shot – no matter how much trouble the company may be in. It was such an unlikely event that the $30 puts weren't even available for trading. However, anyone can call the exchange and make a special request for certain strikes to be listed, which is exactly what this trader did. You must wonder why anyone would request strikes so far from the current stock price that nobody else in the world wanted them – and then bet $1.7 million on it. The trade quickly made the news, leaving everyone scratching their heads and wondering why. Thomas Haugh, general partner of Chicago-based trading firm PTI Securities and Futures, said it best: *"It's not even on the page of rational behavior, unless you know something."* [79]

Another bearish bet hit the tape with a purchase of 1,650 of the $25 puts, representing the right to sell 165,000 shares of Bear Stearns at $25. [80] The option activity was, to say the least, unusual. We didn't know what it was, but we knew that somebody knew.

The rumors began to appear from the shadows. Goldman told clients it would no longer step in for any derivatives deals for Bear Stearns. That's a big problem, as many firms leverage their bets by margins of 50:1. Liquidity was drying up, Bear Stearns was in trouble, and it appears someone knew before it was announced. Within the week, Bear Stearns stock fell below $5, turning the $1.7 million investment into a $270-million windfall – a cool 16,000% in a week. [81] To put the trade on smaller scales, a $500 investment would have netted you $40,000. A $12,500 investment would have turned into one million dollars.

It's not hard to become a millionaire, if you have an actual inside tip and engage in illegal insider trading. The market gives clues every single day to trades being placed on inside information in the form of unusual option activity.

CELGENE ACQUIRES JUNO THERAPEUTICS

On January 16, 2018, Celgene Corporation (CELG) was rumored to be in talks to acquire its remaining stake in experimental drug maker Juno Therapeutics, Inc. (JUNO) to gain access to its CAR-T cancer therapy technology.[82] The rumor alone sent the shares flying more than 56% the next day from $45.60 to $71.37. Six days later, the rumor was confirmed, and Celgene announced it was buying Juno for $9 billion cash, or $87 per share. If you bought 100 shares on the rumor for $4,500, you nearly doubled your money. Not bad for a week's work. Options provide a better way.

On December 20, 2017, about one month before the announcement, Pete announced unusual option activity on CNBC's *Halftime Report*™ showing heavy trading activity in Juno's February $52.50 calls for $2.50. Rather than buying 100 shares for $4,500, why not buy one contract? The worst you can lose is $250 – a claim stock traders can't make – but you stand to make a small fortune.[83] After the buyout announcement, those calls were trading just over $33. A $250 investment turned to $3,300 in a month. Of course, an insider wouldn't just buy one contract. That's why the unusual option activity shows so easily on the tape – provided you know where to look. Rather than spending $250, what if you spent $1,000? You could buy four contracts for a fraction of what you had to pay for the stock, but that turned into a $13,000 windfall. A $5,000 investment turns to $65,000. Impressive? That is great, but we could do better.

Another strategy we teach at our investor education company, Market Rebellion™, is to ladder your selections across different strikes. It creates a little more leverage, and more importantly, allows you to avoid the high volatility that so often accompanies the ATM strikes that are normally purchased. We often run financial models and create various "what-if" scenarios to see where the best plays may be. If you go back to December 20,

2017, when Pete was making the announcement, the same February contract had $70 calls trading for 40 cents. A $1,000 investment would buy 25 contracts, and with Juno shares at $87, the calls were worth $17, or over $42,000. Rather than buying one strike, it often pays to diversify and spread just a little bit of money to the higher-strike calls.

BLACKSTONE BUYS HILTON

On Tuesday, July 3, 2007, The Blackstone Group announced it would buy Hilton Hotels for $26 billion cash, or $47.50 per share, which was a 40% premium over the previous day's closing price.[84] The day before, however, shares climbed over 6% ahead of the announcement, which isn't that uncommon. When news is that big, even some stock buyers will step in ahead of the announcement. But the week before the stock traders knew, our *Heat Seeker*™ captured unusual option activity. We issued an alert for our subscribers and capitalized with a 10-fold profit on the trade.[85] Interestingly, one of the traders responsible for buying shares was Raj Rajaratnam, the insider we talked about in Chapter Two, and this was, in fact, one of the very trades that prosecutors charged was insider trading. The benefit of trading on unusual option activity is that you can capture bigger profits by using options over the stock, but you'll never run the risk of being charged with a crime if you only trade on publicly available information.

CHECKING INTO HILTON — AGAIN

On CNBC's *Halftime Report*™ for April 10, 2018, we found more unusual option activity in Hilton Hotels (HLT). The stock was trading for $75, down $1.15, but someone came scrambling in to buy 11,000 of the April $75 calls – just two weeks prior to expiration.[86] The average daily volume was imperceptible on the chart, probably fewer than a 200 per day, so 11,000 was in the stratosphere. We issued alerts for our subscribers, and I even announced on CNBC that I bought the April $75/$80 vertical spread, which meant I bought the April $75 calls but sold the $80 calls, which I chose to do as a hedge against volatility and time decay. I said I'd hold them for about five days.

The next day, the stock gapped up to close at $79.61, up nearly 7%, doubling the price of the long calls. It later traded as high as $82.99 five days later. What caused the jump?

Goldman Sachs swapped Marriott for Hilton on its "Conviction Buy" list. Most analytic firms use buy, sell, or hold, but Goldman added this fourth tier. The idea being that only the stocks with the best chance of outperforming the S&P 500 will make the list. The point is that unusual option activity isn't just limited to takeovers, earnings, and FDA announcements. Those are some of the biggest, but any information that will move the stock will get reflected in the option market long before the news arrives.

D.R. HORTON BEATS EARNINGS

During CNBC's *Halftime Report*™ on July 25, 2018, I announced that 4,300 Weekly $41 calls were purchased for homebuilder D. R. Horton, Inc. (DHI). The company was releasing earnings the next day, so it looked like someone knew they'd beat expectations. The calls were part of a bull spread with shares at $39.42. Open interest in that strike was only 183 contracts before the trade occurred, so these were clearly opening trades. The next day, the stock gapped up to $41.39 on the opening bell and closed at $43.84.

It wasn't a terribly big gap in price, just 5% on the opening bell and nearly 12% on the close, but options create a lot of leverage. However, there's another side that people overlook when dealing with unusual option activity. Those options weren't priced for those gaps because few people knew about it, so they traded for a lot less, and that's another source of leverage. One of the key reasons unusual option activity can be so profitable is that few people know about it, so the options often remain cheap. Those calls rose to $3.10, nearly six times their initial purchase price. The stock only rose about 12% by the end of the trading day, showing how quickly options can outperform their underlying shares.

However, it's important to understand that options have an expiration date, and there are a couple of key scenarios where you could be correct that the underlying stock's price will rise – but still lose on the call. First, the stock's price may not reach your strike. If you purchased the $44 strike, for instance, it expired worthless. Second, you may have paid too much for implied volatility, which is a topic covered in Chapter Six. For example, the July $41 calls were trading for about 50 cents prior to the news announcement. As you'll discover in Chapter Five, that contract would need the stock price to reach $41.50 just to break even. What if the option had been trading for $4 instead? Then you'd need the stock price to reach $45 before any profits are made. With the stock closing at $43.84, the $41 call was theoretically worth $3.84, but because you paid $4, you were left with a loss – even though the stock price rose and your contract expired with intrinsic value. Successful trading isn't just about finding the right information. It's also about applying the right strategy at the right time.

On the next page is a screenshot of the alerts we sent to our subscribers regarding DHI.

We also flagged unusual option activity for the July $40 calls on June 15, 2018, which wouldn't have been successful.

HOME PREMIUM SERVICES EDUCATION NEWS CRYPTO COMPANY

Date	Ticker	Type	Stock	Details	Sector
09/18/2018 2:54:30 PM	DHI	Bullish Call Buying	43.41	2,000 October 45 calls bought for 0.68 above open interest of 344 contracts. Stock 43.41.	Construction
07/26/2018 10:35:09 AM	DHI	Bullish Call Roll	42.72	1,500 September 45 calls bought for 1.00 above open interest of 23 contracts; 1,500 27July 42.50 calls sold for 0.58 below open interest of 20,241 contracts. Stock 42.72.	Construction
07/25/2018 12:23:52 PM	DHI	Bullish Call Spread	39.42	4,300 27July 41 calls bought for 0.52 to 0.54 above open interest of 183 contracts, 4,300 27July 43 calls sold for 0.15 to 0.15 above open interest of 940. Stock 39.42. EPS *tomorrow* before open.	Construction
07/24/2018 12:00:16 PM	DHI	Bullish Call Buying	41.02	3,100 August 42.50 calls bought for 0.91 above open interest of 8 contracts. Stock 41.02. EPS 7/26 before open.	Construction
07/12/2018 10:35:10 AM	DHI	Bullish Call Buying		15,700 27July 42.50 calls bought fast for 0.64 to 0.81 above open interest of 56 contracts. Stock 41.20.	Construction

HOME PREMIUM SERVICES EDUCATION NEWS CRYPTO COMPANY

Date	Ticker	Type	Stock	Details	Sector
06/15/2018 2:51:27 PM	DHI	Bullish Call Buying		15,000 July 40 calls bought at the same time from 3.35-3.65 above open interest of 42 contracts. Stock 42.75.	Construction

WENDY'S RIDES ON ARBY'S

Takeovers don't just benefit the target companies. Sometimes, other companies are connected to the deals, and their share prices can rise too. Our scanners alerted us to unusual option activity in Wendy's (WEN) in late October 2017. Was the hamburger chain a takeover target? Not exactly.

On November 28, 2017, Arby's announced it would acquire Buffalo Wild Wings (BWLD) for $2.9 billion in cash, a 7% premium, sending the shares soaring.[87] However, Roark Capital Group owned 81.5% of Arby's while Wendy's owned the remaining 18.5%. After the news, Wendy's stood to gain about $450 million from the deal.[88]

- **October 24**: 4,100 December $15 calls were bought for $0.61 to $0.65 against no open interest with shares trading at $15.05

- **November 15**: 10,700 February $14 calls were bought for $0.85 to $1.15 above open interest of 877 and shares at $14.40

- **November 22**: 5,100 May $14 calls were bought for $1.10 to $1.15 above open interest of 5 contracts with shares at $13.92

The day Arby's announced the Buffalo acquisition, Wendy's climbed from $13.70 to $15.44 – a 12.7% rally in one week, and the stock eventually broke $17 a month later. All of the calls listed above roughly tripled in value.

FIREEYE (FEYE)

The week of August 20, 2018, was a low point for FireEye, Inc. (FEYE). The cybersecurity company had fallen sharply since its earnings report a month earlier and was one dollar off its 52-week low. But an hour after the opening bell on August 23, our *Heat Seeker™* program flagged unusual option activity. Traders quickly opened bullish positions in two strikes expiring on September 7 with shares trading at $15.13.

- 4,300 Weekly $15 calls were purchased for $0.34 to $0.54 above open interest of 231 contracts

- 2,400 Weekly $15.50 calls were bought for $0.18 to $0.29 above open interest of 356 contracts

About two hours after the activity was spotted, Pete announced on the *Halftime Report™, "We're seeing a buy and a buy. That's always interesting because it shows somebody out there is pretty bullish on FireEye."*

Those calls soared in price along with FireEye shares after Pete's comments. But then they got another boost later in the afternoon on news reports that the digital-security firm had helped Google and Facebook identify disinformation campaigns linked to Russia and Iran, respectively. The social media networks came under intense congressional scrutiny over concerns of political interference the following month. FireEye opened at $14.90 that day before later spiking to $16.38 in the same session.

The $15 calls traded as high as $1.57 by the end of the day, more than four times their initial purchase price. The $15.50 calls traded up to $1.09, or six times their original price. The stock gained just 7.2% at the same time.

ISHARES MSCI TURKEY FUND

Most of the time when we see unusual option activity, the catalysts usually involve specific corporate news – earnings, mergers, FDA announcements, or litigation. However, as long as the news will drive prices, the paper trail can precede macro-economic issues as well.

On Aug. 10, 2018, U.S. equities fell sharply along with other indexes around the globe after the Turkish lira plummeted 17% against the dollar to a record low. Many economists said contagion from the currency's plunge could spread to other countries and threaten multiple asset classes in markets worldwide. But bearish option activity began to flow heavily a month earlier in the iShares MSCI Turkey Fund (TUR). In July 2018, *Heat Seeker*™ identified two downside trades in the same contracts within the span of a week, both part of bearish rolls:

- On July 12, 2,428 January $26 puts were bought for $2.85 above open interest of 50 contracts, sold from 2,024 January $32 puts sold for $6.60 below open interest of 2,028 contracts with shares at $26.40

- On July 17, 6,000 January $26 puts were purchased for $2.40 to $2.45 above open interest of 2,458 contracts, rolled from 6,854 January $30 puts sold for $4.50 below open interest of 6,782 contracts with shares at $27.40

TUR dropped nearly 15% on Aug. 10 to close at $21.42, but those puts traded up to $7.10 on August 10, or about three times their last purchase prices.

THE SEPTEMBER 11 TERRORIST ATTACKS

Unusual option activity is a way for outsiders to track the footprints of insiders, and the previous examples show we can track anything from stock transactions to macro-economic events through ETFs. However, it's proven to be even more powerful.

Prior to the September 11 attacks, Pete and I noticed heavy put buying on United Airlines (UAL) and American Airlines (AAL) on Friday, September 7, prior to the following Tuesday attacks.[89]

The unusual activity, however, didn't begin there. The month before, there was heavy put buying in these two airlines with the number of puts being 25 to 100 times larger than expected. However, these put purchases weren't balanced with call purchases. Without any pending news, you'd expect the number of puts traded to be roughly equal to the number of calls. This statistic is easily tracked by the CBOE's put-call ratio, which is often used as a technical indicator. These trades were not likely caused by large institutional funds rotating in or out of sectors. If they were selling airlines, all the airlines would be down. Why only American and United? Why not Delta, Southwest, and JetBlue?

The activity, however, heated up in the week prior to the attacks. On September 6 and 7, the CBOE reported 4,744 put options were traded compared to just 396 calls. That's a put-call ratio of nearly 12:1. We didn't place trades based on the information, as we saw no logical reason for there to be such large put buying on two airlines that were well capitalized, no earnings coming due, no merger talks that may fall through, and no pending litigations. After the attacks, we realized there may have been something more sinister to the unusual option activity. Was it possible the terrorists were buying puts to finance their activities, knowing these stock prices would fall?

After all, such a horrific event will likely cause the airlines to ground its planes, and an airline with no planes means no revenue. Investors would surely sell shares on the news – and they did. It may have taken years of planning, but only takes seconds to place a trade. But on this fateful day, it was American Airlines Flights 11 and 77, and United Airlines Flights 93 and

175 that crashed. After the fact, it became evident why these two airlines may have been singled out with the unusual put buying.

We phoned the FBI to report the highly suspicious activity, and they were receptive to our concerns, and it was part of the probe launched by the National Commission on Terrorist Attacks. Some reports, however, came back saying they found the trades to be purely coincidental because a newsletter publisher had faxed these recommendations to subscribers based on fundamental reasons. Those trades accounted for 95% of the put volume.

We were told differently.

The FBI said it traced the trades to a number of accounts in Hamburg, Germany, which was the location of the now infamous Hamburg terror cell where many of the terrorists were trained prior to coming to the U.S. for flight training.

The magic of the markets is that they give the incentive for everyone in the world to cast their opinion on a stock's value. When people are voting with dollars, nobody will intentionally place a trade they think will lose money. When someone has information – legal or not – that will affect stock prices, it will get filtered into the market. Unusual option activity gives everyone access to the collective opinions of the world by bringing these trades into the spotlight. We can use these trades for profits. We can use them to predict macro-economic events. But there may be an even bigger, unexpected benefit: Unusual option activity may help to uncover those who not only undermine the integrity of the market, but also those who try to challenge our freedom.

Pete and I made a career from trading unusual option activity, and it's been more rewarding than we ever imagined. It allowed us to create, grow, and sell Mercury Trading. It allowed us to do the same with tradeMONSTER™. And now, CNBC has created a segment during their *Halftime Report*™ which allows us to share with our viewers some of the unusual option activity we're seeing. We've spent years testing, analyzing, and trading to figure it out. So, you may be thinking, if the information is so valuable, why do we share it?

First, the option market is still relatively small. No matter how many people trade from our information, it's usually not going to be enough to move the prices to reflect the true value of the inside information. Big price moves normally only happen once the news is announced. For us, it's about showing the world that our methods work, and the only way to do that is to share it. Second, we're at a point in our career where we feel it's time to give back. It's a philosophy our parents and coaches instilled, and it's exciting to know we're making a difference for investors.

The idea behind the search for unusual option activity isn't that difficult. We're just looking for option trades that are unusually large without any apparent reason to account for it. If a particular stock has an average of 100 contracts trading per day, but a trade for 5,000 contracts was just placed, it'll get our attention. However, that alone isn't enough information. Unfortunately, many of today's platforms give traders the ability to search for option trades that are larger than normal, and they place trades based solely on that information. Then they wonder why it rarely pays off. The problem is that large trades alone don't tell the story, so we want to share with you some of the things we look for before determining what we trade.

Some of the terms in this chapter may be unfamiliar to you. That's okay, but it shows the importance of education, as we can't describe how a system works if you don't understand the language. We'll cover these in detail in later chapters, but we want to uncover the methodology for unusual option activity.

Options are used for far more than insiders trading on illegal information. They were designed to hedge risks, and anyone looking to transfer risk can buy option, and anyone willing to accept risk can sell them. The options market makes the overall market more efficient by transferring risks to those who are willing to accept it. Therefore, most of the large downside trades, even unusually large trades, are probably better explained as a hedging transaction by a hedge fund – and possibly even an insider. Just because Bill Gates buys 100,000 put options doesn't mean he thinks Microsoft is heading south. Instead, they were probably purchased for protection on long shares of stock. In that case, it's actually a bullish position. If you base your analysis strictly on large volumes, you'll end up with a lot of false signals, and even worse, may end up on the wrong side of the trade.

F.R.A.M.E. YOUR TRADE

The idea behind unusual option activity is simple: Find unusually large option trades, as that's where the smart money lives. However, it's the starting point – not the ending point. We must dig further for answers. Bullish positions can be created by using put options, and bearish trades can be created with calls. If someone told us that an unusually large order for call options just traded for a particular stock, and that's the only information we had, it's virtually worthless. There are far more reasons why it's probably not suspicious. We created our F.R.A.M.E. methodology to guide you through the entire process – from evaluating opportunities to making, managing, and exiting the trade.

THE F.R.A.M.E. METHOD

FILTER TO FIND POTENTIAL TRADES

RESEARCH VIABILITY OF POTENTIAL TRADES

ANALYZE OPTION MARKETS TO FIND BEST STRATEGY

MAKE AND MANAGE YOUR TRADE

EXIT YOUR TRADE

Filter: Was the trade larger than average orders? Was the trade large in terms of dollars? Was the trade short term?

Research: Will earnings be announced soon? Are there pending court cases, FDA announcements, or other market-driving news that could explain the trade?

Analyze: Was the trade executed on the offer? Was the trade greater than the open interest? Was the trade tied to a spread? Was the trade tied to shares of stock? How far is the strike away from the stock's price? What's the implied volatility?

Make and **Manage** Your Trade: Should the trade be hedged, as with a vertical or diagonal spread? Should you roll the position? Should you collect premiums against your contracts?

Exit Your Trade: Should you hold the position another day? Is the risk-reward ratio becoming unbalanced? Should you sell half and keep half? You can exit trades in many ways and for many reasons. Successful traders consider them all.

Through years of tracking unusual option activity, Pete and I have come up with a checklist of points we go through before considering if the activity of interest is enough to trade on. Unfortunately, there is no master checklist because each trade is different. However, we can outline some of the key elements that must be present before we'll consider a potential trade based on unusual option activity:

FILTER, RESEARCH, ANALYZE

- ✔ WAS THE TRADE GREATER THAN THE OPEN INTEREST?
- ✔ WAS THE TRADE EXECUTED ON THE OFFER?
- ✔ WAS THE TRADE LARGER THAN AVERAGE ORDERS?
- ✔ WAS THE TRADE LARGE IN TERMS OF DOLLARS?
- ✔ WAS THE TRADE TIED TO A SPREAD?
- ✔ WAS THE TRADE TIED TO SHARES OF STOCK?
- ✔ WAS THE TRADE SHORT TERM?
- ✔ HOW FAR IS THE STRIKE AWAY FROM THE STOCK'S PRICE?
- ✔ WHAT'S THE IMPLIED VOLATILITY?

WAS THE TRADE GREATER THAN THE OPEN INTEREST?

In Chapter Five, we'll talk about opening and closing transactions, and why they're important for unusual option activity. Let's say ABC stock usually has an average of 100 contracts traded per day, but an order just occurred for 5,000 contracts. Is it meaningful?

Not if they're closing transactions. People trading on inside information want to get into the market – not out – and that means they must be placing opening orders. In other words, they'll be buying calls or puts. However, as we'll cover in that chapter, open interest isn't updated until the next trading day, so we won't know if they were opening or closing transactions until tomorrow. We could wait for tomorrow and decide then, but there's another way we can identify today if the trades were opening or closing, and that's to see if the unusual order is greater than the current open interest.

It's not hard to identify large trades, but it is hard to identify if they're meaningful, and that means they must be opening transactions. If a large order is executed, and it's larger than the current open interest, it must be an opening trade. For example, let's say today's open interest is 1,000 contracts, but a trade just went through for 5,000 contracts. It can't be a closing order, as there were only 1,000 open that day. Does that mean tomorrow's open interest will be 6,000? Not necessarily, as some of the 5,000-contract order could have been filled by other traders closing theirs. None of that matters because the one thing we need to know is whether the order to buy 5,000 contracts was an opening trade. We know it must be since it was greater than the number of open interest at the time of the trade. When people are in possession of inside information, it only makes sense to trade big. Bank robbers aren't going to hold up a bank for $100, and people trading on inside information aren't going buy a handful of contracts. If an insider is going to take the risk, they will trade big. It's not uncommon to see trades for 5,000, 10,000, or far more contracts.

Considering each contract controls 100 shares, a 10,000-contract order controls one million shares of stock. Few traders will place a single order that large, so most of the time, these insider trades will be larger than the current open interest. When that happens, we know they're opening trades, and that's important information.

WAS THE TRADE EXECUTED ON THE OFFER?

For any stock or option, there are two prices – a bid and an offer, also called the asking price. The bid price represents the highest price someone is willing to pay at that moment. The offer, on the other hand, shows the lowest price for which another trader will sell. Therefore, if you're trying to buy an option, you'll generally purchase it on the offer. On the other hand, most of the sell orders are executed on the bid.

Another thing we look for is that the trade must be a buy, so it must occur on the offer. It shows the trader laid out money for the right to buy or sell the shares. People trading illegally on inside information aren't going to be selling options. When you sell an option short (one you don't already own), the most you can make is the amount you receive, so it's a strategy that has a small, limited profit. To pass the unusual option test, the trade must have occurred on the offer.

WAS THE TRADE LARGER THAN AVERAGE ORDERS?

Another checkpoint is that the trade must be larger than average. We look at several averages, some short term and some long term. For example, we may look at a running five-day moving average, which calculates the average number of contracts every five days. To qualify as unusual option activity, the suspicious trade must beat the averages. After all, "large" is relative.

For example, we may find that 5,000 contracts traded at a certain strike and met the first three criteria. It was an opening order, occurred on the offer, and was greater than the open interest. So far, so good. However, when we check it against the averages, we may find that trades of this size occur with some regularity. These large orders may be infrequent, but they're not rare, and there is a difference. Florida hurricanes happen infrequently, but they happen nearly every year. When a Category 5 sweeps along the coast, weathermen aren't scratching their heads in disbelief about how unusual that is – even though they're infrequent. But what if a polar bear went strolling along the coast? That would be unusual. That's how unusual option activity must be viewed. For some stocks, it's common to have options with low volumes or open interest, but they always seem to get one or two large trades each month. Now it's not so interesting, and unless it passes other tests, we're probably going to let it go. To identify the truly unusual option activity, we're looking for trades that beat the averages. We're not looking for infrequent. We're looking for rare.

WAS THE TRADE LARGE IN TERMS OF DOLLARS?

Not only do we consider the size of the trade relative to volume and open interest, but we also look at it in terms of dollars. Sometimes traders pounce on a trade just because they see large volume, but they never stop to think if it's really significant. For instance, we may see 2,000 contracts trade on an option that only has 100 open interest. If the trade was executed at five cents, it only represents a $10,000 investment. We're not saying it's not interesting or that we wouldn't investigate further, but it's just not going to set off the same alarm bells as if there were more dollars being invested. On the other hand, if that same trade was for a $5 option, now it represents one million dollars, and the trade is far more interesting. Lots of people may be willing to put $10,000 down on something that has a mild chance of success over the short term. Few will invest one million dollars.

This is why the Bear Stearns trade we talked about in Chapter Three was so significant. It was only a 30-cent option, but it was 55,000 contracts, so it represented nearly $1.7 million.[90] Keep in mind that was for a strike 35 points out-of-the-money (OTM) with only ten days until expiration. That got our attention. In the world of investing, everything is relative. Yes, 10,000 shares of stock may seem like a big trade, but if it's for a penny stock it's not all that impressive. On the other hand, one share may not sound like a lot, but if it's for Berkshire Hathaway, it will cost $300,000. Trade volumes are important, but you can never forget to measure them in terms of dollars. Ultimately, that's what traders are after, so it only makes sense to include that measurement in the decision.

WAS THE TRADE TIED TO A SPREAD?

If we find that a large trade hits the tape that meets the previous qualifications, it's a great sign, but we still have more digging to do. We'll also check to see if it's tied to a spread. As you'll learn in Chapter Ten, spreads are any number of option strategies where the trader buys one option and simultaneously sells another against it. In other words, the trader will be holding both long and short contracts at the same time. One of the key reasons for entering a spread is to reduce the amount of money you must spend. For example, if the $100 call is trading for $20, but the $105 call is trading for $17, you can buy the $100 call and sell the $105 call and only spend the $3 difference to buy the spread. In exchange, your profit is limited to the difference in strikes, or $5 in this example. If the trader isn't willing to spend $20 per call, paying $3 per spread is better than nothing.

For any unusually large trades, our software will search every expiration and strike to see if it was part of a spread order. For instance, we may see 5,000 contracts traded on the March $30 call, and that may pique our interest, but upon further inspection, we might find that 5,000 contracts also traded on the March $35 call. Now it looks like the buy of the March $30 call was part of a spread. We don't often act on unusual option activity that's tied to a spread because the trader is intentionally limiting profits, and that's something that you wouldn't expect from someone trading on inside information. However, will we consider spread orders as potential unusual option activity?

Sure, but it normally only happens with high-priced stocks, say in the hundreds or thousands of dollars per share. With these price tags, the options will also be high priced, and the traders may be better off buying many spreads rather than buying a few high-priced calls. One of the main reasons for using options over shares of stock is to get significant leverage. But if the options are high priced, the leverage benefits disappear. For those times, insiders may use spread orders. In fact, Pete and I use spreads for the same reason, and that's why we teach spreads as part of our unusual option activity.

For individual traders, searching for all spread combinations can take an inordinate amount of time, but it's critical for weeding out false alarms. Further, searching for spreads isn't always as easy as just looking for another matching trade at a different strike. For instance, maybe 5,000 contracts traded at the $100 strike, but there are no other strikes with a 5,000-trade order. But if we look closer, we may find the $105 strike had an order for 2,000 contracts and another for 3,000 contracts at the same time for a total of 5,000 contracts. Now it appears that the trader received multiple fills on the $105 strike, and we'll presume it was the other side of a spread trade. The basic rule is that we'll ignore spreads if executed on cheap options, say under a couple of bucks. There's no reason for using a spread in these cases, so even if it's a large trade, we're probably going to let it go. But if the options are high priced for a short-term expiration, we'll probably consider it as a potential trade on insider information.

WAS THE TRADE TIED TO SHARES OF STOCK?

Just like any calls or puts cannot be tied to other strikes, they also can't be tied to the underlying stock. If someone trades 10,000 puts, it may look like there's pending negative news. But if the trader also bought one million shares of stock, it's most likely part of a protective put strategy. By purchasing shares and buying puts, it'll behave just like a call option. However, it's also super expensive, so it destroys the leverage. The main reason insiders turn to the option market is to gain leverage, so they're not interested in buying shares. For any dollar amount they spend on shares, they may control 10 or 20 times the number of shares by using options. If they're willing to trade on inside information, it only makes sense to make the most use of your dollars and not include shares of stock as part of the trade. Just as with spreads, our software will search through all trades at the time of the unusual option order to see if it was tied to a stock transaction. It doesn't just apply to put options. Sometimes, hedge funds will buy call options to hedge short shares of stock. If a large purchase of call options is matched to a short stock trade, it's not going to make the cut.

WAS THE TRADE SHORT TERM?

In the stock market, timing is everything, and it's especially true for unusual option activity. So another checkpoint is to see if the trade occurred in a short-term contract. That doesn't mean the trade must occur in the front month or front week expiration, but it should be close. In most cases, inside information begins circulating very close to the time of the announcement, so that's when the option buying begins. Even though companies may plan for buyouts, mergers, and acquisitions months or years in advance, there's no sense in buying the shares or options until the announcement is near. We may see an unusually large trade, but if it occurred in an expiration that's six months from now, it's probably not from inside information. Although it would warrant further checking, it's not as interesting because it's probably just a hedging transaction. If that same trade, however, occurs in an option expiring in two weeks, it's far more likely to be based on inside information.

HOW FAR IS THE STRIKE AWAY FROM THE STOCK'S PRICE?

Our computer program also checks to see how far the purchased option strike is away from the current stock price. If the stock is currently trading for $100, and we see an unusually large order for the $90 call, it's doubtful it's due to insider information. Again, when people are trading on inside information, they know the answer, so it only makes sense to get the leverage and buy the cheaper, out-of-the-money (OTM) contracts. On the other hand, if the unusual activity occurs at the $110 strike, that definitely raises suspicions. Why would somebody want to buy a short-term contract that's $10 OTM? The easy answer is that they likely know something. And if the strike is even further OTM, say the $120 strike, it gives us even more confidence that somebody must know something – and the information is expected to be powerful. As we'll talk about in option strategies, we use the unusual activity as information, but it doesn't mean we need to trade the same contract and expiration where the unusual activity is occurring. It's just the signal, and it's up to us to make adjustments. But the further OTM we see traders lining up, the more aggressive we'll get with the strategy.

WHAT'S THE IMPLIED VOLATILITY?

As you'll learn in Chapter Six, an option's implied volatility tells a lot about the trade. The implied volatility is the volatility number that's required to feed into a pricing model in order to make it equal the option's current market price. Under normal conditions, an option will usually trade at implied volatility levels that are pretty close to the stock's current volatility. When insider trading heats up, traders are willing to bid option prices to much higher levels, and that raises the option's implied volatility. If the stock is trading at 20% volatility, and the unusual option activity occurs at 25% or 30% volatility, it's not as significant. If that trade, however, occurred at 70% volatility, then it will make the top of the list.

We also must consider the implied volatility for the trade we're investigating. As mentioned previously, just because unusual option activity occurs at that $100 strike, it doesn't mean we have to trade that same strike. If the implied volatility is through the roof, we'll have to adjust our strategies. Implied volatility is also used for another reason. Once we cover the Greeks, you'll see that an option's price may move far more than suggested by an option pricing model. Our computer programs search for this, so if we see, for instance, an at-the-money option moves $1.50 for a one-dollar move in the stock, it can only be explained by implied volatility. Understanding implied volatility and the role it plays in option pricing is crucial for identifying which trades are truly unusual.

So far, we've discussed the key points we look for to *uncover* potential insider trading. We're not done yet, as we've only tackled F.R.A. of our F.R.A.M.E. method. To potentially profit from the information, we need to add M. and E. – making, managing, and exiting the position.

TRADING THE INFORMATION

Once we've located an option that's passed all the checkpoints, we're ready to place a trade. Remember, it's perfectly legal to trade on this information, as we're finding these opportunities based on publicly available information. It's information available to everyone, and that's all that matters. However, few people know where to find it – and even fewer know how to interpret the numbers. That's where the advantages lie with trading unusual option activity. We get an enormous edge, as few people are able to sort through such massive amounts of data – and make the proper interpretations. Once we find opportunities, how do we trade them?

In almost all cases, we prefer to use options because they offer higher leverage with limited risk. It's the perfect combination for speculation. As with all strategies, however, there are tradeoffs, and there may be times when the option implied volatilities are too high, and we're not able to find an option strike priced at acceptable volatility levels. Alternatively, the shares may be cheap, and we may not get a big advantage by using options. For these times, we may just buy the shares rather than the options. It's rare, but it does happen. Once we've found unusual option activity, however, there's a process we use to find the right strike and strategy.

Let's start with choosing a strike price. Most of the time, we don't trade the same strike and expiration where the unusual activity is occurring. As option traders pile in to purchase the same contract, the extrinsic value gets bid up to abnormally high levels – and sharp skews become present. No matter how good any opportunity may be, if you end up overpaying for it, it negates the entire reason for getting into the trade.

A common mistake by new traders is to assume there's something magical about the particular expiration and strike where the unusual activity has occurred. The problem is that these strikes are often overloaded with extrinsic value. Trading these strikes will sometimes put the odds against you, and in the worst case, may create a losing trade even though the stock moves in the anticipated direction. All of these options are tied to the same underlying stock, so they'll all respond, just to different degrees. Each expiration and strike has different prices, different deltas, different gammas, and different thetas. By mastering option strategies, you can usually find a better month or strike to trade.

One thing is for sure: If the option is in-the-money at expiration, it'll only be worth the intrinsic value. That's ultimately all that matters in the end.

Choosing a strategy is more art than science. Many times, I'll buy one strike and expiration while Pete may use another. Other times, we may actually use different strategies. I might buy a call, while Pete may use a vertical spread. We're acting on the same information but applying different interpretations and risk tolerances. That's okay, and every trader is free to make those adjustments, but here are some guidelines we suggest for selecting your strategies.

First, if you're able to afford the outright purchase of an option, do it. Pay the money and buy the long call or put. Inside information is potentially powerful market-moving information, so there's no sense in using other strategies that limit your gains – if you can afford it. Naturally, those dividing lines will be different points for different people. Some may not want to pay more than $3, for instance, for a speculative option trade while others may pay much more. Traders have their own guidelines, and it's up to you to find your comfort level.

However, no matter how much you may prefer to buy the outright option, there will be times that you just won't be able – or willing – to spend that much.

When you're dealing with higher-priced stocks, option prices rise. And because so many of today's stocks trade into the hundreds or even thousands of dollars, option prices can get very expensive. But when you couple that with high extrinsic value, they can get launched into the stratosphere. For example, on July 19, 2018, Amazon closed at $1,813 with one week to go until the next earnings announcement. Previously, Amazon had released several fabulous earnings reports, and the stock had moved up sharply after each one, and traders were expecting a repeat performance. The at-the-money (ATM) $1,812.50 strike was trading for $53 –

with only eight days until expiration. To avoid paying that much, traders start buying the cheaper out-of-the-money strikes, but that means the high extrinsic value eventually gets built into them too, which ends up pushing their breakeven points to outrageously high levels. On the same day, the $1,912.50 strike – 100 points out-of-the-money – was trading for $16. The stock would need to climb nearly $116 – just to break even.

Inside information can have the same effect on stocks. It doesn't matter how the intrinsic value gets pumped into the options, just as long as it's there. It doesn't matter whether people are expecting a great earnings report, a positive FDA announcement, or a buyout. The point is that the market is expecting a large move and extrinsic values get bid up to very high levels. When you're in situations like these, you can always turn to vertical spreads. No matter how expensive a stock may be, and no matter how high the implied volatility may be, you can always buy a five-dollar spread for less than $5.

Probably 90% of the time, we trade either the outright long call or long puts, or we trade vertical spreads. We'll cover these strategies in detail in upcoming chapters. If you know them well, you'll be in a great position to capitalize on unusual option activity. Traders often ask why we'd use vertical spreads when they limit profits. First, while we prefer to not limit profits, vertical spreads may provide opportunities when long calls and puts are simply too expensive. It's always better to have some position than no position.

Second, were okay with limiting profits, as that's part of a disciplined approach. If we buy an out-of-the-money vertical spread for 50 cents and it trades to its maximum value of $5, it's a 10-fold increase on our money. Things could be worse. Even if we just bought the outright options, we'd probably close them long before a 10-fold increase in profits. Vertical spreads allow you to take smaller trades that still make great returns. When Pete got into the business in 1992, the average S&P stock was $40 per share. Now it's $115 per share.

With those higher prices come higher option prices. Vertical spreads allow you to trade any of them for next to nothing, no matter what the cost, no matter what the volatility.

THE DECISION FOR CLOSING

To succeed with options, it comes down to discipline. Trading on unusual option activity that might be based on inside information is a binary event: It either happens or it doesn't. You're placing the trade in anticipation of a single announcement that's going to move the market, which is different from long-term investing. Most of the time, once the announcement is made, we'll exit the position. There are, however, exceptions, and we'll cover those once we get to strategies. The main thing to understand now is that you must develop a discipline to follow. There are, however, some decisions that always stay the same. For example, if short options are trading for nearly nothing, we'll always close them out.

When Pete and I were on the trading floors, we used to watch other traders unwilling to buy back short options that were trading for next to nothing. We never thought it was a good idea, so we developed a different discipline. Our reasoning was based on the dynamics of risk and reward. If we sell an option for one dollar, and it's now trading for five cents, the additional amount we can make going forward is just the five cents – but the liability stays the same. As the option's price shrinks, there comes a point where it just doesn't make any sense to continue holding it short. Of course, everything is relative, so if we sold the option for a higher price, we may not wait for it to fall to five cents. As a basic rule, we'll close these options if we've collected at least 85% of the premium. For instance, if we sold the option for $8, we'll buy it back for $1.20.

> **TO SUCCEED WITH OPTIONS, IT COMES DOWN TO DISCIPLINE.**

Other traders in the pits would say we were wasting money by buying back options that were nearly guaranteed to expire worthless. They have a point, as those costs do add up. There's a big difference between $1.20 and zero, especially over thousands of trades. However, there's also a big difference between guaranteed and *nearly* guaranteed. It's especially true in the biotechs where companies may be one drug or FDA announcement away from making the stock pop – or drop.

On February 29, 2000, biotech Geron Corporation (GERN) closed at $51.80.[91] Many traders in our pit were short the $55 calls with only a few days until expiration. They made the bulk of their profits – but refused to close them out. The next day, the company released promising results on a cancer vaccine, and the stock spiked 27% to close at nearly $66:

That one announcement ended careers for many. For others it launched them. One of the traders in our pit became nearly an overnight partner with Spear, Leeds & Kellogg. Less than a month before, he bought 500 contracts of the $12.50 strike back when the stock was trading under $10. He was paying nickels and dimes for the short-term options that sellers thought were *nearly* guaranteed to expire worthless. And they were right. They were nearly guaranteed. Spikes like these aren't anything new for biotechs, especially at that time, as the hunt for the cancer cure was red hot.

On May 4, 1998, EntreMed (ENMD) closed just over $12. That night, the company announced the results of a drug trial that showed large tumors on mice shrank, and eventually disappeared, when exposed to their treatment.[92] The next day, the stock opened for trading at $83, nearly 600% higher. And no, that's not a typo. The company has since changed its name to CASI Pharmaceuticals (CASI):

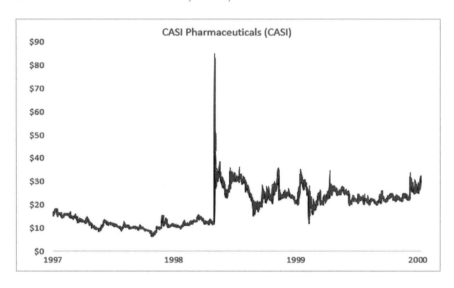

While CASI has never been optionable, it still shows how large price gaps can be, and it put many short sellers out of business. Of course, these spikes aren't just limited to biotechs, but they can be among the most dramatic. That's why we have a simple rule: Buy back short options if they're not worth much. You never know what's going to happen with the stock, but you do know you can't make much more on the option. When possible, base trading decisions on things you know, not on things you think will happen – even if they're nearly guaranteed.

Similarly, if we're using a vertical spread, a strategy we'll cover in Chapter Ten, the most you can make is the difference in strikes. If we're holding the $100/$105 vertical spread, the most it could ever be worth is the $5 difference. If it's trading for $4.50, it's not worth holding until expiration to capture the remaining 50 cents. The decisions to buy, sell, hedge, or roll have room for debate. But it never makes sense to remain in a position – whether long or short – when there's not much profit remaining.

Finding unusual option activity is easy. Interpreting it is difficult. But once we find trades that are significant, it's time to devise a strategy. If you want to join us in the hunt for unusual option activity, you must understand the tools we'll be using, and that means you must understand options. You must understand how they work, how they're priced, and how they respond to changes in the stock's price, time, and volatility. When you understand these essential concepts, you'll see why there isn't a financial asset more perfectly suited for investing, trading, speculating – or trading on inside information. That's why the option market heats up when inside information is leaked. When it does, you'll be in the right F.R.A.M.E. of mind to profit from it.

Ch. 5

LONG CALLS & PUTS

Option strategies come in different shapes and sizes, from simple to complex, but they're all created from just two building blocks – call options and put options.

When inside information is circulating the markets, it shows up in the option market long before it shows up anywhere else. However, you're not required to use options to profit from it. If it appears the news is good, you could just buy the shares, and if it looks bad you could short the shares. Using shares, however, has two big drawbacks. First, they're expensive, so you'll need a lot of money to take a position. Second, there's a tremendous amount of risk if the stock's price moves in the opposite direction for any reason. There's always other news that could overshadow the benefits of the inside information.

Options give you the best of both worlds. For very little money, you can take bullish or bearish positions. Second, they greatly limit the amount you could lose. These are the main reasons unusual option activity shows up in the option market. The *smart money* knows it's a much better place to capitalize on the information. There's an added benefit, however. Because the option market is not as widely used, it makes it an easier place for the insiders to hide. If the insiders bought the shares, the price would rise before the announcement. By purchasing options, they can continue to load up on positions without affecting the stock's price too much – and without tipping the information off to the majority of the crowd. For unusual option activity, while we occasionally buy shares of stock, we mostly buy calls and puts, but we'll also use vertical spreads and diagonal spreads, which are covered in later chapters. As you'll see they're combinations of two calls or two puts. No matter which strategies you use, you must understand calls and puts. They're the essential building blocks from which all other strategies are created.

THE LONG CALL

Probably the simplest and most common of all option strategies is the purchase of a call – especially for those who illegally trade on inside information. In stock market lingo, if you buy an asset, you're "long" the asset, so buying a call option makes you "long the call."

If you buy a call, you have the right, but not the obligation, to buy shares of stock, for a fixed price, over a given time. By purchasing a call option, you've locked in a potential purchase price but are not committed to ever buying the shares. It's simply a right to buy, and it's entirely up to you to make the decision. It's your "option" to choose. The idea may sound complicated, but you've probably used similar things to call options if you've ever been shopping during the holidays. They're actually quite easy.

I'LL TAKE A RAIN CHECK

Let's say you go to Best Buy for a Fourth of July sale to buy a television for $1,000 – only to find it's sold out. No problem, you can just come back in a few days and see if a new shipment arrived. However, that presents a risk. The sale may be over, and you'll end up paying a higher price. Is there a way you can lock in today's sale price but not be obligated to buy should prices fall?

Because of the inconvenience, the store manager may offer you a rain check, which is just a coupon saying the store will honor the sale price for a given time. In other words, you have the right to purchase the same television set for the fixed price of $1,000, perhaps over the next 30 days. However, it's not an obligation, and that means you can't lose on the deal. No matter what happens to the price during the next month, you'll never pay more than $1,000. If the price is lower when the new shipment arrives, forget about your rain check, pay the lower price, and you're ahead. However, if prices rise, simply present your rain check and pay the lower $1,000 price. The rain check ensures you won't pay more than $1,000 over the next month. It's a perfect solution.

Call options work in a similar way. Not all stocks will have listed options, but if they do, it's called an *optionable* stock. Almost every popular stock you can think of will be optionable. If a stock isn't optionable today, it could become optionable if news occurs that creates enough demand for it.

Option quotes are listed in a grid, which is called the *option chain*. If you have an option broker and type "IBM" in the quote box, you'll see the current price of IBM shares. Below that, however, you'll see an array with various expiration dates across the top and different strike prices running up and down. As you'll learn, each strike price and expiration creates different sets of risks and rewards. It's up to each trader to determine which is best. We'll discuss this in more detail once we get into strategies. Depending on the expiration date, strike, and strategy, you can select the "rain check" you'd like to own:

IBM CALL OPTIONS				
STRIKE	JANUARY	FEBRUARY	MARCH	APRIL
$135	15.10	15.60	16.15	16.70
$140	10.65	11.65	12.60	13.50
$145	6.65	8.00	8.75	9.60
$150	3.55	5.10	6.35	8.00

HOW MANY SHARES DOES EACH CONTRACT CONTROL?

Generally, each option contract controls 100 shares of stock, which means if you exercise your call, you'll buy 100 shares of the underlying stock. If you purchased two contracts, you'd control 200 shares, and so on. However, as markets have evolved, and investors' needs changed, so have contract sizes. Today, there are a handful of stocks that have *mini contracts*, which only control 10 shares. If these smaller contracts gain popularity, they'll eventually be offered on other optionable stocks. Regardless of the number of shares each contract controls, the mechanics are the same. For this book, we'll always assume the contract controls 100 shares of the underlying stock unless otherwise stated.

Unlike rain checks (that are handed out for free), you must pay for options. If you look at the previous table, the IBM April $150 call is trading for $8. That $8 price is called the *premium*. However, it is the price per share, and because each contract controls 100 shares, you must multiply it by 100, which means you'll pay a total of $800, plus a few bucks for commissions.

The IBM April $150 call gives the buyer the right, not the obligation, to buy 100 shares of IBM for the fixed $150 price at any time between today and expiration in April. That fixed price of $150 is called the *strike price*, as that's the price where the deal was "struck." It serves the same purpose as the $1,000 price written on the rain check in our Best Buy television example.

If you wish to buy shares of IBM, your purchase price is locked in at $150 through the expiration date in April. Because your purchase price remains locked in, call options make money when the underlying stock rises. Buying calls is therefore a *bullish* strategy.

Remember, you're not required to ever buy the shares – even if you're trying to collect a profit. It's a right, not an obligation. If you choose to use your call option to buy the shares, just give your broker the instructions, which is called *exercising* your option. It's easy to do. Just click a few buttons on your broker's platform, and the next day you'll own 100 shares, and your account will be debited for $150 per share, or $15,000 – no matter how high the actual shares of IBM may be trading. Because the strike price is the price you'll pay upon exercise, it's also called the *exercise price*. If you hear the terms strike price or exercise price, they mean the same thing, and sometimes we'll flip back and forth between the two terms. Once you understand the basics of call options, you'll see that holding a call option is similar to holding a rain check. The difference is that rain checks are handed out for free, but call options must be purchased.

TOTAL CONTRACT VALUE

Once you know that each contract controls 100 shares of stock, you can easily figure out the *total contract value*, which is just the amount of dollars the contract controls. If you own one IBM $150 call that controls 100 shares, the total contract value is 100 shares at $150 per share, or $15,000. In other words, if you exercise the contract, you'd pay $15,000 to receive 100 shares of IBM. Because of this, the total contract value is also called the *exercise value*, as it represents the total dollars you'd pay to exercise the option. Even though most traders never exercise their options, the total contract value is an important concept, as it shows the amount you're not spending to control shares of stock. For example, if IBM is trading for $150, you could buy the shares for $15,000 right now. Alternatively, you could buy the $150 call, controlling the same number of shares, for $800. You're effectively borrowing $15,000 between today and expiration. If you exercise the contract to buy the shares, you'll spend $15,000 at expiration – not today. Call options therefore provide a special kind of leverage not seen in the stock market, as you're mathematically borrowing money without actually borrowing anything.

WHEN DO OPTIONS EXPIRE?

Unlike shares of stock, all options have an expiration date, and after that date, you can no longer buy, sell, or exercise your contracts. One of the confusing things about expiration dates is that stock options technically expire on Saturday following the third Friday of the expiration month. However, Saturday is included as part of the legal definition so that the contract is valid for clearing purposes only. As a retail investor, the date to pay attention to is the last trading day, which is the third Friday of the expiration month. Because of this, you may hear traders talk about "expiration Friday" to distinguish it from the true contract expiration of Saturday. It's an important distinction since some trading platforms will show the option expiring on Saturday while others show Friday. Always remember that the last day to do anything is the third Friday of the expiration month. If that day lands on a holiday, the last trading day will usually be one day earlier, but your broker's platform will always show you the last day to trade. The third Friday seems like an odd date to hold a standardized expiration, but it's the one day of the month that corresponds to the fewest holidays or other events that would interfere with the expiration date.

Conventional option contracts are valid for up to nine months, but in 1990, the Chicago Board Options Exchange (CBOE) listed Long-Term Equity Anticipation Securities, or LEAPS, which are contracts lasting up to three years. And of course, there'll be a host of expiration dates in between.

In 2005, the CBOE listed *Weekly* options, which begin trading on Thursday and expire the following Friday. Most of the popular stocks will list Weekly options, which means investors may have 52 expirations each year. For any weeks where a standard expiration would occur on the same Friday as a Weekly, only the standard contract will trade. In other words, you'll never have two different contracts expiring on the same date.

Some options, such as many index options, expire on Wednesday. Regardless of the contract you're trading, your broker's platform will clearly show the expiration date. The most important point to understand is that there is never anything you can do on Saturday, no matter what the platform may say. The expiration months are determined by the exchanges through a rather convoluted process, which is called the *expiration cycle*. It's not necessary to cover the process, but just realize that each optionable stock may have different expiration months available. However, one thing all optionable stocks have in common is that they'll list the current month and the following month, which is called the near-term contract. If it's currently March, and the March contract hasn't expired, you'll see March and April expirations for every optionable stock. The remaining expirations depend on the expiration cycle and whether it has Weeklys or LEAPS. The main point to understand is that different stocks may have different expiration months. When you're looking in your brokerage platform, or websites showing different option quotes, what you see is what you get.

STRIKE PRICES AND DOLLAR INCREMENTS

For any given expiration month, you'll see many strike prices listed. In our previous example, we assumed you bought the IBM April $150 call. However, there will be many different strikes to choose from than we showed in the previous table.

For example, the current 30-day option on IBM has 30 different strikes ranging from $125 to $170. However, for that same expiration date, Amazon.com has over 100 strikes ranging from $1250 to $1860. The reason for the big difference is that Amazon is more volatile, which means its price can move greater distances – up or down – over the same time. However, if any stock's price ever closes below the lowest listed strike or above the highest listed strike before expiration, the exchanges will roll out new strikes. The range of strikes may adjust over time.

Different stocks may also have different strike-price increments. Stocks priced below $50 will generally trade in $2.50 increments, so you may see strikes of $30, $32.50, $35, and so on. On the other hand, stocks priced between $50 and $200 will usually trade in $5 increments while any stocks priced above $200 normally trade in $10 increments. As always, there are exceptions to the rules, and you may see some stocks, especially with short-term expirations, trade in 50-cent or one-dollar increments. Just as with expiration dates, what you see is what you get.

When we get into strategies, we'll explain why you may wish to choose one strike over another. For now, don't think of any strike as better than another. Instead, think of each as a different tool. Each strike and expiration date has benefits and drawbacks, and it's up to you to figure out which tool is best for the job. You may select the April $150 call while another trader chooses the March $120 call, and both could be justified in their decisions. It's not a question of right or wrong. It's a question of which combination offers the best set of risks and rewards for you. When we get to strategies, we'll give you some tips and guidelines on choosing your strikes.

STANDARDIZED CONTRACTS

Rain checks are flexible, and the terms can be completely negotiated by you and the store manager. He can make the purchase price and expiration date anything he wishes. If the television is on sale for $1,000, he can write that amount on the rain check. If it was $999.99, no problem, just write that number instead. He's also free to make it good for any number of days agreeable to both of you. Rain checks are privately negotiated and fully customizable. In the option market, however, the terms aren't so flexible. Instead, options are *standardized* contracts, and each conforms to a limited number of terms. That's why there's only so many strike prices or expiration dates from which to choose. Think of a standardized contract like the "cookie cutter" contracts you may see at an office supply store. They're generic, and the user fills in blanks for things like buyer's name, price, purchase date, and other basic information. The legal jargon remains the same. Option contracts work the same way. You can select different expirations and strike prices, but the rules on expiration, exercising, contract size, and other mechanics remain the same. The only thing the market decides is price.

While standardization creates limitations, it also creates benefits. The big benefit is that it makes the contracts easily exchangeable, or fungible, as it's called in financial terms. That's just a fancy way to say my 100 shares of IBM are identical to yours. We could swap certificates, and it wouldn't make a bit of difference to either of us, any more than if we exchanged $20 bills. My IBM April $150 call is identical to yours regardless of where or when it was purchased. Because they're the same, we can easily buy and sell them with other traders. If you own the IBM April $150 call and want to sell it to collect your profits, you don't need to sell it back to the person you bought it from. You can sell it to anyone who wants to buy that contract. While standardized contracts have limitations, they're powerful because of the speed and ease at which they can be bought and sold.

THE LONG PUT

Now that you understand call options, put options will be easy. Put options work much like call options, but they give you the right to *sell* shares of stock, at a fixed price, over a given time. Notice the definition is identical to that of a call option except the put option allows you to sell shares rather than buy. New traders make the mistake of thinking that put options are the opposite of call options, but they're far more alike than opposite. In fact, the only difference is that put options make money if the stock price falls while call options make money if the stock price rises. All other rules regarding the contracts are the same. We tell traders to think of calls and puts as northbound and southbound lanes of a highway. The lanes move in opposite directions, but other than that difference, all the exits, speed limits, and other rules are identical. The two opposing lanes have far more similarities than differences. Think of puts as being more like calls rather than opposite.

While call options are like rain checks, put options are comparable to insurance policies. For example, if you have an auto insurance policy, you're not required to use it – even if your car is damaged. You have the right to choose. On the other hand, if your car is totaled in a hurricane, you have the right to "sell" your car back to the insurance company and collect cash in exchange.

To understand how put options work, let's say you own 100 shares of IBM and buy the IBM April $150 put. You're long the put. At any time between now and expiration, you have the right, not the obligation, to sell your shares and receive the $150 strike price. If IBM's price rises at expiration, your put expires worthless, and you could sell your shares in the open market and receive a higher price. On the other hand, if IBM's price falls below $150, you could exercise your put option and receive $150 per share, or $15,000, for your 100 shares. The put option ensures you cannot receive less than $15,000 for your shares at expiration, and that's what makes it like an insurance policy. Put options make money when the stock price falls because you're locking in a price to sell. The further the stock price falls, the more valuable the put becomes.

Of course, you're not required to buy shares of stock in order to buy a put. Instead, you could just buy the put, and it will gain value as the stock price falls. Buying put options is therefore a *bearish* strategy. At a later time, you could sell it in the open market for a profit and exit from the contract. The idea behind calls and puts is exactly the same. Both are locking in a price today over a designated period of time. For calls, you're locking in the price to buy. For puts, you're locking in the price to sell. Call option prices rise when the underlying stock price rises, while put option prices rise as the underlying stock price falls. The directions are different, but the mechanics are identical.

INTRINSIC & EXTRINSIC VALUES

Whether you buy calls or puts, you must pay for them, and the price you pay is called the premium. It's now time to take the next

step in understanding options and strategies by realizing that all
option premiums can be broken down into two parts – intrinsic
value and extrinsic value. When new traders first learn about
these two values, they sometimes complain that it's a mindless
mathematical exercise. Who cares that we can divide the premium
into two parts? Isn't it enough to know the total price?

Intrinsic and extrinsic values make *all* the difference in selecting
strategies. They are the essence of strategies. All option
strategies make use of intrinsic value or extrinsic value – and
sometimes both. To find the right strategy, you need to know
where the value's coming from. Otherwise, you may end up with
a strategy that looks like a great deal, only to find it's not what
you thought. It's an easy trap to fall into if you're focusing on
the wrong value.

Think of it like the check you receive after lunch. The total
charged to your credit card may be $30, but it's not just the price
of the chicken salad you ordered. It also includes tax. The $30
total price can be broken down into two parts: To you, the $30
price mattered most. To your accountant, it was the tax. Each
of you has different needs, so each is concerned with a different
portion of the total check.

That's how you must think of option prices. You're quoted a
single price, but it's really the combination of two different
prices – intrinsic value and extrinsic value. While these are
critical concepts for all strategies, you'll find out later they're
the difference between life or
death when devising strategies
for unusual option activity.
Ok, maybe not that severe, but
certainly the difference between
profit and loss. Your broker's
platform will show these two
values to you, and they will

> **INTRINSIC AND EXTRINSIC VALUES MAKE *ALL* THE DIFFERENCE IN SELECTING STRATEGIES.**

change over time, but to interpret them, it helps to know how the values are calculated.

Always start by finding the intrinsic value, as you need that value to figure out the extrinsic value. No option trader or pricing model in the world can figure out the extrinsic value first. Don't bother trying. The amount of intrinsic value can only be found by knowing the current stock price and the strike price. The easiest way to figure out if an option has intrinsic value is to think of the "immediate benefit" being conveyed in the option. For instance, if you own a $150 call and the stock is trading for $155, the option has $5 of intrinsic value. Because you have the right to pay $150 with the stock at $155, there's an immediate $5 benefit being conveyed in the option. If the stock price rises to $160, the $150 call has $10 of intrinsic value. For call options, all strike prices *below* the current stock price have intrinsic value because they give you the right to pay less than the stock is currently worth. The amount of intrinsic value is just the difference between the strike and stock price.

The only thing that can change an option's intrinsic value is the stock's price. If IBM rises one dollar to $161, the intrinsic value rises one dollar to $11. If IBM drops one dollar to $159, the intrinsic value falls one dollar to $9. As the stock price changes, so does the intrinsic value. Because there's no theoretical limit on how high a stock's price can rise, there's no limit on how much intrinsic value a call option can have. One of the keys to understanding options is that all option prices must always reflect all intrinsic value, if any is present.

Put options work the same way – but in the opposite direction. They'll have intrinsic value if the stock price falls below the strike. If you own the IBM $150 put when the stock is trading for $145, that put has $5 worth of intrinsic value. Again, think about the "immediate benefit" conveyed in the contract. The $150 put gives you the right to sell shares for $150 that are only worth

$145 – that's a $5 benefit – so the put has $5 of intrinsic value. If IBM's price drops one more dollar to $144, the $150 put now has $6 of intrinsic value. For put options, all strike prices *above* the current stock price have intrinsic value because they all give you the right to sell shares at a higher price than the stock is currently worth. Just as with calls, a put option's intrinsic value rises and falls with changes in the stock's price. The further the stock price falls, the more intrinsic value your put option contains. Unlike call options, however, put options have a theoretical limit on the amount of intrinsic value, as a stock's price can't fall below zero. If you bought the $150 put, the most intrinsic value it could ever have is $150, and that would only happen if the stock's price was zero. Intrinsic value is always the relationship between the option's strike and the current stock price.

EXTRINSIC VALUE: WHAT'S LEFT OVER

Once you calculate an option's intrinsic value, the extrinsic value is easy. It's the amount that's left over. Let's say IBM is trading for $155, but the $150 call is currently trading for $6. The call has $5 worth of intrinsic value, but it's trading for $6. There's one additional dollar over and above the intrinsic value. That's the extrinsic value.

This $150 call option has $5 of intrinsic value and $1 of extrinsic value. An interesting property of options is that as the intrinsic value increases, the extrinsic value decreases. Let's say IBM rises to $156, and the $150 call is now trading for $6.70. The call increased the intrinsic value to $6 but decreased the extrinsic value to 70 cents. The further the stock climbs, the more the intrinsic value will rise, and the extrinsic value will fall.

Not all options have intrinsic value. If there's no immediate benefit conveyed in the option, there's no intrinsic value. For those strikes, the option's entire price is made up of extrinsic value. For call options, all strikes above the current stock price have no intrinsic value. For puts, all strikes below the current stock price have no intrinsic value.

However, just because an option has no intrinsic value doesn't mean it has no price. Traders are willing to pay for them if time remains on the option because there's always a chance it could generate intrinsic value in the future. Because extrinsic value is present only because time remains, you'll often hear the extrinsic value called *time value*. Let's say IBM is trading for $150, and the $155 call is trading for $4. This call has no intrinsic value because it's giving you the right to buy the shares for more than they're currently worth. That's not an immediate benefit, so the call has no intrinsic value, and the entire $4 cost is made up of extrinsic value. If the $145 put is trading for $3.50, it also has no intrinsic value, as it's giving you the right to sell shares for less than they're currently worth. That's not an immediate benefit, so there's no intrinsic value, and that means the $3.50 cost is made up entirely of extrinsic value.

Any time you see an option trading for intrinsic value and no extrinsic value, it's trading at *parity*, which is just a fancy term meaning the call option is equivalent to shares of stock, or the put option is equivalent to short shares of stock. If IBM is $150 and the $140 call is trading for $10, it has $10 of intrinsic value and no extrinsic value, so it's trading at parity.

TIME DECAY

Prior to expiration, all options will have extrinsic value. It may be a lot, or it may be a tiny amount. Because the extrinsic value is zero at expiration, a portion of the option's price will wilt away with the passing of each day.

For example, if you paid $6 for the IBM $150 call, but the stock is $155 at expiration, the $150 call is worth exactly the $5 intrinsic value. Even though you paid $6 for the call, you can only sell it for the current $5 price. You lost $1, or 17% just from the passage of time. Because a portion of the option's price – the extrinsic value – decays over time, options experience *time decay*. That means some or all of your option's price will disappear each day as you get closer to expiration. *However, the only portion of an option's price that's decayable is the extrinsic value.* You do not lose intrinsic value from the passage of time. Could you lose the entire $6? Yes, but only if the stock price closes at $150 or below on expiration day.

On the other hand, let's say you bought a $155 call for $3. With the stock at $150, there's no intrinsic value, so that option's price is all extrinsic value. If the stock price closes at or below the $155 strike at expiration, you'll lose 100% of the price paid. When you bought the option, it was all extrinsic value, and at expiration, it all disappears. The only way it could have made money is if it generated intrinsic value. The stock price would have to climb above the $155 strike. What about put options?

Remember, they work just like call options but in the opposite direction, so they retain intrinsic value only if the stock price falls below the strike at expiration. If you bought the IBM $150 put for $6, but the stock closed at $145 at expiration, the put has $5 of intrinsic value, so that's all it's worth. Because you paid $6, you lost one dollar's worth of value, or 17%, from the passage of time. Instead, if you bought the $145 put for $2 and the stock closed at any price above $145, you lost the entire $2 premium paid. The only way this put could be worth anything at expiration is if the stock price fell below $145.

THE ONLY PORTION OF AN OPTION'S PRICE THAT'S DECAYABLE IS THE EXTRINSIC VALUE.

Time decay isn't necessarily bad. You can think of it as the price of the insurance policy. For calls, it's the price you pay to guarantee you can't take losses below the strike. For puts, it's the price to pay to guarantee you won't take losses above the strike. Extrinsic value, like intrinsic value, is a trader's tool. Depending on the strategy, you must manage both values. Sometimes you'll want more extrinsic value, but that means you must accept more time decay as a cost. How do you control the amount of extrinsic value you're paying?

By changing to different strikes, you can alter the amount of time decay that will affect your option. Remember, no option strike or expiration is better than another. Instead, they're tradeoffs in risk and reward. Time decay is one of the tradeoffs. Depending on your needs, you may want an option rich with intrinsic value while other times you may need one loaded with extrinsic value. Part of the trick to making any strategy work is to properly identify the intrinsic and extrinsic values. If you don't, you may find that the strategy lost money – even though the stock performed exactly as you thought.

GETTING YOUR MONEY BACK: THE BREAKEVEN PRICE

We just showed that as time passes, your option's price decays a little bit. The extrinsic value is the maximum amount an option can lose from the passage of time. However, if the stock's price climbs above the strike price, the option gains intrinsic value. Therefore, for your option to make money, you need it to gain more intrinsic value than it loses in extrinsic value. A simple calculation called the *breakeven price*, helps traders see just how high the stock needs to climb by expiration in order to get their money back. For call options, just add the option's price to the strike price. For puts, subtract the option's price from the strike price.

For example, if you bought the $150 call for $6, your expiration breakeven point is the $150 strike + $6 cost, or $156. That means the stock price must be $156 at expiration just to get your money back. With the stock at $156 at expiration, the $150 call would be worth exactly $6 and you'd just break even. On the other hand, if you paid $8 for that same strike, you'd need the stock to climb above $158 by expiration before you'd break even. The more extrinsic value, the more stock price movement you need before you'll earn a profit.

On the other hand, if you bought the $150 put for $6, your breakeven point is the $150 strike - $6 cost, or $144. If the stock falls to $144, the $150 put is worth $6 of intrinsic value, and you just broke even. The breakeven price shows that options are a race against time. For call options, you don't just need the stock price to rise. You need it to rise far enough to offset the loss of extrinsic value. Remember, however, each option strike is a tool. Depending on the strikes chosen, you'll get different amounts of intrinsic and extrinsic value. For example, with the stock at $150, the $130 call may be trading for $21, which makes the breakeven price $151, just $1 above the current stock price – and much lower than the $158 breakeven price of the $150 strike. For that benefit, you had to pay the $21 price.

Any time you have an option trading at parity, its breakeven price will be equal to the current stock's price. If the IBM $140 call is trading for $10, its breakeven price is $150 – the same price as the stock. At that point, it's no longer an option – it's behaving like shares of stock. If the IBM $155 put is trading for $5, its breakeven price is $150, again the same as the current stock price. It's trading at parity, so it's behaving like short shares of stock. Options rarely trade at parity unless they're close to expiration.

MONEYNESS: CLASSIFICATIONS MADE EASY

To make things easy with strategies, traders classify all options into one of three categories: in-the-money (ITM), at-the-money (ATM), and out-of-the-money (OTM). Now that you understand intrinsic and extrinsic values, these terms will be easy. First, any option that has intrinsic value is an ITM option. It's easy to remember: Just associate word IN-trinsic with "in" the money. If an option isn't ITM, it's OTM. The ATM strike is the one whose strike matches the current stock price. An ATM option has no intrinsic value, so technically it's OTM. However, we distinguish it as many option strategies call for a strike that's closest to the current stock price, and it's just easier to say the ATM option. However, in practice, it's nearly impossible to find an option strike that exactly matches the current stock price, so the ATM option may technically be slightly ITM or slightly OTM.

For example, let's say IBM is trading for $151, the $150 call would be the ATM strike, even though it's technically $1 ITM. It's the strike that's closest to the current stock price, so we call it the ATM strike. The $145 call would be ITM by $6. The $140 call is $11 ITM. On the other hand, the $155 call is $4 OTM. Let's try some examples with puts.

If IBM is $151, the $150 put would be the ATM put, even though it's technically $1 OTM. The $155 put would be $4 ITM, and the $145 put is $6 OTM.

Option classifications of ITM, ATM, and OTM, are called an option's *moneyness*. They're just simple ways of describing an option's strike in relation to the current stock price, and they make strategies easier to understand. At-the-money options have the greatest amount of extrinsic value, which means they also experience the greatest amount of time decay. Remember, that's not necessarily bad. Sometimes you want the ATM. Other times you don't. The table below shows some call and put prices with the stock at $100. The $100 strike in the center (bold) is the ATM strike. The shaded boxes are ITM while the others are OTM. Notice that the $100 ATM strike always has the most amount of extrinsic value, and the extrinsic values decrease as you move away – up or down – from the ATM strike:

STOCK = $100						
STRIKE	CALL PRICE	INTRINSIC VALUE	EXTRINSIC VALUE	PUT PRICE	INTRINSIC VALUE	EXTRINSIC VALUE
$90	10.22	10	0.22	0.06	0	0.06
$95	5.70	5	0.70	0.53	0	0.53
$100	2.37	0	2.37	2.21	0	2.21
$105	0.68	0	0.68	5.54	5	0.54
$110	0.13	0	0.13	10.03	10	0.03

OPTION VALUES AT EXPIRATION

New traders often hear that all options expire worthless. It seems to make sense because the option has expired, and if it's no longer alive, it must be worthless. However, any intrinsic value remains with the option at expiration. If you own the IBM $150 call and the stock closes at $155 at expiration, your option is worth exactly $5 going into the closing bell. You'd want to be sure to sell it before the market closes, unless you're going to exercise the call and buy the shares. All extrinsic value, however, does disappear at expiration. No matter how much extrinsic value was on an option when you bought it, it will be zero at expiration. Keeping these points in mind, option prices are easy to figure out at expiration: If they're ITM, they're worth their intrinsic value. If they're OTM, they're worthless.

OPTION SELLERS: THE SHORT CONTRACT

Up to this point, we've covered the long call and the long put – traders who buy options. But where do options come from? Just as with shares of stock, for every buyer there must be a seller. The only reason you can buy an option – whether call or put – is because another trader sold it to you. The buyer is *long* the contract while the seller is *short* the contract. Sometimes you'll hear the seller called the *writer*, which is a term borrowed from the insurance field. If you buy auto insurance, your agent, or the seller, *writes* the policy.

As option traders, there are only two things you can do: You can buy an option, or you can sell an option. Because there are two types of options – calls and puts – there are ultimately four basic positions: 1) long call, 2) short call, 3) long put, 4) short put. Every option strategy in the world is created from these four basic positions. You may hear some complicated sounding strategies, such as a short iron condor, broken-wing butterfly, or double diagonal spread, but when you break them down, they're nothing but combinations of long or short calls and puts.

Options are therefore created out of thin air. It's a similar process as trying to find a friend to bet with on an upcoming football game. If the Chicago Bears are playing the Denver Broncos and you want to bet $10 the Bears will win, the only way you can do that is to find another person who's willing to take the other side of the bet. You need a seller. If you find someone, a bet is created, and this process can go on indefinitely.

The stock market works differently. There, a company issues a fixed number of physical certificates, or shares, that are circulated in the open market. Options, however, have no certificates. Instead, the only way you can create an option contract is for a buyer and seller to agree on a price. The option exchanges just make it easier to match buyers and sellers. What happens if you sell an option?

Option buyers have rights, but option sellers have obligations. Once you understand the buyer's rights, the seller's obligations become easy to figure out, as the seller is just on the opposite side of the deal. For instance, if you buy a call option, you have the right to buy 100 shares. Therefore, if you sell a call option, you have the obligation to sell 100 shares. You're just on the opposite side of the trade.

If you buy a put option, you have the right to sell 100 shares. Therefore, if you sell a put, you have the obligation to buy 100 shares. Both traders can't be buyers, and both can't be sellers. Both can't have rights, and both can't have obligations. Instead, one side has rights, while the other has obligations. It's the only arrangement that allows the contract to work. For any option transaction, the buyer pays a fee to get some type of right. The seller receives that money in exchange for accepting an obligation:

	CALL	PUT
BUYER	RIGHT TO BUY	RIGHT TO SELL
SELLER	OBLIGATION TO SELL	OBLIGATION TO BUY

It's important to understand that as an option seller, you really have a *potential* obligation. It's up to the option buyer to exercise the contract. If that happens, you'll get a notice from your broker, which just shows up in your account the following day. These notices from your broker are called *assignments*.

For instance, if you sold an IBM $150 call, you may get an assignment notice from your broker saying you have sold 100 shares of stock from your account. In exchange, you received the $150 strike price per share in cash, or $15,000 cash. It all happens automatically. On the other hand, if you sold a $150 put, you may receive a notice from your broker saying you've been assigned and have purchased 100 shares of the underlying stock for $150 per share. Your account will show you're long the stock and your cash has been debited for $15,000. The long position has the right to exercise, but short positions will get assigned only if the long position exercises. The short option holders therefore have a potential obligation, as they can't force an option assignment.

You can't call your broker and say, "I'd like to be assigned on my option now." It's up to the long position to exercise, and if that happens, then you have the obligation to deliver.

At the most basic level, options are a market of rights versus obligations. You're either spending money to get a right, or you're receiving money to accept an obligation. However, don't think that obligations are bad. If you've ever traded shares of stock, you've placed orders to buy or sell, and those were legal obligations too. Instead, they were necessary transactions to create profits by buying low and selling high. However, in the stock market, you never received cash for accepting obligations. In the option market, you do. Depending on your needs, sometimes you'll want rights to do something, and other times you'll want cash for accepting an obligation. There is no good or bad, right or wrong, better or worse. Instead, long and short options are like chess pieces that can be maneuvered to create strategies that are far more efficient, safe, and rewarding at accomplishing your financial goals.

LONG AND SHORT: WHO'S ON FIRST?

The terms long and short can get confusing because traders use them for two different definitions: First, they can describe whether you have a right or obligation – did you buy or sell the option? Second, they can be used to describe the outlook – are you bullish or bearish?

For example, if you buy a call or put, you're long those options. In this sense, "long" just means you paid money to have some type of right. On the other hand, you could have sold the call or put, which would make you the writer, and you'd have obligations. You'd be "short" these options. Long and short can be used to describe whether you bought or sold the option.

However, the terms "long position" and "short position" can also be used to describe your outlook – whether you're bullish or bearish. A long position means you're poised to make money if the underlying stock price rises. A short position means you'll profit if the underlying price falls. Why are they confusing?

If you bought a put option, you're long the put, but you have a short position – you want the stock price to fall. If someone asks you how you're positioned, you should say "short," but that doesn't mean you're short puts. You're long puts, but it's creating a short position. We know, it's beginning to sound like Abbott and Costello: "Who's on first, what's on second, I don't know is on third." For option traders, you do need to know.

In the movie *The Big Short*, an unsettling account of the 2007-2008 housing credit crisis, several firms were convinced the housing market would collapse, so to profit from that outlook, they dumped a lot of money into short positions – a big short. However, they did it by purchasing credit default swaps – a long contract. The key words are "position" and "contract." If someone asks how you're positioned, think bullish or bearish. If they ask whether you bought or sold the option, think long or short. Abbott and Costello couldn't have come up with better terms.

OPENING AND CLOSING ORDERS

Whenever you place an option order, you must designate whether it's an opening or closing transaction. Most of today's platforms will do this for you automatically, but you still need to understand what it's telling you. It's also a good backup check to be sure the order is entered correctly.

An opening order means you're either initiating a position or adding to the size of an existing position. Closing transactions are just the opposite. You're either reducing the size of an existing position or closing it out entirely. For example, let's say you have no Microsoft August $100 calls in your account. If you place an order to buy these calls, regardless of how many, it's an opening order. If you placed an order to buy five calls, your broker's platform would show the order like this:

Buy 5 Microsoft August $100 calls (to open)

It's an opening order because you've gone from zero to five. It was an initiating trade. Later, let's say you decide to buy two more of the same calls. It will also be an opening order because you've increased the size of your current position from five to seven. At another time, you wish to get out of some of these contracts, so you place an order to sell four. The order would look like this:

Sell 4 Microsoft August $100 call (to close)

It's a closing transaction because you're reducing the size of an existing position. You had seven, sold four, so now your account would show you're long three of these calls. Finally, if you wish to exit entirely, you could close out by selling three more contracts, which would also be a closing transaction since you're exiting entirely. Once it executes, you'll have no more of these calls in your account.

Understanding an opening or closing transaction is important for two reasons: First, some brokers still require that you select the type of trade from a dropdown menu. If you choose *open* when you meant *close*, you'll increase your position, not decrease it. You need to understand how to place the order. Second, it's only the opening trades that have rights or obligations, not the closing ones. For example, if you place an order to buy one Microsoft August $100 call to open, you have the right to buy the shares of Microsoft for $100 per share. However, if you later place an order to "sell to close," it's not a short position. You don't have the obligation to sell shares for $100 – even though you sold a call. The reason is that you sold to close, not to open.

Conversely, if you initially sold the Microsoft August $100 call to open, you'd have a true short call. You'd have the obligation to sell 100 shares for $100 per share. But if you later "buy to close," you don't have the right to buy 100 shares of Microsoft – even though you bought the call. That was a closing transaction.

Whenever you hear traders talk about rights or obligations, long and short contracts, or long or short positions, they're always referring to those traders who have open positions. Opening transactions get you into the market. Closing transactions take you out.

OPEN INTEREST

Traders new to options find it odd that we must specify whether we're opening or closing. Why do we need to do this for options but not shares of stock?

The reason is that options are derivatives, and they're not actual certificates floating around in the market like shares of stock. Instead, they're created whenever a buyer and seller agree on a price. To track the number of contracts currently open for delivery, the *open interest* is tracked by the Options Clearing Corporation, or OCC, an organization we'll cover shortly. Open interest is reported one time each day on the opening bell. During the day, trades may or may not affect the open interest, but you won't know what the new number is until tomorrow's opening bell. How does open interest change?

When a contract is first listed, the open interest is zero because no trades have taken place. As orders are placed, open interest will either increase or decrease depending on whether the trades are opening or closing transactions. Open interest only increases if the buyer *and* seller are placing opening orders and entering into the contracts. Open interest will decrease if both traders are entering closing orders and exiting from the contracts. And if one trader is opening while the other is closing, the trade has no effect on open interest as outlined below:

BUYER	SELLER	EFFECT ON OPEN INTEREST
BUY TO OPEN	SELL TO OPEN	INCREASE
BUY TO CLOSE	SELL TO CLOSE	DECREASE
BUY TO OPEN (CLOSE)	SELL TO CLOSE (OPEN)	NO CHANGE

Open interest begins at zero and usually peaks near the halfway point of the contract's life. After that, you'll normally see open interest begin to decline. It might decline to zero, but statistically, about 10% of all contracts are exercised, so you may see a small amount of open interest remaining at expiration.

Open interest is important to understand, as it's one of the keys we use to see if an option trade qualifies as unusual activity, as covered in Chapter Four. However, open interest is usually defined as a measure of liquidity, which is true, but nearly all education firms teach that you should avoid contracts with little to no open interest. That's false. Why?

Market makers and Electronic Communication Networks (ECNs) are always standing by ready, willing, and able to buy and sell contracts. If the March $50 calls currently have no open interest, but the current quotes are good for at least 100 contracts, it doesn't make sense to say there's no liquidity. As long as there's an active market with bids to buy and offers to sell, it's a liquid market. As an analogy, you may not have $100 cash in your wallet right now, but that doesn't mean you have no money. A quick trip to an ATM, the swipe of a credit card, a cash transfer from a brokerage account, or even a loan from a friend can be transferred instantly through PayPal or Facebook. Store owners aren't the least bit concerned whether you have cash on you. They're just concerned with whether you can get the cash on you. Option traders should have the same view.

Remember, the only way the exchanges make money is to execute trades. If you want to buy 100 contracts, even if there's currently no open interest, you can be sure the trade will get done – and fast. Open interest is a measure of the current open contracts, not the number of contracts that could ever be traded.

It's important to keep these points in mind, as many of the strikes we'll use to capitalize on unusual option activity may have little-to-no open interest. It's done to avoid unfavorable skews, which is a topic we'll cover in Chapter Eight. Don't be fearful of strikes with low open interest. The bigger fear is that you missed a great opportunity because you thought the market couldn't create the contracts.

EXERCISING CALLS AND PUTS

Long options have the right, not the obligation, to exercise. But if you choose to exercise, here's how it works: If you exercise one call option, you'll purchase 100 shares and pay the strike price. If you exercise one $100 call, you'll receive 100 shares of the underlying stock and pay a total of $10,000, plus a couple of bucks for commissions. If you exercise five $100 calls, you'll receive 500 shares of stock and pay $50,000 plus commissions. You're not required to exercise all contracts that you own. If you own 10 call options, you're certainly free to exercise any number of them. The only thing you can't do is exercise for fewer than 100 shares (unless you own a mini contract which controls 10 shares). If you wanted to own fewer shares, say 50, you must exercise one call and immediately sell 50 shares in the open market. It's one of the many limitations of having a standardized contract.

If you exercise one $100 put, you'll sell 100 shares of the underlying stock and receive a total of $10,000 cash, minus commissions. If you don't own the shares, you'll end up selling shares you don't own, and that's a short stock position. Remember, only about 10% of traders exercise options, which means the remaining 90% are just closed in the open market. It's important to understand that the long contract can exercise for any reason at any time – even if it doesn't appear to make financial sense. Can a long position exercise an OTM contract? Yes, the long option can exercise at any time for any reason. But why would anyone do it?

EXPLAINING THE UNEXPLAINED EXERCISES

Now that you understand the basics of options exercises, let's uncover some reasons why you may see the weird, wacky, and unexplained exercises. For instance, let's say you're short a $100 call and the stock is trading under $100 going into the closing bell on expiration Friday, so you decide not to close it. Why spend the commissions, right? The stock closes at $99.90, so it looks like you're in the clear. On Monday morning, however, you find you've been assigned. What happened?

Most brokers allow traders to submit option exercises after the closing bell, usually as late as 5:30pm ET. Let's say the stock released earnings after the close and is trading for $110 in the after-hours market. The owner of the $100 call thought it expired worthless, but if he exercises, he can sell the shares for a profit. He exercises – and you get assigned.

It can happen with puts too. If you were short the $95 put and the stock closed at $100, it doesn't mean you can't get assigned. If the company released earnings and the stock is trading for $90 in after-hours trading, you're probably going to get assigned on Monday morning. However, it doesn't take big changes in the stock's price for you to get assigned on an OTM option.

Let's say a hedge fund buys 1,000 $100 call options, fully expecting to exercise them at expiration. That's 100,000 shares at $100, or $10 million worth of stock. Why buy the calls? Maybe they didn't have the cash today, or perhaps they wanted to just control the shares but get through a few earnings reports first. There are many reasons why a fund manager may buy calls even though the long-term expectation is to own the shares. At expiration, the stock is $99.90, but the fund manager is long 1,000 of these calls. They're OTM, but is it really better to just buy the shares in the open market? If there's 15 minutes until the closing bell, placing an order for 100,000 shares at market will almost surely bump the price over $100. Further, the fund will probably get multiple fills at various prices, which means it's now difficult to track the average cost basis on the shares. Instead, why not exercise the call, and get all 100,000 shares at the nice round price of $100? The point to understand is that even though an exercise may not appear to make financial sense, the trader on the other side most likely has a good reason for doing it. You may not know why, and it doesn't really matter. The thing you need to know is that the long position may exercise at any time for any reason. How can you prevent these unwanted assignments?

Close your short options on expiration day.

Get in the habit of closing any short options on expiration day. If they have intrinsic value, you'll collect the cash. If they're OTM, most brokers won't charge a commission greater than the proceeds. For example, if you buy back a short call for 10 cents ($10 total for the contract), and the broker normally charges a $7 commission, you'll only be charged $7. You won't pay anything, and you won't receive anything, so it's just the same as if the contract expired worthless. But at least you'll get something in return: You're 100% certain you won't be assigned. It's an easy habit to form, and it beats having to explain the unexplained exercise.

CAN YOU EXERCISE OPTIONS BEFORE EXPIRATION?

While you're allowed to exercise any long option at any time, it's usually not a good idea to exercise until expiration day.

For call options, there's an easy rule: If the stock isn't going to pay a dividend, it's never to your advantage to exercise the option early. If you do, you'll throw away all the extrinsic value – and end up holding shares that could lose more money than the option. For example, let's say the stock is trading for $102 and your $100 call is trading for $5. It has $2 of intrinsic value and $3 of extrinsic. If you sell the call to close, you'll collect $5. If you exercise it, however, you'll pay the $100 strike and receive shares worth $102, which gives you a $2 "paper" gain, or unrealized gain. By selling the call you received $5 for certain, but by exercising you're only up $2 on paper. Where did the $3 go?

You threw it away. You don't get to sell your call and exercise it too. You get one or the other. If you sell the call, you collect $5. If you exercise, you're up $2, so you're better off not exercising. But losing money is only part of the damage. By exercising a call early, you'll end up holding the expensive shares of stock, which may end up losing more than the call could have ever lost. By exercising early, you're throwing money away – and accepting more risk. It's not the best financial strategy. What if the stock does pay a dividend?

That's the only time it may be advantageous to exercise a call option early – maybe. Even then, you should wait as long as possible. The day the stock trades without the upcoming dividend is called the *ex-date*, and on that day, the stock's price is reduced by the dividend amount. For example, if a $100 stock pays a $1 dividend, and if the stock's ex-dividend date is today, it will open for trading at $99 – unchanged. It's unchanged because the drop wasn't due to supply and demand, but because it paid a dividend. However, if you were holding an ITM call option near expiration, it would also lose $1 because the stock's price dropped $1. By exercising early, you cancel the effect. However, that's assuming you didn't lose more extrinsic value than you gained from the dividend. As a basic rule, if the call's extrinsic value is greater than the dividend, it's not going to be advantageous to exercise early.

For example, let's say the stock will pay a one-dollar dividend tomorrow and your $100 call is trading at parity, or $10. If you don't exercise, your call will be worth $9 tomorrow. If you exercise, you'll spend $100 but receive stock worth $99, but you'll collect the dollar dividend, so you're even. Exercising a call option early for a dividend isn't necessarily done to make a gain, but to avoid the loss. However, all of this assumes you wanted to own the shares. If not, just sell the call to close and take the $10. Exercising in this case made sense because your call had no extrinsic value. But what if it was trading for $12 instead?

If you exercise early, you're collecting the dollar dividend, but throwing away $2 of extrinsic value. You're worse off by exercising – and you're holding the shares, which is always the big danger. If the stock makes a big enough drop, you would have been better off keeping the call. For those rare times you may think of exercising a call option early for the dividend, exercise it the day before the ex-date. Don't ever exercise a call option earlier than necessary, as you want to avoid holding the shares as long as possible.

There are some advanced methods you can use where you could keep the call option, and come out better than collecting the dividend, and we teach them at Market Rebellion™. However, for this book, we're focusing on strategies for unusual option activity, and exercising a call for the dividend will rarely be an issue.

Put options are a different story, assuming you're holding the shares too. If you exercise a put, you're getting rid of the shares and collecting cash. It's the opposite set of transactions from exercising a call, so it has the opposite effect. For put options, dividends are never the issue. If a stock pays a dividend, the put option's value will increase, at least theoretically. We say theoretically because the market anticipates these regular dividends, and they're already factored into the put's price. But the point is your put is not going to lose money just because a stock pays a dividend. Instead, the only time to consider exercising a put option early is if it has gone extremely deep ITM, and it looks like there's no chance the stock's price will rise above the put's strike by expiration. For example, let's say you're holding a $100 put and the stock has fallen to $70 with 30 days until expiration. If you think there's no way it will rise above the $100 strike by expiration, you might as well exercise it today and receive the cash early. The only benefit, however, is that you'll gain a little bit of interest by getting the cash into your account 30 days sooner, which by today's standards is close to nothing.

Exercising options early can make financial sense in certain situations. However, the benefits are limited. Just because you may hear someone tell you that it's advantageous to exercise a call option early to collect a dividend doesn't necessarily mean you should do it. You'll end up being a little better off by the amount of the dividend – but you're now holding the shares of stock, and that always presents the bigger risk.

THE OPTIONS CLEARING CORPORATION (OCC)

By now, you probably have a burning question: If you buy options and exercise them, how can you be sure the short contracts will follow through with their obligations and actually deliver? It seems that if you own the IBM $150 call and exercise it, but IBM is trading for $200, the short position may tell you to take a hike. When the option markets were set up, they realized this could be a potential problem, so they came up with a brilliant solution. A clearing firm called the Options Clearing Corporation, or OCC, is a highly capitalized and regulated agency that acts as a middleman to all transactions. Whether you buy or sell an option, you're really transacting with the OCC – not another trader. The OCC acts as the buyer to every seller and the seller to every buyer. That doesn't mean, however, that the OCC is placing trades with every trader in the market. Instead, if you exercise an option, the OCC randomly selects a brokerage firm that also has a trader who holds the short contract. That brokerage firm is notified by the OCC, and in return, randomly selects an individual trader who is short the same contract. It's this trader who ends up with the assignment. If you exercise an option, ultimately it will be paired with another trader. You'll never know who it is, and it doesn't matter. You just know the exercise will go through. The OCC guarantees it. Ever since its creation in 1973, not a single exercise has ever failed to go through. It's the OCC that provides efficiency – and confidence – to the option market.

AUTOMATIC EXERCISE: A HIDDEN DANGER

In most cases, the long option holder gets to decide if an option will be exercised. Whether it's a call or put, if you bought the option, it's your right to make the decision. However, the OCC has a process called *exercise by exception*, more commonly known as *automatic exercise*, and it can set a trap for unsuspecting traders. On the option's expiration date, the OCC automatically exercises any open contracts that are at least one cent ITM. It's done to speed up the clearing process. Because nearly all ITM contracts will be exercised, rather than having every option broker make requests for every ITM contract, the OCC assumes the option owners want them exercised.

However, remember that as the option buyer – whether call or put – you're never required to exercise. If, for some reason, you end up with an ITM option after the closing bell on expiration Friday and don't want to exercise it, just phone the broker and say so. Doing so, however, you'll sacrifice any intrinsic value that may be in the option. Some brokers allow traders to place these instructions as late as 5:30pm ET, so be sure to check with your broker on their policies. But the point is that you can't wait until the exercise goes through, phone the broker and say that's not what you wanted. You must place the instructions shortly after the closing bell on expiration Friday.

Here's how automatic exercise works: Let's say you own a Microsoft $100 call and the stock closes at $100.01 or higher on expiration Friday. The call will get automatically exercised and you'll own 100 shares of Microsoft on Monday morning, unless you instructed the broker otherwise. If you don't have the cash, you'll have to deposit at least 50% of the purchase price within two business days. Of course, you could choose to sell the shares on Monday morning, but there's no guarantee that the price will be what you paid.

If you own a Microsoft $100 put and the stock closes at $99.99 or lower, it will automatically get exercised, and you'll sell 100 shares of Microsoft, unless you instructed the broker otherwise. If you don't hold the shares in your account, you'll be short 100 shares on Monday morning. Why?

The exercise is always for shares of stock.

If a long put goes through automatic exercise, you must deliver shares. If they're not in your account, you'll sell shares you don't own, and that creates a short stock position.

To be clear, your options will never be automatically exercised prior to expiration. While you, as the option buyer, have the right to exercise at any time prior to expiration, the OCC will automatically exercise only on the expiration date, and only if the option is at least one cent ITM.

Here's where a trap can get sprung. Let's say you own a $100 call, and the stock is trading for $98 on expiration Friday. It's been trading there most of the day, so looks like it's going to expire worthless. Just 15 minutes before the closing bell, you take off for the beach. Unbeknownst to you, the stock rallies and closes at $100.01 or higher. On Monday morning, you're going to be the proud owner of 100 shares of stock. If the stock opens at that same price on Monday morning, it's not the worst thing to happen. You can simply sell the shares on the opening bell.

But let's say the rally was because the stock is releasing earnings before the opening bell on Monday, and speculators were betting they were going to be great. Instead, they're horrible, and the stock drops down 30%, leaving you with a large loss. The loss may even be larger than the amount you paid for the call option. An automatic exercise is the only time traders can lose more than the amount they spent on the option. That doesn't mean it's wrong when we said the maximum amount an option can lose is the amount you paid. The option can never have negative value, so the amount spent is the absolute worst you can lose. But what happens with automatic exercise is that the option gets converted into shares, and the shares can certainly lose more than the option was worth. If you have any long options that are OTM on expiration day, be sure you're watching them all the way into the closing bell. If they're OTM, they won't be automatically exercised.

Many of today's brokers, however, have some safeguards in place. For instance, if you have a long call that's ITM at expiration but don't have the cash to pay for the trade, they may block the exercise rather than creating a long position you may not be able to afford. If you have a long put that's ITM at expiration but don't own the shares, they may block the exercise rather than creating a short stock position in the account. However, these proactive measures are the exception, not the norm. Always check with your broker for specifics on their rules for automatic exercise.

We don't teach this to our traders to scare them. Instead it's to inform them. Like any field, risks and dangers are neutralized if you understand the rules. As Warren Buffett said, *"Risk comes from not knowing what you're doing."* If you understand the rules of automatic exercise, you'll never get caught with unwanted surprises.

HOW DO OPTIONS MAKE MONEY?

The basic idea of making money with options is easy, and it works the same for trading shares of stock – buy low, sell high. As the stock price climbs above the strike price, the option gains intrinsic value. However, as the stock price is rising, time is also ticking away, and each passing day decreases the option's extrinsic value a little bit. An option's price is the sum of two different forces: First, a rising stock price is driving the option's price higher while the passage of time is pushing it lower. If the underlying stock price rises sufficiently high so that it offsets the extrinsic value, your option gains value.

> *"Risk comes from not knowing what you're doing."*
>
> – Warren Buffett

However, unlike a rain check where you either "use it or lose it," you're not required to exercise a call option to make money. It's a common misconception that to profit from a call option, you must eventually exercise the option and buy the shares of stock – even if just long enough to turn around and sell the shares. Instead, the contract's price will rise as the underlying stock price rises. Rather than exercising the call and buying the shares, you could also choose to sell your contract in the open market and collect the cash.

Let's say you bought a $100 call option for $3. As the stock price rises above the strike, the call gains intrinsic value. If the stock is $105, the $100 call must be worth at least the $5 intrinsic value, but perhaps there's another dollar's worth of extrinsic value for a total of $6. At that time, you may decide to sell your call. You paid $3, sold for $6, so doubled your money – even though the stock's price only rose five percent. Why would another trader buy your call? For exactly the same reason you did – he thinks the stock's price will be rising even higher. At any time prior to expiration, you can choose to sell your call option in the open market without ever having to exercise it to buy the shares.

Put options make money in the same way except they gain intrinsic value as the underlying stock price falls. If you buy the $100 put for $3, that contract becomes more valuable as the stock price drops. That's because you have the right to sell shares for a higher price than the current market price. If the stock is $90, for example, the $100 put is worth at least the $10 intrinsic value. Just like call options, if there's any time remaining, the put option will be worth more than the intrinsic value. At that moment, you could choose to sell your put and collect your profit. You never need to exercise a call or put option to collect a profit. Instead, you can sell the option in the open market. If you sell the option for more than the price paid, you'll earn a profit. Otherwise, you'll take a loss. Just as with shares of stock, profit comes from buying low and selling high. The difference is that stock prices gain or lose value based on the performance of the company. Options gain or lose value based on the performance of the stock.

THE OPTION ADVANTAGE

Let's say it's January, IBM is trading for $150, and you believe the stock's price is poised to rise substantially during the next six months. Prior to understanding options, the only choice you had was to buy shares. If you buy 100 shares, you'll spend $15,000, which is a lot of money, and with today's market volatility, it also means you could lose a lot. Do you take the risk? Or avoid the opportunity? It's a tough decision, but that's where call options come to the rescue.

Regardless of the expiration date and strike you choose, options provide many benefits over shares of stock. Let's look at some of them.

The first benefit is limited losses. For example, if you buy the IBM June $150 call trading for $8, the most you could ever lose is $800. Had you purchased 100 shares of stock for $15,000 instead, there's no way you could guarantee $800 would be your maximum loss. Call options therefore provide a form of insurance, as they allow you to fully participate in all future stock price increases while greatly limiting your potential losses. This insurance property serves as a great form of risk management. Stock traders may spend $15,000 for the shares and think they'll exit if the position loses a certain amount, say $2,000. If the stock takes a hit, however, and losses begin to mount, it's difficult to place that sell order and lock in a guaranteed loss. Instead, traders often hang on to losses hoping to gamble their way out of a bad situation – only to watch the losses grow bigger. Hope is never a good strategy. By purchasing a call option, you know up front with 100% certainty what your maximum loss could ever be. The option won't allow you to lose more.

OPTIONS PROVIDE MANY BENEFITS OVER SHARES OF STOCK.

The second benefit is the long call provides leverage. In this example, you're controlling $15,000 worth of stock by spending only $800, and that means a better return on your investment, or ROI. If the stock rises from its current $150 price to $165 at any time during the next six months, you'll capture the $15 gain just as if you purchased the shares. However, as a stock owner, you earned $15 on a $150 investment, or 10%. On the other hand, if you paid $8 for the call, that same $15 increase represents an 88% gain. Options allow your money to work harder for any given increase in the stock's price.

The third benefit is that by only spending a small fraction of your money to control the same number of shares, options allow you diversify your portfolio. For example, if you have a $50,000 account value, you're not going to control too many different companies. Instead, you'll end up with concentrated positions – lots of money sitting in very few stocks. Options allow you to control shares of quality companies but by spending a small fraction of the stock's price. Options supercharge your performances while providing insurance against losses.

A fourth benefit is that the option will gain dollar for dollar at expiration for stock price increases. However, if the stock price falls, the option won't lose dollar for dollar. The basic reason is that the option can only lose a small, fixed amount (or $800 in this example). As the stock price falls, the option loses less and less. For stock owners, you'll gain and lose dollar for dollar with changes in the stock's price. For option traders, it means you'll make all the gains as the stock price rises – but won't participate in all the losses. That's the insurance quality of the option coming to your rescue. We'll cover these advantages in greater detail in the stock replacement strategy, but keep these points in mind if you're new to options. The option advantage can be summed up easily: ***Options give you options***.

Ch.6 THE GREEKS

To successfully trade options, you don't need to understand why things work, but you do need to understand how things work. For many of the strategies we'll be talking about, there are four essential "Greeks" every option trader must understand – delta, gamma, vega, and theta. These are four of many mathematical measurements used by option traders, which are generated by option pricing models.

They sound complicated, but they're designed to make things easier. Don't worry about the calculations, as your broker's platform will show them to you. What's important is that you know how to interpret them, as they'll be important for understanding how we select strategies for unusual option activity. Many of the decisions on which strategy, strike, and expirations to use will revolve around these Greeks. Each of the Greeks is a sensitivity measurement that shows how sensitive your option is to changes in some other variable. In most cases, they'll measure the change in your option's price.

DELTA

To understand an option's delta, it helps to understand a stock's delta first. When you own shares, your profit and losses rise and fall dollar for dollar with changes in the stock's price. If you purchased shares for $100 and the price rises to $101, you earned one dollar, and if the price falls to $99, you lost one dollar. Your profits and losses always mirror changes in the stock's price. The reason is simple: Your profits and losses are being measured by the very thing you're holding.

Options, on the other hand, don't work that way. Option prices are tied to the stock, but they're not the stock. If the stock price rises one dollar, in most cases, your call option isn't going to rise one full dollar. The reason is complex, but it's based upon how likely it is for the option to expire ITM. For example, if a $100 stock rises one dollar, you shouldn't expect the Weekly $130 call trading for five cents to rise by one dollar too. That would be too good to be true, and option strategies would be simple. Just buy the highest strike you can for nearly nothing, and it's like you're holding shares of stock. Instead, that stock could probably rise $10, and that $130 call option's price probably won't budge. Why? Because traders don't think it will expire ITM, which means it's most likely going to be worthless at expiration. If that's true, why pay a full dollar more for it just because the stock price increased? The $130 call will have very little sensitivity to changes in the stock's price.

At the other extreme, deep ITM call options will be highly

sensitive to changes in the stock's price. If the $100 stock rises one dollar, the Weekly $90 call will probably rise the bulk of that, perhaps 90 cents or more. Because the strike is so deep ITM, it has a high probability of expiring ITM, which means it will most likely be exercised into shares by someone. If it's going to be shares of stock in the future, traders will treat it like shares of stock today, or at least close to it. The reason it probably won't trade exactly like the stock is because there's still a little bit of extrinsic value remaining. If the stock rises one dollar, the intrinsic value for all ITM call options will also rise one dollar. However, the extrinsic value moves in the opposite direction, so the net effect is something less than one dollar. The $90 call will gain one dollar's worth of intrinsic value, but may lose 10 cents of extrinsic value, which means the option's price will only rise 90 cents.

To make trading decisions easier, it would be nice to know how sensitive your option's price is to changes in the stock's price, but the relationships aren't so easy to do in your head. If a $100 stock rises one dollar, how much will your six-month $90 call rise? What about the 30-day $100 call? Or the one-year $105 call? It's not so easy to figure out what your expectations should be.

Fortunately, these relationships are easy because of a mathematical formula that shows the relationship between the change in the stock's price and the expected change in an option's price. This relationship is measured by the Greek letter *delta*. If you're looking at option quotes on your broker's platform, you should see a column showing the delta:

INTERNATIONAL BUSINESS MACHS COM

▾ ◼ 151.50 -0.11   -0.07%   Ext Hrs 151.50 0.00 (0.00%) @ 16:41:19

Open	High	Low	Close	52 Week Price
152.01	152.3888	151.16	151.61	137.45 - 171.13

∿   Sep-28-18   Oct-05-18   Oct-12-18   **Oct18**   Oct-26-18   Nov-02-18   Nov-09-18

Bid	Ask	Intrinsic Value	Extrinsic Value	Delta	Gamma	Theta	Vega	Open Interest	Strikes
				Call					**Nov18 (50 days)**
17.20	17.50	16.50	0.85	0.8728	0.0126	-0.0408	0.1194	775	135
12.70	12.90	11.50	1.30	0.8168	0.0183	-0.0447	0.1512	986	140
8.55	8.75	6.50	2.15	0.7232	0.0259	-0.0488	0.1894	2.7k	145
5.20	5.35	1.50	3.775	0.5806	0.0327	-0.0512	0.2200	4.3k	150
2.82	2.88	--	2.85	0.4096	0.0342	-0.0472	0.2190	8.5k	155
1.33	1.38	--	1.355	0.2490	0.0289	-0.0365	0.1804	2.5k	160
0.58	0.62	--	0.60	0.1340	0.0198	-0.0243	0.1250	1.7k	165
0.26	0.30	--	0.28	0.0703	0.0120	-0.0154	0.0795	199	170

Source: E*TRADE. For educational purposes only. Not a trade recommendation.

While there are several definitions of delta, for our purposes in this book, the easiest is to think about delta as the *percentage change* in the option's price relative to the change in the stock's price. To make things easy, we'll give separate examples for calls and puts.

Call options have *positive* deltas, which means call option prices move in the same direction as the stock. They rise and fall with changes in the stock's price, but generally not to the same degree. The sensitivity, or delta, depends on the strike and the time to expiration.

Delta is always measured as a number between zero and one. At-the-money call options, regardless of the time to expiration, have a delta of roughly 0.50. Because each contract controls 100 shares, however, some platforms will show this is as a delta of 50, but the interpretation is always the same. It shows the *percentage change* for the option's price for the *next* price change in the underlying stock, provided that change is relatively small. The keyword in that definition is the word "next," as delta doesn't stay constant. The current delta you see on your screen only applies for the next price change in the underlying stock.

For example, let's say the stock is trading for $100, and you purchased the ATM $100 call for $3 with a delta of 50. If the stock immediately rises one dollar to $101, that option's price will increase by only 50%, or 50 cents to $3.50. It will not rise by one full dollar to $4 as new traders often suspect. On the other hand, if the stock's price fell one dollar to $99, the option's price would drop by 50% of that change and trade for about $2.50.

To make the concept easier, most options traders define delta as the change in the option's price for a one-dollar change in the stock's price. That way, delta shows by how much the option's price will change. In other words, a delta of 50 means the option will gain or lose 50 cents if the stock price immediately changes by one dollar. However, delta works for any change in the stock's price, provided the change is relatively small. If the $100 stock rose by 40 cents to $100.40, the $100 call's price would increase by 50% of that amount, or 20 cents, and trade for $3.20. It would trade for $2.80 if the stock's price fell by 40 cents. Delta, however, changes over time for a variety of reasons. The two biggest factors are the moneyness (how far the option is ITM or OTM) and time to expiration.

As a call option moves deeper ITM, its delta increases. For example, if the underlying stock is $120, the $100 call price might be $21, but the delta will no longer be anywhere near 50. It may have increased to 90. If the stock price immediately rises one dollar to $121, that call option's price will gain about

90% of that amount, or 90 cents, and rise to $21.90. As the stock price continues to climb, or as time passes, eventually the option's delta will reach the maximum level of 1.0, or 100, which means it will rise and fall dollar-for-dollar with the stock as the stock price climbs higher. At that point, it's no longer an option – it's stock. Deep ITM options are highly sensitive to changes in the stock's price. That'll be important to remember when we get to the stock replacement strategy.

Out-of-the-money options, on the other hand, have very little sensitivity to changes in the stock's price. If the stock is $100 and you buy the $120 call for one dollar, it may have a delta of only 20. If the stock price immediately rises one dollar to $101, the call's price will only increase about 20 cents to $1.20, and if the stock's price fell one dollar, it would trade for about 80 cents. If an option slips far enough OTM, it's delta will eventually reach zero, at which point the delta can't fall any lower. The stock price could continue to fall, and it wouldn't make a difference to the option's delta. Just remember that call option deltas range between zero and 100, with ATM options being about 50.

The concept to understand is that an option's sensitivity to changes in the stock's price depends on whether it's ITM, ATM, or OTM. As the stock price climbs, call options gain sensitivity, and as the stock price falls, they lose sensitivity. It rarely stays the same. The only time delta remains the same is if the call's delta is 100 and the stock continues to climb, or if an OTM call delta is zero and the stock continues to fall. But inside these extremes, deltas are always changing with each tick of the stock's price. It may not be a lot, and you may need to measure it to several decimal places to see the changes, but it's always changing. Because shares of stock always rise and fall dollar-for-dollar with itself, the underlying shares always have a delta of 1.0, or 100. It never changes.

DELTA AS A PROBABILITY

Delta also has another helpful interpretation. While not mathematically perfect, an option's delta is roughly the probability for an option to expire ITM, which is to say it'll end up with at least some intrinsic value. At-the-money options have a delta of about 50, so there's roughly a 50% chance they'll expire ITM. They behave like coin flips, and about half will expire ITM and half will expire OTM. Out-of-the-money options have low deltas, so they have a correspondingly low probability of expiring ITM. In-the-money options have high deltas, so there's a good chance they'll end up with intrinsic value. This is just one of many reasons why professional traders tend to stick with ITM options rather than the OTM options so often used by retail traders.

Delta is an important concept for option traders. For some strategies, you may want the option to mimic the shares of stock, in which case you'll buy a deep ITM call option. Other times, you may not want the option to be sensitive to changes in the stock's price, so you may lean toward ATM or OTM options. Like strategies, deltas are tools. By understanding delta, you'll get a much wider range of possibilities to choose from, and that makes the strategies more versatile than just using shares of stock alone.

DELTA FOR PUT OPTIONS

Now that you understand how call option deltas work, the idea for put options is exactly the same – just in the opposite direction. Put options have *negative* deltas, which means they behave like short shares of stock. For example, if you short 100 shares at $100, you'll earn one dollar if the stock price drops to $99, and you'll lose one dollar if it rises to $101. But you're always gaining and losing dollar-for-dollar with changes in the stock's price – just in the opposite direction. Short shares of stock, therefore, have a delta of -100. It never changes. Like call options, put options don't behave exactly like a short stock position. They'll gain value as the stock price falls and lose value as it rises, but it's rarely dollar for dollar.

At-the-money puts have a delta near -0.50, or -50 per contract. If the stock is $100 and you buy the ATM $100 put for $3, it will gain or lose about 50% of the stock's price change but the put's price will move in the opposite direction. If the stock price immediately rises one dollar, the put's price will *fall* to $2.50. Conversely, if the stock price falls one dollar to $99, that put's price will rise to $3.50. Again, negative deltas just mean the option's price change is opposite that of the stock.

As with call options, these numbers aren't limited to just one-dollar changes, but they must be relatively small in order for deltas to give accurate predictions. If the stock price immediately rises by 60 cents, the put's price would fall by 50% of that amount, or 30 cents, to $2.70, and would increase to $3.30 if the stock price fell by 60 cents. Aside from the inverse relationships, the idea behind deltas for put options is exactly the same as deltas for call options.

For strategies, think of delta as "direction." If you think the underlying stock is going to rise, you want positive deltas as part of your strategy, and if you think the price will fall, you want negative deltas. While we won't be covering them in this book, there are option strategies that profit if the stock price stays relatively quiet, as they profit strictly from the passage of time. For those strategies, you want to initiate your positions as *delta neutral*, or to have deltas close to zero. But the point to understand is that the delta of your position tells the direction you need the stock price to move in order to profit. This is an important concept, as some strategies can have deltas that change depending on the stock's price. Your position may have positive deltas today but change to negative deltas next week. Even though you initiated the position with positive deltas, if it's currently negative, you'd need the stock price to fall to generate profits. Delta tells the necessary direction to generate gains. The level of the delta shows by how much your option's price will change if the stock moves in that direction.

Now, here's where things get tricky with puts: ITM put options have deltas *less* than -50, say -80 and eventually reaching -100 if the stock price falls far enough. Most people think -80 is a bigger number, but it's not. The sensitivity is greater, but -80 is smaller than -50. The only way to move from -50 to -80 is to *subtract*, and that means the numbers are getting smaller. For calls and puts, deltas increase as the stock price rises, and deltas decrease as the stock price falls. Keep this in mind, or gamma will get confusing.

THE EFFECT OF TIME ON DELTA

In the previous section, we showed that changes in the stock's direction will change your deltas. Well, time can also change your deltas. It may seem like a strange idea that time can change an option's sensitivity to stock prices. However, think back to the earlier definition where we said that an option's delta is roughly the probability for it to expire ITM and it will make sense. Let's say the stock is trading for $100, and you're holding the $95 call with 30 days to expiration. Is it guaranteed to expire ITM? Not at all, and therefore the option's delta isn't going to be 100. Let's say the delta is 80. Now let's fast-forward and say there's 10 days until expiration. Are you now more confident that the $95 call will be ITM? You should be, which means the option's delta has increased, perhaps to 90. Now let's say only 10 seconds remain until the closing bell on expiration Friday, what do you suppose the delta is now? It's certainly going to be ITM, so the delta will be 100. The delta increased from 80 to 90 to 100, but the stock price never moved. It was time that changed the delta.

The effect of time depends on whether the option is ITM or OTM. As time passes, all ITM options have their deltas increase to 100 at expiration because the market is becoming more confident they'll expire ITM. We get the opposite effect for OTM options. As expiration approaches, the deltas for OTM options will eventually fall to zero.

This is why our definition of delta always assumed that the stock must make an "immediate" move in order for delta to give an accurate prediction of what will happen to the call's price. If you buy a call with a delta of 40 and the stock price rises one dollar – but it doesn't occur for several weeks until expiration Friday – don't expect your option to pick up 40 cents. It's not going to gain anything. A lot of time passed, and the delta changed.

For example, let's say it's January and you decide to use a call option with a delta of 85. The March $90 call, however, has a delta of 75. You could get a greater delta by choosing a lower strike, but that would also require that you spend more money. Instead, perhaps you could choose the February $90 call and find the delta is right where you need it. Remember, your broker's platform will show you these deltas, but it helps to understand which direction you need to look to find them. The table below shows the effect on delta for various strikes and expirations, assuming the current stock price is $100:

CALL DELTAS WITH STOCK AT $100			
STRIKE	30 DAYS	90 DAYS	240 DAYS
$90	97	86	77
$95	82	71	65
$100	51	52	53
$105	21	33	41
$110	5	18	30

Notice that with the stock at $100, the ATM $100 strike maintains a delta of about 50 regardless of the time to expiration. However, for any given expiration, the deltas increase as you move to lower strikes because each successively lower strike has a greater chance of expiring ITM. Deltas decrease as you move to higher strikes for the opposite reason. For any expiration, the higher the strike, the lower the probability for it to expire ITM, so the lower the delta.

Now take a look at the effect of time. With 30 days to expiration, the $90 strike has a 97 delta, but as you increase the time to expiration to 90 days, the delta drops to 86. With more time remaining until expiration, you're less confident that that option will expire ITM, so the delta must decrease. With 240 days until expiration, the delta drops further to 77.

However, we get the opposite effect with OTM strikes. With 30 days to expiration, the $110 call has a delta of 5, but if you increase the time to 90 days, it increases to 18. With more time remaining until expiration, the OTM call has a better chance of expiring ITM, so its delta must increase. Increase the time further to 240 days, and the delta increases to 30.

Time's effect on delta works exactly the same for puts, but just remember that ITM puts are at higher strikes, not lower. For any expiration, to increase a put option's sensitivity, you must use higher-strike puts. An interesting property of options is that all options tend to have their deltas gravitate toward 50 as you increase time, an effect some floor traders call *trumpification*.

By understanding the delta and time relationship, you now have another tool at your disposal, which is important when selecting strategies – especially for unusual option activity. You can control your deltas by selecting different strikes, but you can also do it by choosing different expirations. The more tools you have to choose from, the better you can structure your strategies, and the better the risk profiles you can create. Remember, with stock, you get one choice. With options, you get many, but that's assuming you know how to create them. Delta is the first step in understanding the finer points of option strategies.

GAMMA: THE DELTA OF THE DELTA

We previously showed that delta changes as the underlying stock price changes. If you have an ATM call with a delta of 50 and the stock price rises one dollar, you now know that delta will increase. That's good information, but as an option trader, the real question you want answered is by how much. Will it rise from 50 to 55? Or from 50 to 90? The answer is found by another Greek measurement called *gamma*. Gamma shows by how much your option's delta will change for the next dollar move in the stock's price. Consequently, you can think of gamma as the "delta of the delta." Like delta, your broker's platform will show each option's gamma, which may be measured as a decimal, or it may be multiplied by the 100-share contract size. For any long option, calls or puts, gamma is always positive.

Like delta, it's easiest to understand gamma by considering shares of stock first. If you own shares of stock at $100, you'll gain and lose dollar-for-dollar with changes in the stock's price. That's the delta. However, notice that the answer never changes – it's *always* a one dollar change in profit. Because the delta never changes, the gamma is zero:

	STOCK PRICE						
	$97	$98	$99	$100	$101	$102	$103
CHANGE IN STOCK PRICE	-3	-2	-1	0	+1	+2	+3
CHANGE IN PROFITS (DELTA)	+1	+1	+1	+1	+1	+1	+1
CHANGE IN DELTA (GAMMA)	0	0	0	0	0	0	0

In the above table, look at the first row labeled "change in stock price," which shows by how much the stock price has risen or fallen. Easy enough. However, the second row shows the "change in profits," which is the delta. Because your profits or losses are always a *one-dollar change* for each dollar change in the stock's price – whether the stock price moves up or down – the delta is always one. Keep in mind that if the stock price falls from $100 to $99, you lost one dollar. You didn't lose negative one dollar. Therefore, every one-dollar change in the stock price always leads to a one-dollar change in the profit or loss. The last row shows the change in the deltas at each stock price. Because delta never changes, gamma must be zero.

Long shares of stock always have a delta of 100 and gamma of zero. Those numbers never change, and it's one of the reasons stock traders are so limited in their strategies. Options, however, have different deltas, and those deltas change over time, and that means options have gamma. Because gamma can get confusing when talking about calls and puts, we'll start with call options.

GAMMA FOR LONG CALLS

Let's go back to the ATM $100 call trading for $3 with a delta of 50, but let's also add some new information and say your broker's platform shows it has a gamma of 5. If the stock immediately rises one dollar to $101, delta shows the option's price will rise to $3.50, but at that new price, you'll get a new delta. What will it be? Just add gamma to the previous delta. The new delta will be 50 + 5, or 55. Had the stock price fallen to $99 instead, the call's price would drop to $2.50, and the new delta would be 45.

The idea of gamma is simple: Add gamma to delta if the stock price rises one dollar and subtract gamma from delta if the stock price falls one dollar. Just like delta, however, gamma doesn't stay constant. As the stock price changes, or as time passes, gamma changes too. In the previous example, when the stock price increased to $101, the call option was trading for $3.50 with a delta of 55, but gamma will also change. Perhaps it's now 3. If the stock price rises another dollar, the call's price will increase by delta, or 55 cents, to $4.05, but it will generate a new delta of 55 + 3, or 58. If the stock price keeps rising, the deltas will continue to increase until they hit 100. At that point, they can't increase anymore, so gamma must be zero.

Gamma's smallest value is zero and the largest is technically unlimited. However, these super high gamma numbers, while possible, only occur for ATM options, and only when the option is in the final seconds prior to expiration. Although it does happen, it's unlikely for an option to remain exactly ATM going into expiration, so you're probably not going to see your gamma numbers fly off the charts. Most of the time, gamma will be a much smaller number.

At-the-money options, whether calls or puts, have the greatest gamma. That's important to remember once we get to the stock replacement strategy, as we'll make an interesting use of it for short-term unusual option activity. As the stock price moves away from the ATM strike, whether up or down, gamma falls toward zero. If the stock price falls far enough, delta and gamma will be zero, and any further drops in the stock's price won't affect delta. At that point, the option's virtually worthless. At the other extreme, if the stock price rises far enough, delta will eventually be 100 and gamma will be zero, and any further stock price increases won't affect delta. At that point, the call's delta is 100 and can't increase anymore. With a delta of 100 and gamma of zero, it's no longer a call option – it's shares of stock.

PUT OPTION GAMMAS

The idea behind gamma for put options is exactly the same as for calls. Long calls and puts have positive gamma. What makes them tricky for new traders is the idea of adding gamma to negative numbers. To keep things straight, the rule is always the same for calls and puts: If the stock price rises, *add* gamma to your delta. If the stock price falls, *subtract* gamma from your delta. It's always that easy, provided you remember that put options have negative deltas.

For example, let's say the ATM $100 put is trading for $3 with a delta of -50 and gamma of 5. It's the same example we used for the calls, but notice the delta is now a negative number. If the stock price immediately rises to $101, the put's price will fall to $2.50, and its delta will increase to -50 + 5, or -45. However, because traders ignore the minus sign and see the number fall from 50 to 45, they mistakenly think that delta decreased. Moving from -50 to -45 is an increase because you *added* 5 to it.

We know it's confusing, so here's a trick to make it easier. Forget about the minus sign, and just think of delta as the sensitivity of the option relative to the stock's price. Put options become *less sensitive* as the stock price rises. Gamma shows by how much. The sensitivity number should therefore fall from 50 to 45. Now just attach the minus sign and you're back in business.

What happens if the stock price falls? If the stock price had fallen to $99 instead, the put's price would rise by delta to $3.50. Because the stock price fell, we must subtract gamma from delta, so the new delta is -50 - 5, or -55. Deltas have decreased. Alternatively, you can reason that the put is becoming *more sensitive* to stock price changes, and therefore the number must increase from 50 to 55. Just attach the minus sign, and you've got the correct answer.

If the stock price rises far enough, eventually the put's delta will be zero and so will the gamma. At that point, the option is virtually worthless. On the other hand, if the stock price falls far enough, the delta will eventually hit -100 and gamma will be zero, and any further price declines will not change the delta. With a delta of -100 and gamma of zero, the put option isn't an option anymore. It's short shares of stock.

THE EFFECT OF TIME ON GAMMA

In a previous section we showed that time will affect an option's delta. Well, time has an effect on gamma too. The math behind gamma can get a little tricky, so we just want you to understand it conceptually.

If you remember that an option's delta gives you the approximate probability for the option to expire ITM, the effect will become clear. Just ask yourself how the change in a stock's price altered your assessment of the option expiring ITM and you'll at least understand whether gamma is high or low.

For instance, ATM options are the easiest to understand. Think about a $100 stock with the $100 call trading for one dollar on expiration day. As we wind down the day and approach the closing bell, even though the option's price is dropping, the delta will still remain very close to 50. There's still a 50-50 chance for it to expire ITM. Now let's say the stock price rises just one cent from $100 to $100.01 the second before the bell rings. What happens to your assessment of it expiring ITM? If you thought there was a 50-50 chance before, you must now believe there's a 100% chance. In other words, the delta swung from 50 to 100, but it did it nearly instantaneously, which means the gamma is huge. Gammas are always largest for ATM options, but they grow rapidly as you get closer to expiration. Remember, there's no upper limit on gamma assuming you're dealing with an ATM option.

Now let's compare that to the 90-day $100 call. It also has a delta near 50, but what happened to that delta when the stock price moved one cent? Did that one-cent move noticeably change the probability for it to expire ITM? Not at all, which means the delta hardly increased. In other words, gamma is very low. The one-cent move didn't have a big impact on the delta. So how do you get an option position with a lot of gamma? You'd need to use short-term, ATM options. That will be another important point when we cover the short-term stock replacement strategy for unusual option activity.

Always remember that delta and gamma change all of the time, except when deltas are at maximum or minimum values. If the stock price changes, your deltas and gammas will change. The passage of time also affects your deltas and your gammas. To visualize these effects, look at the table below, which shows call gammas with the stock at $100 for various times until expiration:

CALL GAMMAS WITH STOCK AT $100			
STRIKE	1 DAY	60 DAYS	240 DAYS
$90	0	1.9	1.8
$95	0	3.8	2.2
$100	38.1	4.9	2.5
$105	0	4.3	2.4
$110	0	2.7	2.2

The main thing to notice is that the ATM strike always has the greatest gamma regardless of the expiration. For any expiration, as you move away from the ATM strike, the gammas decrease. For ATM options, increasing the time until expiration will decrease your gamma. The effect of time, however, can be mixed for ITM or OTM options, and you may see them rise or fall as you increase or decrease the time to expiration. Delta and gamma may sound confusing at first, but continue working with them, and eventually the concepts will make sense. Understanding them will create many alternative strategies you may have never considered. The more tools you have, the better your option trading results will be.

VEGA

Vega is another essential Greek, and one we must consider when selecting the strategies for unusual option activity. To understand vega, we first must take a little detour and cover the basics of volatility.

Option prices ultimately depend on how far a stock's price may move ITM, which creates intrinsic value. For a variety of reasons, some stocks have the ability to make large moves, while others don't move much at all. These movements can be measured by another mathematical concept called *volatility*. You know it better as the Wall Street roller coaster. Without getting into the details, think of a stock's volatility as the day-to-day fluctuations in prices. Volatility is not a directional measurement, so a high volatility stock doesn't necessarily mean the stock's price is flying higher or sinking lower. Instead, high volatility just means there are a lot of fluctuations – up or down – around some long-term average. If a stock rises from $100 to $120, but it does so by rising 10 cents each day, there's no volatility. But if it made many zigs and zags between those two prices, then you've got volatility.

Volatility is therefore a measure of confidence, or stability, in the stock's price. If there aren't a lot of day-to-day price fluctuations, you can be reasonably sure that tomorrow's price will be similar to today's price. By today's standards, General Electric (GE) is a low-volatility stock. Its price just bobs up and down by a few pennies each day. There are rarely big changes in the stock's price. Remember, however, that doesn't mean the stock can't perform well over time. That's not what volatility is about. A low-volatility stock can have a remarkable return at the end of the year. Instead, volatility is about the day-to-day fluctuations that occur during the year.

On the other hand, Tesla (TSLA) is a high-volatility stock. Anyone who's ever watched the stock knows that tomorrow's price could be far different – up or down – from today's price. In fact, the next hour's price may even leave you wondering what happened while you were at lunch. That's a high-volatility stock.

Low-volatility stocks give you a high degree of confidence of where tomorrow's price will be, while high-volatility stocks leave you guessing.

There's a calculation you can do to figure out a stock's volatility, but your broker's platform will do those for you too. Just realize that volatility is always measured as a percentage, and the higher the percentage, the more the stock's price will jump around. In August 2018, GE's volatility was about 22% while Tesla's was 60%. These figures are called the stock's *historic volatility* because the calculations are based on what's happened in the past. Why does it matter?

The price traders are willing to pay for an option depends a lot on the stock's volatility. After all, it's changes in the stock's price that can ultimately give the most value to an option. No matter how much extrinsic value may be in an option, you know it must be zero at expiration. Intrinsic value, on the other hand, remains with the option. The more volatile the stock, the higher the option's price. It seems counterintuitive. If Tesla's prices are so uncertain, you're more likely to lose on a Tesla option than GE, so why pay more for the option? The reason is that options can only lose a small, fixed amount. That never changes. So once that price is paid, you'd rather see high volatility.

For instance, how much would you pay for a 30-day $100 call whose underlying stock price was guaranteed to not move? In other words, a volatility of zero percent. You wouldn't be willing to pay one cent for it because there's no way it will ever gain intrinsic value. It's worthless. Okay, that's an exaggeration, as there is no such thing as zero volatility, but it helps to make the point. What if there was just a little bit of volatility, say 10%? Now the stock can make some small moves, so the options will have some value, just not a lot. For a $100 stock, 10% volatility works out to most of the daily price changes falling within $1.25

per day. On the other hand, how much would you pay for that same call option if the stock had a volatility like Tesla? At 60% volatility, that same $100 stock is expected to move within $7.50 per day most of the time. Suddenly, that same option becomes extremely pricey.

According to a pricing model, the 30-day $100 call at 10% is worth $1.14. If valued at 60% volatility, its price jumps to $6.85. Higher volatility translates to higher option prices, whether we're talking about calls or puts. The reason is that volatility is nondirectional, so high volatility stocks have the ability to increase by large amounts, which is great for calls, but they can also fall by large amounts, which benefits puts. When volatility rises, call and put options get pricier. Option prices are therefore sensitive to changes in the stock's volatility.

However, options aren't priced according to the stock's historic volatility. If a stock was trading at 10% volatility, but is now the target of heated competition for a takeover, its price isn't going to move at 10% volatility. Who cares what it's been in the past? Options are therefore priced according to what traders think the stock's volatility will be over the life of the option, which is called the *future volatility*, or the *implied volatility*. We don't know what the future volatility will be until expiration arrives, but we can figure out what the market thinks the future volatility will be by looking at option prices. To understand vega, you must understand the difference between the historical volatility and the implied volatility.

HISTORIC AND IMPLIED VOLATILITY

All financial assets have a *fair value*, which is a price that doesn't favor the buyer or seller. It's the price where the buyer and seller are expected to break even over the long run. If the price was below, it would favor the buyer, and it would be to everyone's advantage to buy – you'd end up with no sellers. If the price was above fair value, it would favor the sellers, and the market would end up with no buyers. But when an asset is priced at fair value, it's not biased toward buyers or sellers. The price is fair. Just because the price is fair, of course, doesn't mean that buyers and sellers always break even. Most of the time, one side wins and the other loses. Figuring out which side of the trade is the right one, however, should be based on what everyone thinks will be happening in the future, and option prices show us a lot of where traders think prices are heading. It doesn't change our ability to figure out what an option's fair value should be.

The calculations can be daunting, and it took decades to solve the puzzle. It was finally done in 1973, when Fisher Black and Myron Scholes created the now famous Black-Scholes pricing model. It was no easy feat, and the Nobel Prize was awarded to Myron Scholes for his work in 1995. Unfortunately, Fisher Black died shortly before, and the prize is not awarded posthumously.

While there are many pricing models, the Black-Scholes model continues to be the premier model in the industry. This is a very complex model, hence earning a Nobel Prize, and you don't have to understand all of the formulas that drive it. You can find this pricing model readily on the Internet by searching for Black-Scholes pricing model. Using this model, we can enter five different variables (six if you include dividends) and from those, the model tells us what a call and put option are theoretically worth. The five factors are the stock price, exercise price, risk-free interest rate, time remaining until expiration, and, you guessed it – volatility. For example, let's say the stock is trading for $100, and we want to know what the 30-day, $100 call and put are worth. We'll use 2% for the risk-free interest rate, which can be found by looking up the 30-day T-bill rate. We look up the stock's historic volatility and find it's 20%. Using these five factors, the model says the $100 call is worth $2.37 and the corresponding put is worth $2.21 as shown in the following table:

FACTOR	VALUE	CALL PRICE	PUT PRICE
STOCK PRICE	$100		
EXERCISE PRICE	$100		
RISK-FREE INTEREST	2%	$2.37	$2.21
TIME TO EXPIRATION (DAYS)	30		
VOLATILITY	20%		

That means if you look up the option quotes on your broker's platform, you'll see the call and put trading at these prices, right? Not at all. In fact, they're most likely not going to be these prices. Let's say we look up actual option quotes and find the call and put are trading for $3.51 and $3.35, respectively. Is the pricing model wrong?

Not at all. It's giving us perfectly accurate option prices – assuming the volatility will be 20% over the next 30 days. That's the volatility we entered, so those are the prices it's giving in response. That doesn't mean traders will use 20% to currently value the option. Maybe there's an upcoming earnings report, FDA announcement, pending court decision on a class-action lawsuit – or maybe people trading on inside information. With this unexpected news hanging over the stock, traders *think* there's a higher chance for the stock to make a bigger move than 20% volatility would suggest, so they're willing to pay more for the calls and puts. Today's prices are always a reflection of what people think they'll be worth in the future. Traders are reflecting their suspicions that something big will be happening with this stock in the next 30 days that warrants a $3.51 call price and $3.35 put price. If they didn't think it was worth it, they wouldn't be willing to pay the price. How can we account for these prices?

If you look at the five factors in our model, we can't change the stock's price. It's trading for $100 right now, so we must use that value. We're also valuing the $100 strikes, so we can't change the strike price. The risk-free interest rate hasn't changed, so we must leave that at 2%. And finally, the time to expiration hasn't changed, so we must use 30 days. What else is left? What's the only variable that isn't set in stone? It's volatility. That's why traders say volatility is the only true variable in an option's price.

To make the model balance with a $3.51 call price and $3.35 put price, we need to change the volatility. We're now just working the model in reverse. Rather than giving the model a volatility number to generate call and put prices, let's give it the current market value for the call and put, and figure out which volatility would be necessary to make those prices true:

FACTOR	VALUE	CALL PRICE	PUT PRICE
STOCK PRICE	$100		
EXERCISE PRICE	$100		
RISK-FREE INTEREST	2%	$3.51	$3.35
TIME TO EXPIRATION (DAYS)	30		
VOLATILITY	?		

The model would tell us that a volatility of 30% is required to make the call worth $3.51 and the put worth $3.35. So even though the stock is trading at 20% volatility historically, we would say the market is *implying* the future volatility will be 30%, and that's called the *implied volatility*. The stock's historic volatility is 20%, but the implied volatility, as shown by the option market, is 30%.

Now that you understand volatility, we can tackle vega.

Vega shows by how much these option prices will change if we change the implied volatility by one tick (or one percentage point). For example, increasing it to 31% or dropping it to 29%. Those are one-tick changes in volatility. Vega isn't a Greek letter, as the Greeks don't have a letter "V" in their alphabet, so it was chosen to sound like one. Just remember that "V" is for volatility. Like all Greek measurements, it assumes we're talking about an instantaneous change – not next week. Vegas are always positive for long calls and puts. With the call and put priced at $3.51 and $3.35, your broker's platform would have shown the vega for each was 0.11, or 11 by multiplying by the 100-share contract size. If we increase the volatility to 31%, the call and put prices should therefore rise by 11 cents, and the model shows that's true:

FACTOR	VALUE	CALL PRICE	PUT PRICE
STOCK PRICE	$100		
EXERCISE PRICE	$100		
RISK-FREE INTEREST	2%	$3.62	$3.46
TIME TO EXPIRATION (DAYS)	30		
VOLATILITY	31%		

Vega therefore shows how sensitive your option prices are to changes in the market's perception of volatility. Depending on your strategy, it may present certain volatility risks. Perhaps you want volatility to remain stable, so you may wish to "stress test" the strategy and figure out what would happen if volatility rose to 35%, 40%, and 50%? Like all the Greeks, vega only shows the answer for small changes in volatility. That's why we limit the definition to one tick. If vega is 11, it doesn't mean your options will gain 22 cents if you increase volatility by two ticks, and 33 cents if you increase it by three ticks, and so on. Once you change volatility to 31%, you'll get new vega numbers. Sometimes, the numbers will stay reasonably close. Other times, they won't. You need to know how sensitive your positions are to changes in volatility, but it's difficult to tell by just looking at the prices. Vega makes the answers easy.

When we start talking about unusual option activity, you can imagine that ATM and OTM options get bid up to very lofty levels. The problem with buying these options is that all of that volatility will drop upon the news announcement. It's that big drop in volatility that causes traders to lose money – even though the stock price may have increased. As mentioned in Chapter Four, to avoid paying exceptionally high volatility, there are times we may buy the actual shares instead.

For example, let's say a $100 stock has some unusual option activity present, and the 30-day $105 call is priced at $6. Is it a high price?

We hope you're catching on and realize there's no way to know based on that information. The only way we can tell is to figure out the corresponding volatility, and that means we need to know the option's *implied* volatility. Let's enter the option's market price of $6, and let it solve for the volatility:

FACTOR	VALUE	CALL PRICE
STOCK PRICE	$100	
EXERCISE PRICE	$105	
RISK-FREE INTEREST	2%	$6
TIME TO EXPIRATION (DAYS)	30	
VOLATILITY	70%	

The model tells us 70% volatility is required to make the option worth $6, so the call is trading at an implied volatility of 70%. Again, this means the market is implying that the stock's volatility over the next 30 days will be 70%. To find out if that's a high number or not, just compare it to historical stock prices. If the stock is currently trading at 20%, and the highest was 50%, then 70% is an extremely high-priced option – even though it only costs $6. Why does it matter? Aren't we going to make money if the stock price rises sharply? Not necessarily.

Buying options with high implied volatility is like taking a football bet with a high point spread. You can have all the confidence in the world that your team is going to win, but if Las Vegas has a 14-point spread against them, your chances of winning have been reduced. The larger the spread, the lower the chances for your team to win. That's how an option trade works, as the extrinsic value is like the point spread. The larger the extrinsic value, the greater the expiration breakeven price, and the extrinsic value is solely determined by the volatility.

For example, let's say the big news is announced the next day, and the stock is trading for $107. It's a big move for that stock in a day, given that it normally trades around 20% volatility. The $105 call, however, may now be trading for $3.80, so you lost $2.20, or 36%, even though you were correct that the stock would soon make a big move. With the stock at $107, the $105 call has $2 of intrinsic value, and $1.80 of extrinsic value. Why did it have $6 worth of extrinsic value yesterday, but only $1.80 today?

Because the news is out. Traders were willing to pay $6 for the extrinsic value yesterday when the news was unknown. Now that the news is out, they know exactly the effect the news has on the stock's price, so it's no longer a mystery. Option traders call this sharp drop in extrinsic value the "volatility pop" or the "volatility crush," which just means there was a big drop in the volatility level that traders were willing to pay after the news was announced. What volatility is the option trading at now? We can go back to the pricing model and use the following information:

FACTOR	VALUE	CALL PRICE
STOCK PRICE	$107	
EXERCISE PRICE	$105	
RISK-FREE INTEREST	2%	$3.80
TIME TO EXPIRATION (DAYS)	29	
VOLATILITY	21.6%	

The implied volatility is now 21.6%, or about 22%, which makes it back in line with the 20% volatility before the news was announced. This might seem like a dramatic example, but it pales in comparison to actual numbers you'll see when you're dealing with people trading on inside information.

Understanding the difference between historic volatility and implied volatility is important once we get into strategies. If we spot unusual option activity, it doesn't mean a thing if you choose a strike that has outrageously high implied volatility. Pete and I almost always use different strikes and expirations than the ones where the unusual option activity is occurring for this very reason. Unusual option activity is simply information, and there's nothing magical about that strike and expiration the insiders are choosing. In fact, most aren't option experts, and they may very well be missing a better opportunity. Instead, we use the information, but alter the strategy to reduce the effect of the high implied volatility that's always present in the most active strike. Vega is one of the most powerful keys to unlocking the benefits of unusual option activity.

THETA

Theta shows how sensitive your option's price is to time. In Chapter Five, we said that an option loses all of its extrinsic value by expiration. It doesn't matter how much it began with, at expiration it must be zero. Therefore, a portion of each option's price decays with the passage of time. At-the-money options have the fastest rate of decay because they have the most extrinsic value. If all options must lose all their extrinsic values on expiration day, that means the ATM strikes, the ones with the most extrinsic value, must fall at a faster rate.

As long as there's some extrinsic value, an option will have some portion of its price decay with the passage of time. However, remember it's only the extrinsic value that decays – not the intrinsic value. For instance, let's say the stock is trading for $110 and the $100 call is trading for $12. It has $10 worth of intrinsic value, but only $2 worth of extrinsic value. This option will only lose $2 between now and expiration from the passage of time. If the stock price remains the same at expiration, this call will be worth $10. That doesn't mean the option can't lose the $10 worth of intrinsic value, but it will not lose it from the passage of time. The only way this option will lose any intrinsic value is if the stock price falls. And if it falls all the way to the $100 strike or below at expiration, the option will lose the full $10 of intrinsic value.

If you buy an option, the extrinsic value decays over time. For ATM options, they'll decay slowly at first, and then rapidly once the option gets closer to expiration. Theta shows how much your option is expected to lose from the passing of one day's time. Long options, whether calls or puts, have negative theta. For instance, if you buy a $100 call for $3, your platform may show its theta as -.05, or -5 per contract. That means, all else staying the same, your option is expected to lose five cents tomorrow morning and should trade for $2.95. Remember the big caveat: Theta, like all the Greeks, assumes everything else remains the same, which probably will never happen in an active market. At a minimum, the stock's price will probably be a little different, so that means your option's price probably won't be exactly $2.95. Still, theta is an accurate measure of how much your option's price will lose, assuming everything, including the stock's price, remained the same.

Theta is a helpful number to watch because it shows how quickly your option's price is expected to lose money, and you need to weigh that against how quickly you think the stock's price will rise. To make money on options, you need the intrinsic value to outweigh the loss of extrinsic value. Theta helps you measure those effects.

THETA IS NOT LINEAR

One of the most important principles of option pricing is to understand that an option's price isn't going to decay in a straight line. In other words, it won't decay at a steady rate over time. For instance, if you pay $3 for a 30-day, ATM option, it's not going to lose at a steady rate of 10 cents per day. Instead, it will decay relatively slowly at first, losing less than 10 cents per day for a while, and accelerate as expiration draws closer, eventually losing more than 10 cents per day. The point where the price decay begins to accelerate is when 25% of the option's time remains. For a 30-day call, that means you'll experience the heaviest decay when about eight days remain – and it will accelerate even faster as you get closer to expiration. The following chart shows how a one-month, ATM $3 option will decay as it moves toward expiration:

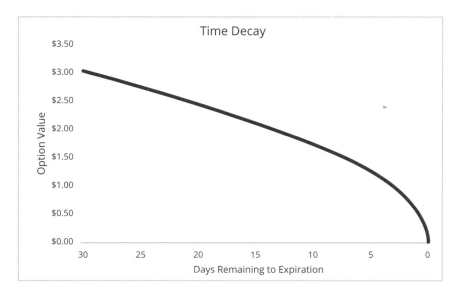

The chart shows it's not a straight line, or linear. Instead, it's curved. You can also understand the effect by looking at the halfway point, when 15 days remain. Most new traders would think the $3 option would lose 50% of its value and be worth

$1.50, but it will only lose about 30% of its value and be trading for $2.10. The reason for this strange rate of decay is that option prices are proportional to volatility, which is proportional to the square root of time. For example, if a one-month option is trading for $1, it seems logical that a four-month option would be worth $4. However, it will only be worth $2. In other words, even though there's four times the amount of time, it won't create a four-fold increase in the option's price. Instead, because the square root of four is two, the additional time increases the option's price by two-fold, or double.

It's an important characteristic to understand because option sellers often make the mistake of selling longer-dated options because they're worth more money, and they believe it's a better deal to sell the more expensive option. But look how the math works out: By selling the one-month option for one dollar, you'll earn an average of 3.33 cents per day. On the other hand, if you sell a four-month option for $2, you're earning an average of 1.66 cents per day – exactly half the amount. Once you understand the relationship, you'll see it doesn't make sense to sell the four-month option for two dollars. Instead, sell the one-month option four times, and you'll collect four dollars – twice as much as if you sold the four-month option once. Of course, you must be practical. If the stock has Weekly expirations and you're only going to receive something that barely covers commissions, say 20 cents, it's not going to make a lot of sense to sell it, unless you're selling a lot of contracts. In that case, you may need to sell an option with a couple weeks or more until expiration before it becomes worthwhile. The essential concept is that you should try to sell the shortest expiration possible.

Keep in mind that only the extrinsic value decays, and the previous time-decay chart applies to ATM options only. If you're using ITM options, the time-decay graph will look very different. If you purchase ITM options with very little extrinsic value, you'll see very little decay. For instance, let's say the stock is $130 and you bought the $100 call for $30.20. The extrinsic value is only 20 cents, so compared to the $3 call, your time-decay chart is going to look like the black line in the following chart:

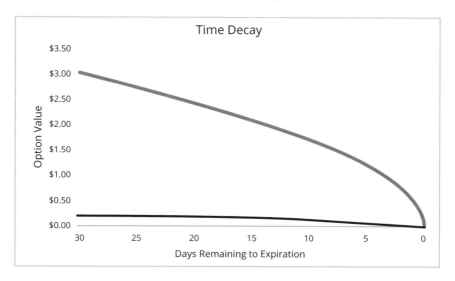

The reason it looks insignificant is because the option only had 20 cents left to decay over a 30-day period. New traders would be fearful of paying $30.20 for an option because they think the entire purchase price is going to decay. Even though this option's price seems expensive if you just look at the price, there's only 20 cents' worth of extrinsic value. It's the value of the insurance policy, so it's the value of the option. Only 20 cents is going to decay over time.

The most important point to understand is that, all things being equal, you should prefer to buy longer-dated options because they're cheaper per unit of time. On the other hand, you should prefer to sell shorter-dated contracts. You'll receive less money per contract expiration, but more money per unit of time. It's far more profitable to sell many shorter-term contracts than to sell one longer-dated one.

Whether you're buying or selling, theta is one of the biggest tradeoffs with options, so it's always part of the decisions. You must understand option pricing if you're to profit from how options are priced. For any option strategy, theta is always a consideration.

THE GREEKS FOR SHORT OPTIONS

Once you understand the Greeks for long options, they're easy to figure out for short options – they're just the opposite. Remember that the buyer and seller are on opposite sides of the transaction so not only will the profits to one be the losses to the other, the Greeks will also be opposite. For example, long calls have positive delta, so short calls have negative delta. Long puts have negative delta, so short puts have positive delta. Long options – calls and puts – have positive gamma, so short options have negative gamma.

POSITION	DELTA	GAMMA	VEGA	THETA
LONG CALL	POSITIVE	POSITIVE	POSITIVE	NEGATIVE
SHORT CALL	NEGATIVE	NEGATIVE	NEGATIVE	POSITIVE
LONG PUT	NEGATIVE	POSITIVE	POSITIVE	NEGATIVE
SHORT PUT	POSITIVE	NEGATIVE	NEGATIVE	POSITIVE

If you're ever in doubt about what's going to happen with a short option, figure out what will happen with the long option and then just flip the answer. If you buy a $100 call with a delta of 50 and gamma of 5, the trader on the other side, the call seller, has a delta of -50 and gamma of -5. When learning the Greeks, focus on the long positions, and once you get that, you'll immediately have the answers for the short positions.

SUMMARY OF THE GREEKS

Delta: shows how much your option's price will change for a $1 change in the stock's price. Delta also shows the contract's equivalent share amount. If a call has 75 deltas and you own 10 of those calls, your position is behaving like 750 shares of stock.

Gamma (the "delta of the delta"): shows how much your option's delta will change for the next dollar move in the stock's price. Gamma also shows the amount of curvature in the profit and loss profile. The more curvature, the larger the gamma.

Vega: shows how much your option's price will change if the implied volatility changes by one tick (one percentage point).

Theta: shows how sensitive your option's price is to one-day's passage of time (time decay). Remember that time decay doesn't occur equally, or linearly. Instead, options decay slowly at first and then rapidly near expiration.

All Greeks show how sensitive your option's price is to some other factor. Gamma is the only exception, as it shows the sensitivities of your deltas – not your option's price. With the exception of delta, all Greeks are maximized ATM.

STRATEGIC APPLICATIONS OF THE GREEKS

By understanding the Greeks, you'll make better strategic decisions. If your primary outlook is that the stock price is going to rise, but you're not very confident about how quickly, your strategy should be centered on high deltas. A simple strategy would be to buy deep ITM calls. They'll have high deltas and low gammas, which means those deltas will remain fairly high, unless the stock price takes a sharp fall. Conversely, if you think that stock's price will make a fast, aggressive move, that's a different story. If that's part of your outlook, you can also use gamma. To do so, you should select a strike price closer to ATM. Doing so, you'll spend less for the option, but if you're correct about how quickly the stock price will move, your deltas will quickly rise. In other words, gamma is going to manufacture the deltas for you automatically. There's no sense in paying for them through intrinsic value. The tradeoff is that if you're right about the direction, but wrong about the speed, the option may lose money. Option strategies with a lot of gamma need fast, aggressive moves in the underlying stock in order to be profitable. On the other hand, strategies with high deltas, whether positive or negative, just need the stock to move in the correct direction, but they'll have a better chance of being profitable regardless of how quickly or slowly the price moves.

Vega can also be used strategically. If you think a news announcement will be accompanied by an increase in volatility, you'll want to use longer-dated options, as they're more sensitive to changes in volatility. On the other hand, if you're trading unusual option activity, most of the implied volatility will disappear upon the news announcement, so you'd prefer to use shorter-dated options.

If you're buying options, you'll want to check the extrinsic value to see how much of the option's price will disappear at expiration. Theta will help you determine how much it will lose daily or weekly. If the extrinsic value is high, you may choose to incorporate some option selling to offset the time decay. For example, you may use vertical spreads or diagonal spreads, which we'll cover later.

AN IMPORTANT POINT TO NEVER FORGET ABOUT THE GREEKS

Whenever we're talking about any of the Greeks, you must remember that these changes are assuming all else remained the same, which is unlikely to happen in a dynamic market. Because traders forget this, they can end up thinking something is wrong with our definitions – or their trading platform. For instance, let's say an ATM $100 call is trading for $3 with a delta of 50. The stock immediately rises to $101 – but the option's price jumps to $4. Is something wrong with delta? Not at all. Instead, the implied volatility changed. In other words, for some reason, traders were now willing to pay $4 rather than the $3.50 as expected by delta, and the only way we could account for that is to say the implied volatility changed. If that changed, then it automatically affected the other variables. In other words, everything else wasn't constant. This is important to understand because it's one of the things our *Heat Seeker*™ program searches for when hunting for unusual option activity. The system will track options to see if the price changes are far greater than implied by delta. If that's true, it suggests there may be other information – potentially insider trading – that's pushing prices higher. A similar effect can happen with theta. Your $3 call may have a theta of 5, which means you'd expect it to trade for $2.95 tomorrow. On the opening bell, the stock price is exactly the same – but the option is trading for $5. What happened? Once again, new information must have arrived that's making traders believe the option is now worth $5 – even though it was only worth $3 yesterday. The only way to account for that is, again, through implied volatility. Remember, all Greeks are outputs from a pricing model, and the model assumes that all other factors remained the same. In the real world, all factors probably changed to some degree, and that means you can get very different results from what the Greeks suggested. Does this mean you should ignore them?

No, but it does mean you must be careful with interpretations. Your car's GPS may say it will take two hours to reach your destination, and that's great information. But it assumes there won't be any heavy traffic, rain delays, flat tires, traffic tickets, or stops to eat. It's making a lot of assumptions, but it's still an invaluable tool for planning.

The Greeks are a trader's most powerful tools. They're the

substance behind the strategies. Unfortunately, traders often ignore them because they look like technobabble that would only be useful to a mathematician playing the stock market. The Greeks are like the instrumentation panel in an airplane – they're your lifeline. They tell you which direction, how high, how fast, and how far. You need to know these answers because option traders, like pilots flying through or above the clouds, have no reference points. If you're long 10 $100 puts, long 5 $105 calls and short 5 $110 calls, with the stock at $103, which direction do you need it to move in order to profit? What will your new delta be? And how much will the position's value lose tomorrow morning? If you don't know these answers, you're likely to shut the position down out of fear. That's regrettable, because the real money is made by staying in positions and managing the risk over time. The Greeks will instantly tell you the answers. By mastering the Greeks, you can master strategies, and that's when you can plan for profits.

Ch. 7 PROFIT & LOSS DIAGRAMS

The Greeks give us guidance, but it's up to the trader to interpret them. Sometimes that's difficult, especially if you're trying to visualize what will happen over a wide range of stock prices. Your deltas may be positive now, but will they always be? Or will they turn negative? At which stock price? That's an entirely different set of questions, and for those, you'll need to use profit and loss diagrams.

If the Greeks are like the instrument panel in an airplane, a profit and loss diagram is full-color radar. They're graphical representations of the profits and losses that will occur across various stock prices, and at different times. Profit and loss diagrams are so powerful that it's nearly impossible to teach options, and even more difficult to trade them, without using these powerful tools. Your broker's platform will automatically draw these charts for you, so there's no need to get out the graph paper and drafting pencil. Just because you don't need to draw them, however, doesn't mean you don't need to know them. By understanding them, you'll find exactly which strategies, strikes, and expiration fit your needs. It's as easy as looking at a picture – assuming you know how to read it.

Let's start with an easy one first and say you bought 100 shares of stock. What does your profit and loss diagram look like? To answer, you'll need to create a table of the various profits or losses at different stock prices. The first row shows that if the current stock price is $85, you'd have a $15 loss if you paid $100. At a stock price of $100, you'd have no gain or loss, which means you'd just break even:

STOCK PRICE	PROFIT/LOSS
$85	-$15
$90	-$10
$95	-$5
$100	0
$105	$5
$110	$10
$115	$15

The following chart is created from the previous table, and the resulting picture is called the profit and loss diagram. The horizontal axis shows various stock prices, while the vertical axis shows the corresponding profits or losses that will occur at those stock prices. To read the graph, select a stock price on the horizontal axis. From there, trace a line up to the profit and loss curve (black line) and look to the corresponding profit on the vertical axis. For example, if the stock price rises to $110, you would make a $10 profit, as shown by the dotted lines:

The picture shows a long stock position rises and falls dollar-for-dollar with itself, and therefore the profit and loss diagram results in a straight line. This is a graphical way of seeing that delta must always be one. If you increase or decrease the stock's price by one, you'll increase or decrease your profit by the same amount. You'll also hear this called a risk graph, risk curve, or risk profile. No matter what you call them, they'll show that options provide much safer profiles.

Long stock is easy to visualize without a diagram because it's dollar-for-dollar up or down. Options aren't so easy, especially for complex strategies, and that's where these charts really help. They're drawn in the same way, but just take a few more steps. The simplest risk graph assumes we're at expiration. For instance, assume you buy a $100 call for $5:

STOCK PRICE	$100 CALL	COST	PROFIT/LOSS
$85	$0	$5	-$5
$90	$0	$5	-$5
$95	$0	$5	-$5
$100	$0	$5	-$5
$105	$5	$5	$0
$110	$10	$5	$5
$115	$15	$5	$10

The table above shows that with the stock at $115, the $100 call is worth $15 at expiration. Because you paid $5, the resulting profit is $10. If we chart these profits or losses for the various stock prices, we'll get the following diagram:

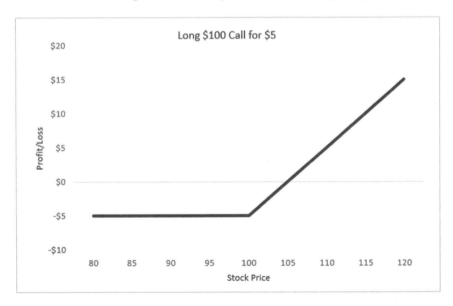

For individual options, we never get a straight line. Instead, they're bent, and the graphs will always bend at the strike price.

If the stock price falls below the strike at expiration, your option expires worthless and the most you can lose is the amount paid. That's why the above graph flattens out for all stock prices below $100 and lines up at a maximum loss of $5.

Wherever the graph crosses the horizontal line at $0 is where the position breaks even. At that point, there are no profits and no losses, so the profit and loss curve lines up at zero. If you purchased a $100 call for $5, your breakeven price is $105, which is where the profit and loss curve crosses zero. For individual calls and puts, whether long or short, you'll always have a single breakeven point. For more complex strategies, however, you can get multiple breakeven points. It's important to understand that when you're looking at expiration graphs, the resulting profits and losses only apply within the final seconds of the option's life on expiration day. They do not apply when there's still significant time remaining on your options.

THE STOCK AND OPTION TRADEOFF

Despite all the advantages that options provide, the benefits don't come for free, and option strategies always involve tradeoffs. To make the most of your strategy selection, you must understand what the tradeoffs are, and profit and loss diagrams will easily uncover them for you. Because option buyers pay an extrinsic value, the breakeven points are pushed a little higher than they would be for the long shares of stock. If we overlay the $100 call purchased for $5 and the long shares of stock purchased for $100, you can see the tradeoff in the call option, as it breaks even at $105 while the stock position breaks even at $100:

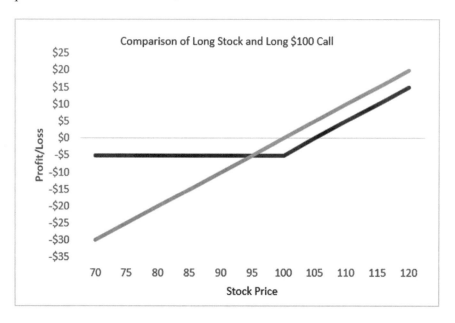

Why would an option trader give up $5 of potential gains? The left side of the chart, the maximum loss, tells the story. The option trader can only lose a maximum of $5 but the stock trader will lose dollar-for-dollar all the way down to a stock price of zero. By altering the strikes or expirations you choose, you can reposition the profit and loss curve nearly anywhere you want. If you don't like the $105 breakeven, perhaps you could buy the $90 call, and that will get the breakeven point much closer to $100. In exchange, you'll pay more for the $90 strike. If you want to pay less for the option, you'll need to accept a higher breakeven price.

The point is that experienced option traders can shift the profit and loss curve up or down, as well as left to right. These are choices that stock traders don't have, and that's one of the reasons stock trading can be so risky. A basic principle of financial risk management is to avoid extreme outcomes, but when you buy shares of stock, you can make it all – or lose it all. That's about as extreme as it gets. By purchasing call options, however, you only sacrifice a little bit of upside, but greatly reduce the risk of the downside. By using options, you'll open up an entirely new world of choices that are simply not available when using shares of stock. The only way to fully understand the benefits – and tradeoffs – is to visualize it through profit and loss diagrams.

OPTION PROFITS AND LOSSES PRIOR TO EXPIRATION

Option profit and loss diagrams are often drawn at expiration, which are like the ones we outlined previously. They form straight lines with a distinct bend at the strike price, or strike prices if the strategy uses more than one strike. The reason is simple because, at expiration, options are either worth their intrinsic value, or nothing at all. While they're easy to draw, they're not all that useful while you're in a strategy. Expiration graphs will show you the maximum and minimum values for different stock prices, but they won't show you what the values are today. When you're in an option strategy, today is what matters most. So how do we draw a profit and loss diagram prior to expiration? We must resort to an option pricing model to see. If you were to graph a profit and loss diagram for a $100 call purchased for $5 but it hadn't expired yet, let's say it has 120 days until expiration, the graph will be a smooth, curved line like the gray line in the following chart:

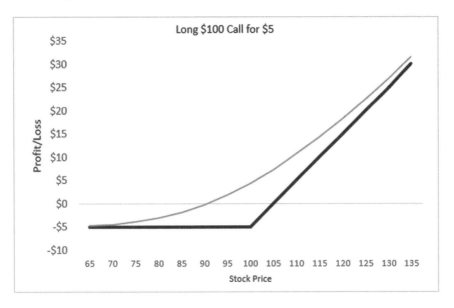

Now there are two lines in the picture, and the risk graph will look something like this in your broker's platform. The gray line shows your profit and losses for today, and is called the *current curve*, while the black line shows your profits and losses at expiration, which is the *expiration curve*. The difference between the two lines is the extrinsic value. Remember, the expiration graph only applies in the final seconds of the option's life. If you're in a position, you'll want to use the current curve to answer most of your questions.

Regardless of which line you're looking at, you read the graph the same way. What would your profit and loss be if the stock price is $115? That depends on whether you're talking about today or expiration. If you want to know what it will be today, trace a line up from the $115 stock price to the current curve (gray line). If you want to know what it will be at expiration, trace a line to expiration curve (black line). As expiration gets closer, the extrinsic value begins to erode, and the current curve will gradually work its way down and eventually mold itself into the expiration curve at the closing bell on expiration day. Theta shows by how much the current curve will decrease each day. You can also see the greatest difference between the current curve and expiration curve is for the ATM strike, and that's a graphical way of showing that ATM options have the greatest extrinsic value – and therefore the greatest theta.

In the prior graph, you'll see that the current curve is curved, and that's another way of understanding gamma. The risk graph for long shares of stock is a straight line. Because there's no curvature, there's no gamma. Option graphs, however, are curved, and that's why deltas don't increase or decrease at a constant rate. The heaviest curvature occurs for the ATM strike, which shows the ATM options have the greatest gamma. However, if the underlying stock rises significantly, the current curve eventually becomes straight and runs parallel to the expiration curve, which can be seen at the far-right side of the chart at a stock price of $135. At that point, your call's delta is 100, gamma is zero, and the option is behaving just like shares of stock.

SHORT SHARES OF STOCK

Short shares of stock are one of the most dangerous positions you can use – and the profit and loss diagram shows why. The position loses dollar-for-dollar as the stock price rises, but because there's no limit on how high a stock's price can rise, there's no limit on the potential losses. Short stock positions truly have an undefined maximum loss:

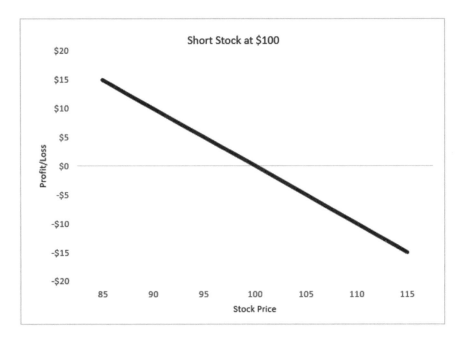

However, short stock positions can also be one of the most profitable, as stock prices often fall faster and harder than they rise. For stocks, it's the staircase up – and the elevator down. Buying put options changes the risks. You can profit from falling stock prices, but without the fear of unlimited losses. The following chart is the expiration profile of a long $100 put purchased for $5:

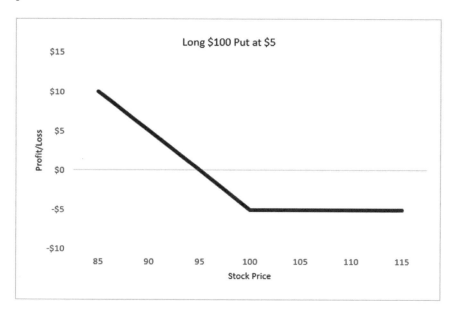

The chart shows the most you can lose is the amount paid, or $5 in this example, but that only occurs for all stock prices above the $100 strike at expiration. On the other hand, you'll profit dollar-for-dollar at expiration just like a short stock trader would – but without the corresponding risks.

ZERO-SUM GAME: IT ADDS UP TO NOTHING

Derivatives were not created as betting tools, but it can help to understand strategies as a bet between a buyer and seller. The loser pays the winner. Derivatives are therefore a zero-sum game, which means if you add up all the gains and losses, they add up to zero. Contrary to what the financial press would have you believe, derivatives don't create financial black holes where money just goes *poof* and vanishes into a cloud of smoke. No matter how sensational the story may be, and no matter how bad losses may be, not one dime is ever lost to the overall economy. Instead, money is just shifted from one person to another, just as with a bet. If one party loses $100 million on a derivatives contract, the financial press points to it as an obvious reason why derivatives should be banned. What they don't tell you is that another party earned $100 million. As Gordon Gekko from the movie *Wall Street* said, *"Money itself isn't lost or made, it's simply transferred from one perception to another."*

The final point to understand about profit and loss diagrams is that the short position's profit and loss diagram is the mirror image of the long position's. If you purchased the $100 call for $5, there's another trader on the opposite side who sold that call for $5, and his profit and loss diagram is the mirror image of yours, as shown by the gray line in the following chart:

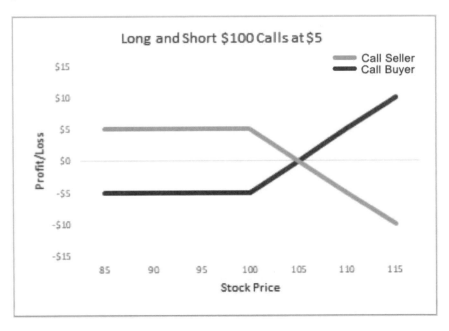

Long and short strategies always share the same breakeven point, or points, if there are more than one strike involved. After all, one trader can't break even but leave the other with a profit or loss. By understanding profit and loss diagrams, you'll instantly have a better understanding of short positions. They're just the opposite of the long positions.

Because everything is opposite between the buyer and seller, the Greeks are opposite as well. Profit and loss diagrams make the difficult, but essential, parts of option trading much easier. After all, a picture's worth a thousand words, and maybe even a thousand Greeks.

8

Ch.

SKEWS, TILTS, & DANGEROUS SMILES

"In a successful organization, no detail is too small to escape close attention." Those were the sage words from Coach Holtz that Pete often used when we were deciding on which option strategy to use for unusual option activity. For any outlook, nearly any strategy can work to some degree. A carpenter can use a wrench to hammer a nail into a wall, or a pair of pliers to remove it. They work, but there are better ways. Options work the same way.

For any strategy, you can select in-the-money (ITM), at-the-money (ATM), or out-of-the-money (OTM) strikes. You can also choose different expiration months, so there are potentially hundreds of combinations. To the inexperienced trader, the choice is easy: Find the expiration and strike with the price that's just right for your budget, and you've got the right option.

It sounds like a good idea, but there's a small detail you're overlooking – a skew curve. It's easy to overlook, as most platforms won't even show them to you. For those that do, few traders know what they mean or how to use them, so they get shrugged off as an insignificant detail. As long as the unusual option activity points to the stock's price heading higher, who cares?

Anyone who wants to profit from it.

Skew curves are one of the main reasons option traders lose money – even if they're correct about the stock's direction. Before we cover some of the main strategies we use to capitalize on unusual option activity, we must spend some time on skew curves. They're a small detail, but not too small to escape close attention.

OPTIONS IN A PERFECT WORLD

In Chapter Six, we talked about an option's implied volatility. That's the volatility number that's necessary to enter into a pricing model so that it generates the option's current market price. In a perfect world, all option strikes across all expirations would trade at the same implied volatility. For instance, if the stock is trading for $100 and the July $100 call is trading at 30% implied volatility, all July strikes should trade at the same implied volatility. After all, each strike is tied to the same stock and expires on the same date, so there's no reason to think the $95 call should be priced at a different volatility from the $100 call, or that either of those should have different volatilities from the $105 call. In other words, if traders think the stock's volatility through July expiration will be 30%, all strikes should be priced at 30%. If we graphed the implied volatilities for various call strikes for a given expiration, we'd expect to get a straight line as in the following chart:

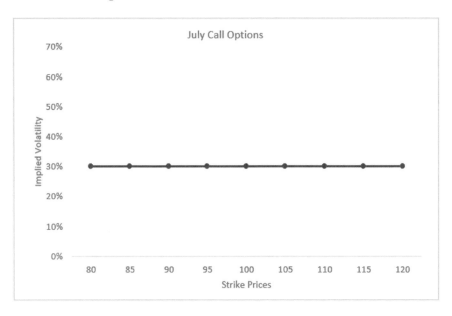

The flat line just shows that no matter which strike you choose, it'll be priced at the same 30% implied volatility. If we graphed the put strikes, we'd get exactly the same perfect picture, but that's because we're assuming a perfect world. In the real world of trading, option prices are not only determined by volatility, but also according to supply and demand for the various strikes. If the July $100 call is trading for $5 at 30% volatility, a pricing model would say the $95 call is worth $6.53, and the $105 call is worth $1.61 – assuming they're both priced at 30% volatility. What if there was a flurry of buying activity for the $105 strike but not the other strikes? Is it possible that its price could rise to a different price, say $3, instead of the $1.61 we'd expect? Yes, and that's when the flat line begins to bend. We'll start to see skews.

OPTIONS IN THE REAL WORLD

Most of the time, different strikes will trade at different
volatilities, sometimes by a little, other times by a lot. Rarely will
they be identical. If we graphed actual implied volatilities for
different call option strikes for a given expiration, we wouldn't
get a straight line, but instead, a graph that looks something like
the following:

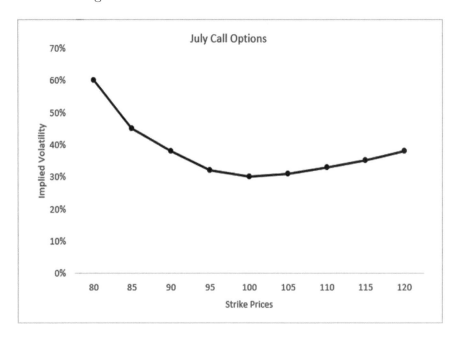

Notice that the numbers are now "skewed," which just means the graph no longer plots as a straight line but, instead, is bent. Consequently, it's called a *skew curve*. Specifically, it's a *vertical skew* since we're looking at a single expiration date but various strikes. If you were looking at an option quote board, you'd see the strikes vertically arranged for a given month. If we looked at a chart for put options, we'd get a similar picture. However, the put curve will usually sit higher than the call curve:

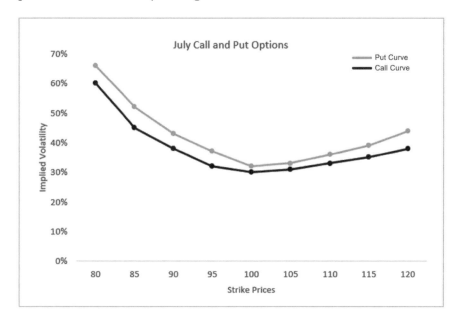

Whether you're looking at stocks or indexes, you'll normally see the lower strikes, whether calls or puts, trade at higher implied volatilities, but put options will usually trade at higher volatilities across the board. The ATM strikes, however, will usually trade for identical values, or at least very close, and the skews get more pronounced from there. Many types of skews occur in the markets, so let's cover some of the basic ones we'll encounter with unusual option activity.

POSITIVE-NEGATIVE SKEWS

Theoretically, any pair of option strikes that are equidistant from the current stock price strike should trade for the same implied volatility, and therefore the same price. For instance, if the stock is trading for $100, the $95 put should trade at the same implied volatility as the $105 call. Both options are $5 OTM, and because there's an equal probability for both to expire ITM, they should trade at the same volatility levels. If the $95 put is trading for $3, the $105 call should also trade for the same price (but that's only true if the risk-free interest rate is 0%). Likewise, the $90 put should trade for the same implied volatility as the $110 call since both are $10 OTM, and so on. In the real world, however, it's usually not true. If the put trades at a higher implied volatility, it's called a *negative skew*, or a *reverse skew*. On the other hand, if the call trades at a higher implied volatility, it's a *positive skew*, or *forward skew*. Most of the time, stock and equity indexes will exhibit negative skews, and the OTM put will trade for a higher implied volatility than the corresponding OTM call. If we graphed only the OTM strikes, we'll get a skew curve that looks something like the following:

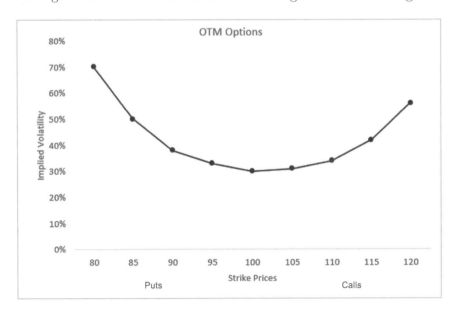

In this chart, the $100 strike is the ATM strike, so all strikes
below $100 are OTM put options, while all strikes above $100
are OTM call options. The chart looks more like a U-shape and
is often called a *volatility smile*. If the $95 put is trading for $3,
but the $105 call is trading for $2.50, there's a negative skew.
Again, because of the negative skew that's usually present, the
corresponding put strikes will normally sit somewhat higher
on the chart, which is easy to see by looking at the ends of
the chart: The far left side sits higher than the far right side.
Rather than a volatility smile, you'll sometimes hear this called
a volatility smirk. Whether a smirk or a smile, what causes the
graph to bend?

Prior to the Crash of '87 (Black Monday), these skews hardly
existed, and the equidistant call and put strikes traded at nearly
identical implied volatilities. After the crash, traders realized that
the downside risk was far greater than any upside risk. Markets can
crash down, but they never crash up. Historically, OTM options
were priced too cheap. Most pricing models assume stock price
changes follow a bell curve, but they actually follow a lognormal
distribution, which means large stock price declines have a higher
probability of occurring than the model would suggest. To
compensate for this risk, sellers began offering OTM puts at higher
prices. At the same time, speculators were aggressively bidding
higher because the crash showed there was always the potential
for tremendous payoffs. As a result, OTM puts have almost always
traded at higher implied volatilities ever since.

For calls, it's normal to see OTM strikes trade at higher implied
volatilities too, as they're great tools for speculators. Buyers are
willing to pay more than an option may theoretically be worth
because it's a cheap way to control shares of stock. For instance,
if the $120 call is theoretically worth 10 cents, it's not hard to
imagine that some traders would be willing to pay 20 or 30 cents
for it – even one dollar seems like a steal. If the pricing model
says it's worth 10 cents, but the market price is 30 cents, the only

way to account for that is through higher implied volatility, and now the right side of the graph is shifted higher too.

However, for the calls, we also get added selling pressure that's usually not seen for the puts. The markets are loaded with people who have IRAs or other tax-advantaged accounts unable to buy calls – but they can sell calls against shares of stock, which is the covered call strategy. Because of these additional sellers, the right side of the smile usually sits a bit lower.

Interestingly, if an OTM put trades at a higher implied volatility, the corresponding call (same strike) must also trade higher too. We're not going to cover it in this book, but there's a mathematical link called *put-call parity*, which keeps the implied volatilities very close to the same. So, the better way to understand the smile is that lower-strike options – whether calls or puts – will generally trade at higher implied volatilities than higher-strike options. That's a negative skew.

While a negative skew is the most common in the equities markets, it's not impossible to see positive skews where the OTM calls trade at much higher implied volatilities than the puts. For instance, you'll often see positive skews in biotech stocks where the potential for upside price bursts is far greater than downside losses. There's an added risk for call sellers, and an added demand for call buyers, so the OTM calls often trade at higher implied volatilities. You can also see positive skews in IPOs where you can see excess buying pressure during the first few trading days. Positive skews are almost always present in commodities markets where there's not much downside risk – but a whole lot of upside risk. Corn farmers, for instance, know how much to grow to meet current demand. But if there's a drought, supply goes down – and price goes up. For commodities, the risk to the sellers is almost always to the upside, and that's why you'll see positive skews.

When unusual option activity heats up, option prices become

negatively or positively skewed, depending on the expected direction of the stock's price. If you're not taking these skews into account, you're missing out on opportunities – or stepping into potential traps.

CHANGING TIMES, CHANGING SMILES

Information changes over time, traders' opinions change over time, and that means volatility smiles can change too. Sometimes, smiles will be relatively flat. Other times, they'll get more U-shaped. During major FDA announcements, for example, when the market isn't sure whether the news will be good or bad, skew curves can get very pronounced and end up looking more like a "V" rather than a smile:

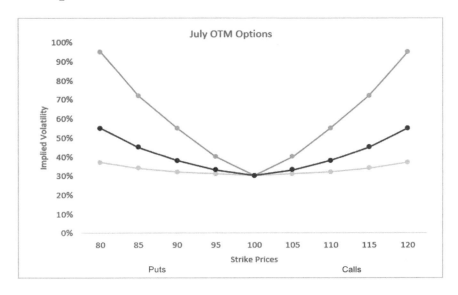

Interestingly, these curves will change over time – sometimes drastically. It may begin relatively flat but get more pronounced over time, or it may do the opposite and flatten.

When any type of news is circulating that could send stock prices higher or lower, such as unusual option activity, skew curves can get very peaked. For instance, if the $105 call has a sudden amount of buying pressure, its price may rise significantly, so traders begin to buy the $110 strike, then the $115 – and on up the chain. As each successive strike gets pushed to higher prices, the skew curve becomes more peaked. Because skew curves can go through dramatic changes, they can have unexpected impacts on strategies. If curves are very peaked, they'll probably relax as expiration gets closer, and that must be taken into consideration.

HORIZONTAL SKEWS

So far, we've covered vertical skews, which means we considered different strikes for a single expiration. Another type of skew occurs when we look at single strike prices across different expirations. For instance, we could look at the $100 calls for January, February, March, and so on. Generally, longer-dated options will trade at higher implied volatilities for the same reason longer-dated bonds have higher yields. They compensate investors for the additional risk over time:

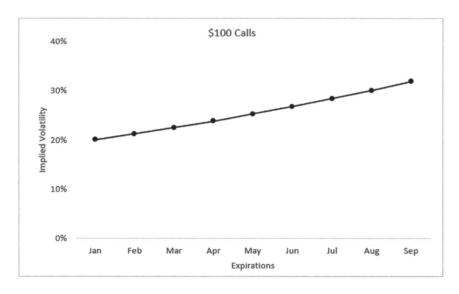

If you were looking at these option quotes, you'd see they appear horizontally on your broker's platform, so it's called a *horizontal skew*, but professional traders often call them tilts.

Horizontal skews can be confusing. Option prices get more expensive as you increase the time to expiration, so just because you see option prices rising across time, doesn't mean there's a skew. Instead, the presence of a skew tacks on an additional premium. For example, if a 30-day option is trading for $3, a pricing model would say a 120-day option would cost twice that, or $6. However, you may see it trading for $7 in the market. The option's price increasing from $3 to $6 is from the additional time, but the extra dollar is from the skew.

Whenever a stock has upcoming news, you'll often see the front-month, or front-week, contract trading at exceptionally high volatility levels. For instance, on September 6, 2018, Palo Alto Networks, Inc. (PANW) was releasing earnings after the closing bell. The stock was trading close to $220, and the $220 strike was trading for $7.80 – with one day until expiration. That's an implied volatility level of 142%. The stock, however, traded historically with a volatility near 25%, so the call option was extremely high priced – even though it was priced under $8. However, that same strike for the following week with eight days to expiration was trading at 63% volatility. With 22 days to expiration, the $220 call was priced at 45% volatility. The horizontal skew curve had reversed, so it's contrary to what we'd normally see, but that's because there was impending big news.

The same thing happens during unusual option activity, and that's why horizontal skews are important to check. Most of the time, the target expiration month will have exceptionally high implied volatility, just as Palo Alto did. Alternatively, the unusual activity may have occurred in a somewhat longer dated option, perhaps 30 or 45 days. To figure out which expiration is the best, we must always consider horizontal skews. Sometimes, we'll use the front-month option. Other times, we may use a longer-dated one. If none of those look good, we may use vertical spreads or diagonal spreads. These decisions, however, are never based on option prices. They're based on implied volatilities, and that's why skews are important to understand.

PUT-CALL SKEW

Another type of skew traders encounter is a put-call skew. Corresponding calls and puts – those with the same strike and expiration – should trade at the same implied volatility, or at least very close. If the July $100 call is trading at 30% implied volatility, you'd expect the July $100 put to trade at the same volatility. However, if the call is trading higher, it's called a positive put-call skew. If the put trades higher, it's a negative put-call skew. Don't confuse these terms with positive and negative skews that we covered previously. Those occur for the strikes that are equidistant from the current stock price.

Put-call skews also play a role in strategy selection for unusual option activity. We may decide to use a vertical spread but if there's a strong put-call skew, we may end up paying too much for the long call strike. In that case, we may be better off selling the put spread, so we can put the skew in our favor. We'll cover vertical spreads in Chapter Ten. For now, just understand that skews appear in many forms, but you must know where to look.

CONSIDER THE SKEW WHEN SELECTING YOUR STRATEGY

New traders often pick the strike where the unusual option activity is occurring, or they arbitrarily select a close strike that seems reasonably cheap. If you do that, you could step into a trap by picking the option with an abnormally high implied volatility. Once the news is announced, the skew curves flatten, and your option could lose money, even though you may have been correct about the stock's direction.

Interestingly, most traders avoid the ATM strike because it's the strike loaded with extrinsic value. However, depending on the skews, sometimes it's the best choice. On the other hand, if none of the option strikes can escape high implied volatility, we may need to choose a different strategy.

The trouble for most novice traders is they don't know about skew curves, so they just focus on the option's price. Once you understand that options are priced in terms of volatility, you'll see that the dollars you're spending have nothing to do with the option's value. As Warren Buffett said, *"Price is what you pay. Value is what you get."* For option traders, the value is always measured by the implied volatility. Every option we buy, every option we sell, and strategy we choose, involves the use of skew curves. It's a small detail, but it's not so small to escape close attention.

Ch.9 THE STOCK REPLACEMENT STRATEGY

Option strategies come in all shapes and sizes, and all are important if you want to custom-tailor the risks and rewards for a variety of situations. For unusual option activity, understanding which strategy to apply is just as important as identifying the opportunity itself. Finding a great opportunity, but applying the wrong strategy, can end up losing you money – even if the stock performs the way you expected. For unusual option activity there are three main strategies we teach: stock replacement, vertical spreads, and the stock replacement covered call. If you learn these strategies, you'll have all the strategies needed to profit from insider activity – while greatly limiting your risk.

Let's start with the stock replacement strategy, as it's powerful, adaptable, and easily customizable to various needs. What makes this strategy so interesting is that it's almost an optical illusion. To most traders, it appears the strategy uses a super-expensive option, which most people think would be risky. The stock replacement strategy, however, is more like buying cheap shares of stock with a small insurance policy attached. Because options are so much cheaper than shares, you can control a lot of stock for little money. If you're not afraid to trade shares of stock, you have absolutely nothing to lose – and everything to gain – by using the stock replacement strategy. It's a superior strategy to long shares of stock, and the profit and loss diagrams show why.

Any time you're trading options, you're effectively trading shares of stock. After all, options are derivatives whose price is tied to the underlying stock. Your strategy therefore depends on what you feel may happen with the stock's price. Will it be a long-term, slow, upward trend? Or an explosive burst? Or maybe somewhere in between? The stock replacement strategy is versatile, and depending on your outlook, you can tailor the strategy to suit your needs. For this book, we're just going to focus on the two most common uses – short term and long term.

Short-term strategies are typically used for unusual option activity. You may think a long-term strategy has no place in the unusual activity toolbox. However, it's not uncommon to see a company's price jump on a buyout announcement, but the acquiring company continues a long-term upward trend for months – or years – after. For instance, look at the price jump on Whole Foods (WFM) on June 16, 2017. Amazon.com announced it would acquire the company for $13.7 billion, or $42 per share – a 28% increase on the opening bell:

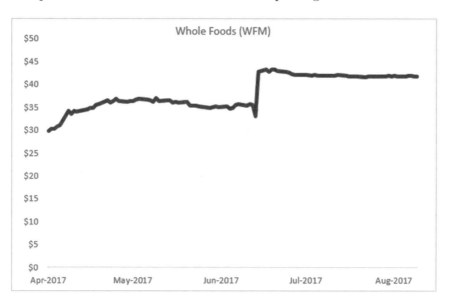

We uncovered unusual option activity in Whole Foods two months earlier and announced it on CNBC's *Halftime Report*™ on April 17. Pete showed that someone bought 5,000 contracts of the November $34 calls, just slightly ITM at the time, but paid a big premium of $3.40. Somebody knew something, and we flagged it.

However, after the announcement was made, investors realized Amazon was serious about expanding, as this was its largest acquisition by a long shot – and an all-cash deal. Previously, it had acquired Zappos for $1.2 billion and Twitch for $970 million, so after making profits on the short-term calls, perhaps the news prompted you to take a long-term position on Amazon. The chart below shows Amazon's strong growth trend continued long after the Whole Foods acquisition:

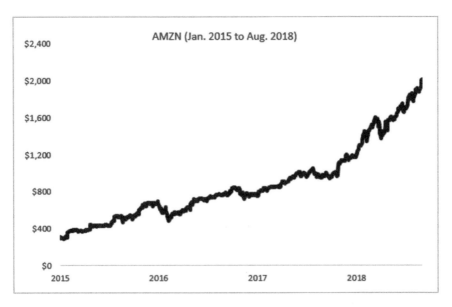

Over the next 14 months, Amazon's stock price rocketed from $987 to $2,012 – a 103% increase. By switching to the long-term stock replacement strategy, you could capture those much larger returns, all while greatly limiting the amount you could lose. Strategies can therefore change depending on what's happening with the target company or takeover company, even if they were uncovered from unusual option activity. Sometimes we may only want the short-term play. Other times, we'll take long-term outlooks. But when we're just trying to control shares of stock, we'll usually use variations of the stock replacement strategy.

CALL OPTIONS ARE EQUIVALENT TO INSURED SHARES OF STOCK

New traders are often fearful of call options. They've been told they're risky, and that they should stick with shares of stock. To capitalize on strategies to their fullest, you must have confidence in how they work, so before we cover the strategies, we want to show that ITM call options are equivalent to insured shares of stock. If you're willing to assume the risk by holding shares of stock, there's no reason you should fear controlling the same shares with an attached insurance policy. And just like any insurance, you can accept a deductible in exchange for paying lower premiums. You can do exactly the same with this strategy, so it's completely customizable to your tastes and preferences. Shares of stock aren't. Sounds strange, we know, but once you understand it's like trading insured shares of stock, you'll have total confidence in the stock replacement strategy.

Let's say you wanted to buy 100 shares of IBM. On July 27, 2018, the stock closed at $145.15, so you'd spend just over $14,500. Not only is this a lot of money to come up with, it poses a big downside risk. Stock, remember, moves dollar-for-dollar up, and dollar-for-dollar down. To guard against falling stock prices, let's say you decide to buy a put option. After all, using put options as a form of insurance against long shares is what they were designed for.

At this time, the November IBM options had 111 days to expiration, and the $130 put was trading for $1.60. By purchasing this put option, your cost basis rises by $1.60 per share, so you've effectively purchased shares of IBM for $146.75. Congratulations, you now have insured shares of stock. If IBM's price falls below the $130 strike at any time between now and expiration, you can always exercise your put and receive $130 per share. Nobody can argue that it's not a safer position. Yes, it's true that if IBM rises and the put expires worthless, you'll lose the $1.60 spent on the put, but that's the idea of insurance. Give up a little bit of the upside in exchange for knowing you're not going to get wiped out.

It may seem unlikely for IBM to drop to $130 – a 10% drop –
during that time, but that's why the insurance only cost $1.60.
If you didn't want to be exposed to that much of a loss, you
could buy a higher-strike put, say the $135 strike, but you'd
have to pay more for it. Different option strikes just give you
different choices, and it's entirely up to you where the sweet
spot is.

You may be wondering if it's worth buying insurance at all.
Just ask anyone who owned Facebook after it released earnings
on July 26, 2018. They not only missed expectations, but also
announced its revenue growth was expected to slow down.
The stock lost 20% of its value, or $120 billion in market
capitalization in a single day. In the IBM example, spending
$1.60 allows you to rest easy knowing the absolute worst you
could lose is 10% on your investment. Purchasing the IBM $130
put is like buying an insurance policy with a $15 deductible.
You're willing to assume the first $15 of the stock's price decline
from $145 to $130, but that's it. The following profit and loss
diagram shows the resulting position of the long shares plus the
long $130 put:

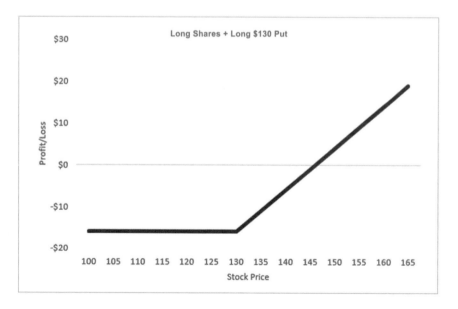

The graph bends at the $130 stock price because that's the put's strike price. For all stock prices below $130, you can always exercise your put and receive $130 cash, which is why you won't sustain further losses below that price. Long shares of stock have a straight line for their profit and loss diagram, but by insuring your shares with a put option, you've bent the graph and limited your potential losses. If you're not uncomfortable holding shares of stock, you shouldn't be uncomfortable holding shares that have a well-defined, limited loss. You're probably thinking this is sounding pretty good, so why would anybody mess with "risky" call options? Pete and I do, and here's why.

Rather than buying the combination of the shares plus the $130 put, we would buy the November $130 call trading for $16. It's the same strike and expiration of the put, but we're using calls instead. The following is the profit and loss diagram for the $130 call purchased for $16:

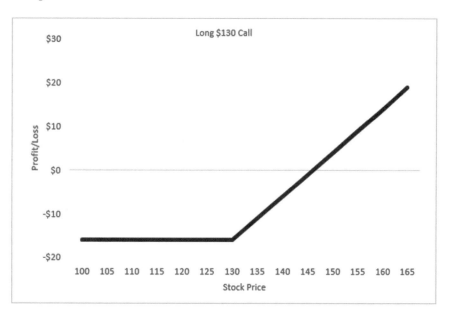

Hold on a minute, it looks exactly like insured shares of stock! There's a good reason – it's equivalently the same thing. In the business, we call the combination of long stock plus a long put the *synthetic equivalent* of a call option. Synthetic positions are just mathematical equivalents that use two different positions to create the mirror image of a third. They're called synthetic positions because they behave in all respects like the one they're designed to mirror, much like synthetic wool looks and feels like regular wool. If you can understand that 0.5 is exactly the same as 1/2 even though the construction is different, that's the idea of synthetic positions. The forms are different, but the values are identical. Synthetic positions is a topic that every professional trader knows well because we can get equivalent positions for far less money. You spent $146.75 while we spent $16 – but we're holding exactly the same thing. The leverage comes because you had to purchase the stock while we took the right to buy the stock. Because both positions, however, control 100 shares of the same stock, both positions behave identically at all price points. Okay, let's put it to the test. Even though the long call may look like stock plus put combinations, how will it compare when we get down to dollars and cents?

By purchasing the shares and the put, your expiration breakeven point is $146.75, so you'll begin generating gains for all stock prices above that. For us, by purchasing the $130 call for $16, our expiration breakeven is $146. We're better off by 75 cents – and we spent less money to have the same benefit. In fact, our position will always beat the stock plus put combination by 75 cents – no matter which stock prices we're talking about.

For instance, let's say the stock rises to $160 at expiration. You, as the insured stock trader, would earn $13.25 ($160 sales price - $146.75 cost) per share. For us, the $130 call option would be worth the $30 of intrinsic value at expiration, leaving us with a $14 gain ($30 sales price - $16 cost). The difference between $14 and $13.25 is, again, 75 cents. Pick any stock price above the $130 strike, and the long call will outperform the stock plus put combinations by 75 cents at expiration. What about the downside?

If you own the shares of stock with the put option and IBM falls below the $130 strike, you'd exercise the put and receive $130 cash, leaving you with a loss of $16.75 ($130 sales price - $146.75 cost). For us, the $130 call expires worthless, creating a loss of $16. Once again, we're better off by 75 cents. This 75-cent benefit keeps appearing, and it's not a coincidence. Why does the long call always win by 75 cents?

Whenever you're comparing option strategies, always keep your eye on the extrinsic value. That's what makes an option an option. Any differences are due to the extrinsic values. In this example, the stock was purchased for $145.15. The $130 call at $16 has 85 cents of extrinsic value. However, the $130 put, trading at $1.60, is made up entirely of extrinsic value. So, the call is lower by 75 cents.

Theoretically, the extrinsic values should be the same for the same-strike options – assuming interest rates are zero. In the presence of interest rates, the same-strike call should trade for a little bit more money than the put. With today's relatively low interest rates, there shouldn't be a big difference between the call and put, but in the real world, there often are discrepancies. It's not uncommon to see OTM puts trade for more extrinsic value than the same-strike call. The reason is that stock traders are often attracted to OTM puts because they create a cheap form of disaster insurance. As a result, these put options get bid to higher extrinsic values, but not the corresponding calls. When that happens, traders are even better off buying the deep ITM call. Not only are we spending less money, but our insurance policy costs less too. What's the tradeoff?

If we compared the profits and losses of our $130 call to the actual shares of stock, we'd underperform by 85 cents for all stock prices above the $130 strike. But if the stock price falls below $130, the call option limits our losses, and we'll outperform the long shares by increasing amounts. The further the stock price falls below the strike, the more the stock trader loses while our losses remain limited to $16. By paying a one-time fee of 85 cents, the extrinsic value, we have insured shares. So the decision to use calls over the stock comes down to this: You can pay $16 to control shares, or you can pay $145 for the stock, take your chances on the downside, and have 85 cents more profit on the upside. It's not a good idea, and now you see why professional traders use call options – and you should too. You'll be making more efficient use of your money – and getting a small insurance policy to boot. Who would have thought that "risky" options could provide such benefits?

If you're not afraid to buy shares of stock, you shouldn't be afraid to insure them by buying puts. And if you're not afraid of that combination, you definitely shouldn't be fearful of ITM calls. It's the same idea, only cheaper. Now that you understand that deep ITM calls are a cheap way to control shares of stock with a small insurance policy attached, we can now show you how to make more efficient use of your money – and capture longer, more profitable trends with less risk by using one of our favorite strategies – stock replacement. We're going to start with the long-term version first, and then we'll show the adjustment we make for short-term outlooks.

THE LONG-TERM STOCK REPLACEMENT STRATEGY

The long-term stock replacement strategy is used anytime you have a longer-term outlook. It may be a three-month swing trade, or you could use it to control positions for years. As we said earlier, there may also be times where a short-term outlook leads to a longer-term position, so that's why we include it when teaching unusual option activity. You never know which opportunities will present themselves, so you need to understand all the choices available.

The long-term stock replacement strategy is conceptually simple

– but very powerful. The idea is to use deep ITM call options as a substitute for long shares of stock. Remember, though, all strikes aren't created equal. Each strike acts like a different tool, and like a carpenter, you need to reach for the right tool for the job. Most traders like to reach for the ATM strikes because they're so much cheaper. However, their price is made up entirely of extrinsic value, and that means your breakeven point is pushed well above the current stock price. As a result, you'll need fast, aggressive stock price moves in order to break even, which means you're less likely to see profits.

Out-of-the-money strikes are even cheaper, but they need even bigger moves from the stock in order to generate profits. They have a lower probability for success.

In-the-money options, however, have high deltas, so they behave more like shares of stock, and if you go far enough ITM to where there's no extrinsic value, they perform *identically* to shares of stock.

The idea of the long-term stock replacement strategy is to find a good balance between intrinsic and extrinsic values. You don't want to spend a lot on the option, but you also don't want it to be loaded with extrinsic value. How do you determine the right strikes?

THE DETAILS ARE IN THE DELTAS

There's a simple rule of thumb: Find the strike that has an 80 to 85 delta, and you'll be in the ballpark. With those deltas, you're far enough ITM that the option won't have a lot of extrinsic value. But if you select higher deltas, you'll greatly increase the option's cost, but won't reduce the extrinsic value that much. In other words, using deltas above 85 results in diminishing returns. You'll spend a lot more money, but you won't receive a lot of additional benefit. Take of look at the wider range of strikes for the IBM November calls (111 days to expiration):

IBM STOCK = $145.15				
STRIKE	PRICE	INTRINSIC	EXTRINSIC	DELTA
$100	45.57	45.15	0.42	92
$105	40.59	40.15	0.44	92
$110	35.61	35.15	0.46	92
$115	30.63	30.15	0.48	92
$120	25.65	25.15	0.50	92
$125	20.70	20.15	0.55	89
$130	16.00	15.15	0.85	82
$135	11.77	10.15	1.62	75
$140	8.18	5.15	3.03	63

We chose the $130 call for this example because it had a delta of 82. However, had we chosen the $125 call instead, we would have increased the price from $16 to $20.70, or by $4.70, but only decreased the extrinsic value by 30 cents. If we chose the $120 strike, we would have increased the cost from $16 to $25.65, or by $9.65, but only reduced the extrinsic value by 35 cents. You can see it's just not worth it. The reason is that each time you reduce the strike by $5, you increase the intrinsic value by the same amount, but you're only reducing the extrinsic value by a small amount. The net effect is that you get a big increase in cost without much additional benefit.

Of course, you're always free to tweak the selection a little bit. In some instances, you may want to push the deltas a little higher or lower. But in all cases, for long-term outlooks, you want to keep the deltas fairly high. Our recommendation is you should be somewhere in the 80 to 85 delta range.

Now that you know the secret to finding an option that behaves like stock – without spending a fortune, what are the benefits of the long-term stock replacement strategy?

BENEFIT #1: LOWER COST

The stock replacement strategy has many key benefits, but perhaps the most obvious is the low cost. In our example, you could buy the stock plus the $130 put for $146.75, a total investment of $14,675 for 100 shares, or you could buy the $130 call for $16, or $1,600 total, to *control* 100 shares – an 89% reduction. You're able to control the same amount of shares, reaping nearly the same benefits, for a much lower cost. This opens the doors to opportunities you may have never had, especially for IRAs or other tax-advantaged accounts where you're limited on the amount of money you can contribute each year. Many of today's investors often want to buy the high-flying popular stocks like Amazon, Netflix, and Apple but simply can't afford them. The door is closed, and the opportunities disappear. Consequently, they often let the tail wag the dog and choose their investments based on what they can afford – instead of those they feel are the best opportunities. For example, consider an investor who thinks next year's winners will be Amazon, Facebook, Google, Netflix, and Apple. However, he buy shares of Bob's Bait and Tackle because it's the only stock he could afford – it's absurd. Not only does it not make financial sense, but it subjects the investor to unwanted risks, simply because price shut him out from the better choices. Not anymore. The stock replacement strategy sharply lowers the cost and allows traders access to the companies where they'd prefer to invest.

BENEFIT #2: BETTER RETURN ON INVESTMENT (ROI)

The stock replacement strategy also provides financial leverage, which is what every investor would like to have – all things being equal. Financial leverage just means that your gains, or returns on investment (ROI), are magnified. When stock prices rise, magnifications are great for the long positions. The problem is that financial leverage is a double-edged sword: It also magnifies your losses. Options provide a benefit because you get the magnification to the upside – but without the corresponding risk to the downside.

Financial leverage is created any time you borrow money to buy an asset. When you borrow money, you're only depositing a portion of the asset's total price, yet you're keeping 100% of the gains. For example, if you put 10% down on a new home, you'll earn all price increases upon the sale. However, because you only put one-tenth of the value down, your leverage will be 10 times as great. If the home's value rises 5%, the return on your money is 10 times as large, or 50%. However, if the home's value falls 5%, your investment loses 50%. No matter what the percentage returns may be – gains or losses – the returns to you will be 10 times greater. That's financial leverage. High leverage means small changes in the underlying price equals big changes to your profit and loss.

Because options are cheaper than shares of stock, they also provide financial leverage. Depending on the strike chosen, you can control the amount of leverage. The leverage comes from the same place it always does – borrowed money. Interestingly, options are a form of borrowing money – but without actually borrowing. It's a mathematical leverage, and that's what creates this second benefit. In our example with IBM trading at $145.15, investors have two choices. Let's say Pete buys 100 shares outright. Instead of buying the shares, I buy the $130 call for $16. Both of us will capture all of IBM's future price increases between now and expiration, but I didn't pay the full $145.

> **FINANCIAL LEVERAGE IS CREATED ANY TIME YOU BORROW MONEY TO BUY AN ASSET.**

However, let's say at expiration, I decide to exercise the call and pay the $130 strike. At this point, Pete and I each own 100 shares, but I didn't fully pay for them until expiration. In other words, I "floated" or "borrowed" the

$130 strike price. Again, I didn't actually borrow money, but it's a mathematical leverage created from the fact that I wasn't required to pay the strike price at the time I bought the call.

Call options, therefore, provide leverage compared to owning shares of stock. For example, by spending $16 for the call rather than $145 for the shares, I'm getting $145/$16, or 9:1 leverage. If IBM rises 10%, the call will increase nine times that, or about 90%. It won't work out exactly because the extrinsic value disappears at expiration, which is the true cost of the option. That's something we pay, but don't get back. By design, however, we keep the extrinsic value small, so the numbers should be close.

For example, if IBM rises 10% at expiration, its price will rise from $145.15 to $159.66 thus making the $130 call's intrinsic value $29.66. Because I paid $16, my return is 85% rather than the 90% the 9:1 ratio would suggest. Either way, it beats 10%.

Stock investors can also get leverage, but it's dangerous, as they must actually borrow money, which is called trading on margin. To trade on margin, you must deposit 50% of the stock's price and will borrow the balance from the broker. If you bought 100 shares of IBM for $145, your account would be debited $7,250 cash and you'd borrow the remaining $7,250 from the broker, for the total of $14,500. Doing so, your leverage is 2:1. Whether the stock price rises or falls, your gains and losses are double those percentages. It's a lot of risk for only 2:1 leverage.

At best, if you're a pattern day trader (PDT), you can get 4:1 leverage, but you must have the position closed by the end of the day. The stock trader must therefore pay $7,250 for 2:1 leverage, the pattern day trader pays $3,625 for 4:1 leverage, but the stock replacement trader pays $1,600 ($16 for the call) and gets 9:1 leverage.

Trading shares on margin, however comes with another big risk. If the stock's price drops far enough, you can end up owing more money than initially invested, which is called a *margin call* or *maintenance call.* For instance, if you paid $7,250 for 100 shares and borrowed the remainder, your equity is 50%, which is found by taking $7,250 divided by the $14,500 value of the stock position. The margin trader must always begin at 50%. However, after the trade is placed, most brokers allow the equity to dip down to 30% before issuing a margin call. If the value of your IBM shares falls from $14,500 to $10,357, your equity is $3,107, which is 30% of the market value. Any further decrease in the stock's price, and you'll be required to deposit enough cash, or sell or deposit other securities, to bring your account equity back to at least 30%. The biggest risk with margin trading is that most traders are borrowing money because they don't have the funds to buy the shares they want. When they get a margin call, they're usually forced to sell their shares to meet the call but that means are selling shares at the absolute worst time – probably the very bottom. That will never happen with the stock replacement strategy. In our IBM example, you'd get 9:1 leverage without the fear of any margin call.

Margin trading also means you'll pay interest on the borrowed money. Because these loans are secured against the shares of stock, the rates are generally cheaper than credit cards, but they're far from free. In mid-2018, for example, E*TRADE™ charged 10.5% for margin balances below $10,000. If you borrowed about $7,260 for this IBM trade, you'd pay $762 interest for the year, or almost $64 per month, which means you'd pay about $235 for 111 days.

The $130 stock replacement call, however, only had a one-time "charge" of 85 cents, or $85 total, which was the extrinsic value. The stock replacement strategy therefore gets 9:1 leverage at a cost of $85, limited downside risk, no margin calls, and saves nearly $150 worth of interest for the year – all for a one-time $85 charge – the extrinsic value.

BENEFIT #3: LIMITED RISK & GAMMA

Options provide greater leverage compared to trading shares

on margin. That alone is a benefit. However, financial leverage is usually dangerous since it also magnifies losses, and in some cases, you can lose more than you have invested in the position. Using the earlier example, if the home price dropped 20%, you'd lose 10 times that, or 200%. That's not true for options.

With options, the most you can lose is the amount you paid, so by purchasing the IBM $130 call, the most you can lose is $16. For that to happen, however, IBM's price would have to be $130 or lower at expiration. In that case you'd just let the option expire worthless and walk away from the deal. If that happens, you're only worse off by the 85-cent extrinsic value compared to the stock trader. That was the value of the insurance policy. Recall that the profit and loss diagram for a long call has a hockey-stick shape, but prior to expiration, it won't be that pronounced, but instead will be curved. The profit and loss diagram below shows a long stock position (gray) compared to the IBM $130 call with 111 days until expiration (black):

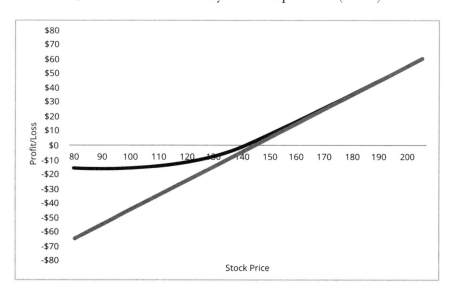

The chart shows the call option's curved profit and loss profile begins to quickly taper off for all stock prices below $130. That curvature is the option's gamma coming to your rescue if the stock price falls.

The stock trader, on the other hand, continues to lose dollar for dollar all the way down to a stock price of zero. However, as the stock continues to climb above its current $145 price, the risk profile shows the call option and the long shares of stock are nearly identical. The two lines overlap, and you can't even see the black curve underneath the gray curve. That's another way of showing that the option and the long stock position are virtually identical for all future stock prices above $145. The $130 call is "mimicking" or "replacing" the shares of stock on the way up – but not on the way down.

So, another advantage to the option trader is that as the stock price rises in your favor, you'll make nearly dollar-for-dollar – just like the stock trader. However, if stock price falls, you won't lose dollar for dollar. Options have an asymmetric payoff profile: It looks like stock to the upside, but not to the downside. That's an enormous benefit, and it's all because of the hidden power of gamma.

BENEFIT #4: DIVERSIFICATION

Except for Warren Buffett, most investors eventually run into cash problems, and that means they run into diversification trouble. Investors like to spread their risk by purchasing many different positions, but also leave some cash on the side for other opportunities – including unusual option activity. However, if you own shares of stock, you're going to quickly run low on cash because you're spending so much money to own the shares. Again, this is a big problem for people with retirement accounts where they're restricted by the amount of money they're allowed to contribute each year.

If you have $100,000 in your account, you may only be able to take positions in six to 10 different stocks. Of course, there are some positions where you won't even be able to afford 100 shares, such as Amazon, currently trading around $2,000. The stock replacement strategy creates new possibilities. Because you're only spending a small fraction of the stock's price, yet virtually controlling the shares of stock, any given account size has the ability for greater diversification.

For instance, let's say you wanted to buy the five FAANG stocks: Facebook, Amazon, Apple, Netflix, and Google. At their current prices in mid-2018, it would cost about $380,000 to buy 100 shares of each. By using the stock replacement strategy with 80-delta calls for June 2019 expiration (328 days to expiration), you could control those shares in these same companies for $87,000, or about 23% of what it would cost to own the shares. As a pattern day trader, you'd pay slightly more at 25% but could only control them for a single day. If you had the $380,000 cash, but used the stock replacement strategy instead, you'd have nearly $293,000 sitting in cash to purchase other securities or take advantage of the market dips that often provide great buying opportunities. In other words, the stock replacement strategy allows you to control the same shares for less money, which means you can spread your money thinner and further diversify through many different stocks. It all comes from being more cash efficient with your trading, and we think there's no better way to get it than by using the stock replacement strategy.

BENEFIT #5: ROLL, ROLL, ROLL!

All clients in our education and subscription services know the phrase too well – "roll, roll, roll!" There's a good reason for it. It's another big advantage that option traders have over stock traders. What is rolling?

Rolling is just an option trader's term for a trade that switches us from one expiration or strike to another. For example, let's say you're holding a March $100 call option and it's about to expire. Rather than waiting for it to actually expire on Friday and buying a new position on Monday, you could roll the position on Friday.

Just place an order to sell your March $100 call and simultaneously buy a new one, perhaps the April $100 call. By using a single order, you can execute both trades at the same time. Once it's executed, you'll no longer have the March $100 call but will be long the April $100 call. You've rolled from March to April. Rolling to a different expiration month is a lot like renewing your auto insurance policy. If it expires on December 31, you don't wait for it to expire and then start a new policy next year. Instead, you renew the policy before it expires. You roll from one year to another.

We can do the same thing by rolling to different strikes. Let's say you own the April $100 call at a price of $6. The call option has greatly limited your risk compared to owning shares of stock but you would still like to protect that investment. Unfortunately, many traders sell at the first sign of profits. They may pay $6 but sell when it gets to $6.50 or $7 because they're so fearful of losing money. In the business, we call this picking up nickels in front of bulldozers. By selling early, they miss out on the big gains that so often occur in the long run.

Take a look at the following chart on Amazon.com from January 2015 to August 2018:

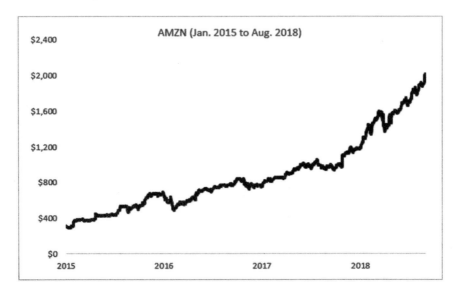

It had enormous price gyrations and certainly big enough to scare most investors out of positions. Yet, during that time, it rose from about $300 to $1,854 – a return of over 68% per year. With this stock, you can get about 3:1 leverage by using the stock replacement strategy, and you can see that adds up to serious money. However, most investors never capture those big trends because they get caught in a small dip and exit the position at a loss. Rolling gives you the best of both worlds. You can limit your losses – but still hang on for explosive returns.

To execute a roll-up, you sell your current call and buy a higher strike with the same expiration. For instance, sell your April $100 call and simultaneously buy the April $105 call. You've increased your strike from $100 to $105 – you rolled up the strike. What's the advantage?

For any given expiration date, lower-strike calls must be worth more money than higher-strike calls. The reason is logical: Lower-strike calls give you the right to pay less money for the shares, which is a benefit. The market recognizes that benefit so it always makes sure lower-strike calls have a higher price than those with higher strikes. For example, without even looking at option quotes, you know the April $100 call must trade for a higher price than the April $105 call, and the April $105 call must be worth more than the April $110 call.

By executing a rollup, you're selling a more expensive option and swapping it out for a less valuable one. That means you'll get cash back from the transaction, or a net credit for the trade. The cash received offsets your purchase price, which further reduces the amount you can lose. However, because you didn't completely exit the position, you still have a call option that can continue earning profits if the stock continues to rise. To see how a roll works, let's say you bought an April $100 call for $6. Your profit and loss profile at expiration looks like this:

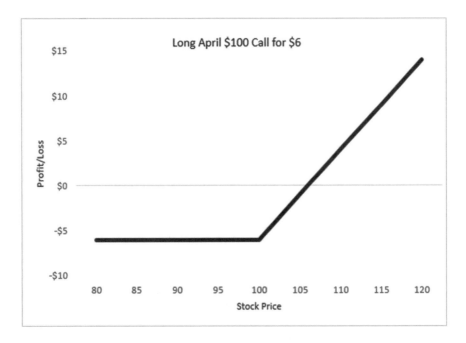

It has the usual hockey-stick shaped graph, limited to only losing $6, but can make dollar-for-dollar at expiration as the stock rises. Even though it has limited downside, it would be nice if we could guard against that $6 maximum loss too. That's where a roll-up comes in.

Let's say the stock rises, and the call option prices have increased in response. Your April $100 call is now worth $8, and you can buy the April $105 call for $4. Rather than selling your $100 call and taking the $2 gain, let's roll the call up to the $105 strike. It's a simple trade where you'll sell your $100 call and simultaneously buy the $105 call. It's a single order that executes both trades. You may have noticed that the trade is a short vertical spread. All you have to do is sell the April $100/$105 vertical spread, which is a strategy we'll cover in the next chapter. The trade looks like this:

> Sell April $100 call and simultaneously
> Buy the April $105 call.

Once the order fills, however, the sale of the April $100 call closes your current long April $100 call, and you'll just be left holding the April $105 call.

Like any order, you can place the trade "at market" and be guaranteed the fill, but you can't guarantee the price. You can also choose to place a limit order, which guarantees a minimum selling price, but you can't guarantee it will fill. Most of the time, we suggest setting a limit order equal to 80% of the difference in strikes. Because you're rolling from the $100 to the $105 call, that's a $5 roll, so you should place a limit order for a $4 credit. Again, that just means the order can't be filled unless you receive at least four dollars. If you were rolling from the $100 call to the $110, you'd usually set a limit equal to 80% of that difference, or $8 and so forth. What benefit did you get from the roll?

By rolling to the $105 call for a net credit of $4, you effectively own the $105 call for a price of $2. It was trading for $6 in the market, but you received $4 back from the trade, and that cash is now sitting safely in your money market account. The most you can now lose has been reduced from $6 to $2. The real benefit can be seen by comparing the before and after profit and loss diagrams. When you initiated the original $100 call position, you were on the black line, which could lose a maximum of $6. After you rolled to the $105 strike, the gray line shows you can only lose a maximum of $2:

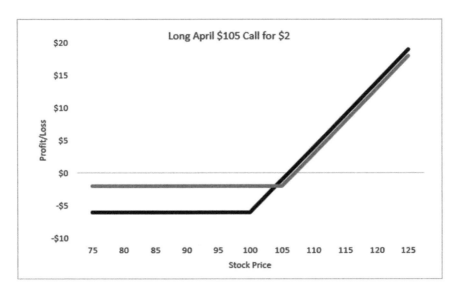

The maximum amount you could lose has been greatly reduced from $6 to $2, a reduction of 66%. That, in and of itself, is a great reason for doing the roll. In addition, because you didn't completely exit the position, you can still continue to earn an unlimited amount as the stock rises. The roll doesn't come for free, and there is a tradeoff: Your breakeven price has been shifted a little bit higher. The $100 call had a $106 breakeven while the $105 call has a $107 breakeven. That one-dollar sacrifice is the "cost" of the roll. It's easy to figure out this cost, as it's the difference in strikes ($5) less the credit ($4). Synthetically, you purchased the $105 put for one dollar.

Think about the tradeoffs. Your maximum loss is reduced by 66%, but you still have the ability to make unlimited gains – just minus one dollar. It's a small cost for a big gain, and that's the power of rolling. By reducing the maximum loss, you reduce the fear, and now can hold on for bigger profits.

Previously, we suggested doing a five-dollar roll for a $4 credit, and now you should see why. If you roll too early, you won't receive much money, say one dollar. You'll barely reduce your losses, but you'll shift your breakeven point forward by $4. It's a big cost for a small gain. At the other extreme, if you wait until you can roll $20 higher for a $16 credit, you're taking too much of a chance for the stock to move against you. While there are exceptions, depending on fundamental or technical events, we generally always roll every time we can receive a $4 credit for a $5 roll. Now let's say the stock climbs higher. What should you do?

Roll, roll, roll! Let's say you can now receive another $4 credit by rolling to the $110 strike. Your order looks like this:

> Sell $105 call and simultaneously
> Buy $110 call
> _____
> Net credit of $4

When the trade is executed, your long $105 call cancels, or closes, the short $105 call. You're just left holding the $110 call, but again, have shifted your curve higher by four dollars. This time, however, something is quite different about the resulting profit and loss diagram. It no longer sits below zero:

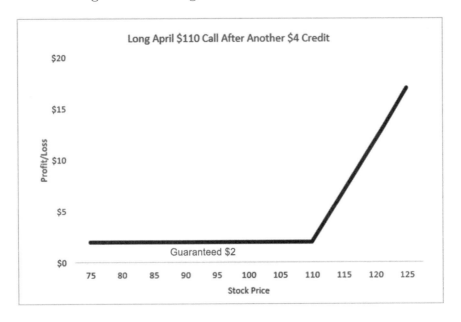

In other words, you can't lose. It's like playing with "house money." Initially, you paid $6 for the $100 call, but you've collected a total of $8 from the two rolls – a 33% return. Better yet, that $800 is sitting in cash, so no matter what happens to the stock's price, you're guaranteed a 33% return on your money – but you might do better – as you still own a call option for possible further gains.

Rolling is one of the most powerful advantages at an option trader's disposal, as you can't do the same feat by using shares of stock. Let's say you bought 100 shares of stock instead. If the stock price rises, you might hedge by selling off a portion, say 25 shares. However, you could only do that four times before you run out of shares. Also, your sensitivity changes. In other words, you used to earn $100 for every dollar move in the stock, but now will only make $75. Sell off another 100 shares and you'll only earn $50 per dollar move and so on.

By using call options, however, you'll never run out of "shares," and you'll never reduce your sensitivity. If you bought your initial call with a delta of 80, each successive roll will keep the deltas about the same level. You can roll the option forever and always maintain around 80 deltas. That's an impossibility by using shares of stock. As a stock trader, you must either continue to let the stock price run, thereby accepting more risk if it should fall, or you can begin to sell shares as it rises. However, you may find that you sold out of the position far too soon. You missed the big money. Rolling your call options up eliminates all of these unwanted outcomes. It's the biggest benefit of long call options, and we make great use of it when staying in long-term positions.

THE SHORT-TERM STOCK REPLACEMENT STRATEGY

The long-term stock replacement strategy rests on a single idea: Select a strike price that's sufficiently deep ITM, which means a high delta of 80 to 85, and your call option will behave more like shares of stock. It won't have a lot of extrinsic value to decay, and your breakeven point will therefore be close to the current stock price. That's a description that sounds far more like shares of stock than an option.

However, when we get qualified signals for unusual option activity, our expectation is that we're about to get major market-moving news. However, there's no guarantee that a qualified signal equates to insider trading. But if we have some expectations on the speed, or aggressiveness, of the stock's price, we're not expecting it to drift up slowly over time. Instead, we may see price spikes of 5%, 10%, or far more in a few days.

That's aggressive. And if that's part of our outlook, why not incorporate it into the strategy decision? For the long-term stock replacement strategy, delta was the secret. For short-term, we'll make more use of gamma.

If you recall from Chapter Six, gamma measures how quickly the deltas will accumulate. If you have an option with a lot of gamma, you don't need a lot of delta, as gamma will manufacture the deltas for you. What you need is a fast, aggressive move from the underlying stock. Perfect – it's exactly what we're expecting when we're trading unusual option activity.

If your outlook is for an aggressive change in the stock's price over a short time, say less than 60 days, we generally use a little different selection process, even though we still call it the stock replacement strategy. It's the same idea, just tweaked a bit for a shorter-term outlook. In Chapter Six, we showed that ATM options have the greatest gamma. Also, the shorter the expiration, the greater the gamma. Therefore, if you're using short-term, ATM strikes, your option will be rich with gamma, which means your deltas will quickly accelerate from a medium number near 50 to a high number if the stock price moves quickly. You won't get that type of acceleration using longer-dated options.

It doesn't mean we'll be right, but that's the whole point of designing a strategy. If we're right, gamma will automatically generate the deltas, and in the blink of an eye, we'll have high deltas which we can roll. If we're wrong, we won't have as much intrinsic value to lose because we didn't buy deep ITM strikes. It provides a better risk-reward setup based on the outlook. If you only use shares of stock, the only thing you can do is alter the number of shares you own, but you'll still have a delta of 100 and gamma of zero, and you can't change them. With options, you can. It's one of the biggest advantages of options, so use it. So, how do we select the strike?

By now, you probably figured out we're going to lean toward ATM strikes. However, we alter it a little bit depending on whether we're using calls or puts. For calls, we'll go slightly ITM and select a strike with a delta near 65. We'll get a little more delta than if we selected the ATM strike, but we'll still have a lot of gamma. For puts, we'll select a strike closer to ATM, so we're hunting for something near 50. Why the slight delta difference between calls and puts?

We have two reasons: First, stock prices tend to fall harder and faster than they rise. Remember, staircase up, elevator down. Fear is a powerful motivator, and panicked investors rush to sell on negative news far faster than they line up to buy on good news. If stock prices are expected to take a sharp nosedive, it makes sense to increase the gamma a bit more by purchasing the ATM strike.

Second, when stock prices plummet, fear causes the extrinsic value on all options to spike to much higher values. When prices are crumbling in front of investors' eyes, they rush to buy puts for protection against further losses. When a rush of buy orders hits the markets, the extrinsic value rises. Because ATM options have the greatest gamma, we'd like to capture that spike in extrinsic value. By understanding delta and gamma, the short-term stock replacement strategy becomes simple: Buy calls with a delta near 65 and puts with a delta near 50, and now your strategy is aligned with your outlook.

Which expiration do we choose? We usually follow the market on this one. If the unusual option activity is in the 30-day expiration, that's most likely within the time frame of the announcement. After all, the *smart money* isn't going to buy a contract that expires before the news becomes public. However, if the activity appears in a very short-dated expiration, say within the week, we may extend it to the following week.

Of course, if you're ever in doubt about the aggressiveness of any potential stock price move, you're always safer to select a call option or put with a higher delta. You'll pay more for it, but you'll also break even sooner. Pete and I have done this on many occasions when we see unusual activity occurring at strikes far away from the current stock price. For instance, if the stock is $100 but there's heavy buying in the $140 strike, it sends a big signal, but we may not want to press our luck that much. If the stock price doesn't reach $140, that option is almost assuredly going to expire worthless. Instead, maybe we'll play the $110 or $120 strikes. If you make adjustments like this, just balance the amount you're willing to spend against the breakeven points. For example, if the unusual activity occurs at the $110 strike, it's not a good idea to buy the $140 strike just to make the option's price cheaper. For those big signals, we'll turn to an even more versatile strategy – the vertical spread.

Ch. 10 THE VERSATILE VERTICAL SPREAD

For option traders, there's nothing more frustrating than thinking you've struck potential gold from unusual option activity but can do nothing about it because the options are too expensive. Even with stock replacement, if you're dealing with $1,000 stocks, you still may need to spend a lot of money to control the shares.

Two of the main factors that affect option prices are the underlying stock's price and volatility. Options are a form of insurance, and just as in the insurance markets, as the price of the insured item rises, so do the premiums. It'll cost more to insure a Ferrari than a Volkswagen. That's exactly how it works for stocks, and for the same reason. All else being equal, you'll pay more for an ATM $1,000 call than you will for an ATM $100 call. If both stocks rise, say 10%, the $1,000 stock can generate $100 worth of intrinsic value into an option while the $100 can only create $10. Higher-priced stocks have a stronger ability to increase an option's intrinsic value, and therefore will cost more money.

For example, let's compare two ATM calls on stocks with very different prices. On September 28, 2018, Amazon (AMZN) closed at $2,003 and its 33-day $2002.50 call was trading just over $88. General Electric (GE), on the other hand, closed at $11.29 and the $11.50 call with the same expiration was trading for 38 cents. Big differences in stock prices mean big differences in option prices. Many traders think this difference is due to volatility, but both stocks are trading with an implied volatility near 34%. The big reason for the price difference in this case is the cost of the shares.

The second factor that greatly affects an option's price is volatility. Higher volatility means there's less certainty about future stock prices, so the more volatility, the larger the premiums. Many times, you'll find unusual option activity, but it will occur on high-priced or high-volatility stocks – sometimes both. For these times, option premiums can get super pricey. From the risk-reward perspective, sometimes it just doesn't make sense to buy an outright call or put option, even though unusual option activity might suggest there is potentially a large move coming. It's hard to justify spending $50 or more on an option that expires in a week just because of some unusual activity. Is there something you can do to take a position without breaking the bank? Options are versatile, and a vertical spread is an option strategy that shows just how versatile they can be.

WHAT IS A VERTICAL SPREAD?

In financial strategies, the word "spread" always means

you're buying one asset and simultaneously selling another. Both assets are related, so the prices play off of each other. In other words, as one value rises, the other falls. There are stock spreads, bond spreads, futures spreads, and many others. They're different in many ways, but they share one thing in common: The trader will be long one asset and simultaneously short another.

For option traders, it usually means we're buying one option and simultaneously selling another option against it. There are many spread strategies and most are named for the way that they appear on the quote board. To place a vertical spread, both options must be calls or both must be puts – not one of each. They must also have the same expiration date. For instance, you might buy a June $100 call and sell a June $105 call, which we'd call the June $100/$105 vertical spread. If you look at a quote board, you'll see those two quotes appear vertically from each other, so traders would say we've spread the long option off vertically.

STRIKES	JANUARY
$100	$10.22
$105	$5.70
$110	$2.35
$115	$0.68

As with all option strategies, you can use calls or puts, and you can buy or sell, so for vertical spreads, there are four combinations you can create:

- Buy call spread
- Buy put spread
- Sell call spread
- Sell put spread

By understanding these four combinations, you'll have one of the most powerful and versatile tools for capitalizing on unusual option activity – the vertical spread.

THE LONG CALL VERTICAL SPREAD

Let's start with "long" spreads, as they're the easiest to understand. To buy a call spread, you'll buy a call at one strike and sell another call at a higher strike with the same expiration date. You're "buying" the spread because it will result in a net debit for the two trades, so long vertical spreads are also called *debit spreads*. The reason for the debit is that lower-strike calls are worth more money than higher strikes, assuming the same expiration date. Because you're spending more money than you're receiving, the trade is a net debit. You paid for it. You own it. Therefore, it's a long call spread.

Let's say the June $100 call is trading for $8 while the June $105 call is worth $5. If you spend $8 for the $100 call but receive $5 for selling the $105 call, you'll spend $3 in total. In trading terms, you bought the June $100/$105 vertical spread for a net debit of $3. Because each option controls 100 shares of stock, the spread will cost $300 plus commissions. As with any option you purchase, the price you paid is the most you can lose. No matter how low the stock's price may fall, your maximum loss is the $3 price paid. However, because you bought the spread, you have an asset, and that means it has the potential to earn money. How much money can you make?

Think back to the rights and obligations covered in Chapter Five. With this spread, you have the right to buy shares for $100 and the obligation to sell shares for $105, and therefore the most you could ever make is the $5 difference in strikes. The most any long vertical spread can ever be worth is the difference in strikes. Because you paid $3, your maximum profit is the $2 difference, or $200 for the spread. It may not sound like much, but considering you paid $3 for the spread, it's a 66% return on your money.

The following is a table showing the profits or losses at expiration for each of the calls. The spread's value is just the combination of them:

STOCK PRICE	LONG $100 CALL	SHORT $105 CALL	SPREAD VALUE	PRICE PAID	PROFIT/LOSS
$90	$0	$0	$0	$3	-$3
$95	$0	$0	$0	$3	-$3
$100	$0	$0	$0	$3	-$3
$103	$3	$0	$3	$3	$0
$105	$5	$0	$5	$3	$2
$110	$10	-$5	$5	$3	$2
$115	$15	-$10	$5	$3	$2

From that table, we can draw the profit and loss diagram, but remember, your broker's platform will draw these for you. Probably the most prominent feature of all vertical spreads is the limited gains and limited losses. That's why the graph flattens out on the left and right sides of the chart. No matter how low the stock price may fall, the most you can lose is the $3 paid. And no matter how high it may rise, you can only make $2:

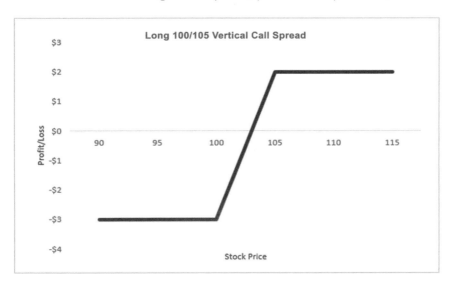

As a quick check, the maximum gain plus the maximum loss must add up to the difference in strikes. In this example, $3 debit + $2 maximum gain equals the $5 difference in strikes. The graph shows the long call spread's maximum value occurs if the underlying stock is at or above the short strike at expiration. In this example, you'd need the stock to be at or above $105 at expiration before it would be worth the $5 difference in strikes. To make money with the long call spread, you need the underlying stock price to rise, so the long call vertical spread is a bullish strategy. Because profits are limited though, it's normally used for *moderately bullish* outlooks. Remember, in this example, the maximum profit is $2 – no matter how high the stock price rises.

The limited gains of the vertical spread sometimes make new traders question the strategy's value. Who wants to limit gains to just $200? As with all strategies, you're not limited to just one spread. If you bought 10 of the $100/$105 vertical spreads, you'd spend $3,000 and could make a maximum of $2,000. You can always scale any strategy to suit your needs, but the biggest benefit of the vertical spread is that they greatly reduce the amount of money you must spend. It allows more people to at least take a position in a trade they may otherwise have been unable to afford – or unwilling to enter. No matter how high priced the underlying stock may be, and no matter how high volatility may be in the options, vertical spreads can always be purchased for very little money. For instance, let's say you were looking at a $1,000 stock with high volatility. The 30-day $1,000 call may be trading for $60 while the 30-day $1,005 call may trade for $57. Even though the individual call options are super pricey, the vertical spread would cost the same $3.

Vertical spreads are versatile, and you're not limited to making a spread only $5 wide. If you bought the June $100/$110 vertical spread, you'd pay more money, but it could also be worth up to the $10 difference in strikes. Depending on option prices and your outlook, you may choose different sets of strikes, but any long spread's maximum value, whether using calls or puts, is always limited to the difference in strikes. Remember, the spread's maximum value is the difference in strikes, but *your* maximum profit is determined after subtracting the vertical spread's cost.

Like individual calls and puts, vertical spreads have one breakeven point at expiration, and the calculation is the same for long calls and puts. Just add the spread's total cost to your long call option, which is the lower strike. In this example, the $100 call plus the $3 debit equals $103, so that's where you need the underlying stock to be to break even on the trade. With the stock at $103 at expiration, the $105 call would expire worthless, and the $100 call would be worth the $3 intrinsic value, exactly the price you paid, and you'd just break even. The long $100 call must make up the spread's total cost before a profit can be realized. Even though the $100/$105 vertical call spread's maximum value occurs for all stock prices above $105, you don't need the stock to reach $105 in order to profit. Any stock price above the $103 breakeven point will generate gains. This vertical spread will therefore be profitable for any stock price above $103 at expiration but have a maximum gain at $105 or above.

THE LONG PUT VERTICAL SPREAD

As with all option strategies, you can create bullish or bearish positions. If buying a call spread is bullish, buying a put spread must be bearish. However, for puts, the pricing works in the opposite direction, and higher-strike put options will be worth more money, as they give you the right to sell shares for a higher price than a lower-strike put.

Vertical spreads are usually listed in numerical order, so your broker's platform may show the $100/$105 vertical put spread. But if you buy that spread, you're buying the $105 put and selling the $100 put. For vertical spreads, the rule is always easy: To buy the spread, you must buy the more valuable strike, which means you're either buying the lower-strike call or the higher-strike put.

Let's say the June $100 put is trading for $5 while the June
$105 put is trading for $7. If you buy the $105 put and sell
the $100 put, it'll create a net debit of $2. As with all vertical
spreads, the price you pay is the most you could lose, and the
most the spread could ever be worth is the difference in strikes,
or $5 in this example. By owning the $105 put, you have the
right to sell shares for $105. By selling the $100 put, however,
you have the obligation to buy shares for $100 per share.
If you buy shares for $100 per share but sell them for $105
per share, the spread's maximum value is the $5 difference.
Because you paid $2, the maximum profit is $3, or $300 per
spread. As with the call spread, the maximum gain plus the
maximum loss must add up to the difference in strikes.

The breakeven point is found in exactly the same way as a
long put. Just subtract the spread's total cost from the higher-
strike put – the one you own. If you paid $2 for this spread,
your expiration breakeven price is the $105 strike minus the
$2 cost, or $103. Just as the long call needs to make up the
spread's total cost before profits are made, the long put must
make up the spread's total cost for the put spread. However,
because put options become more valuable as the stock price
falls, you need the stock price to drop before profits are made.
The following table shows various profits and losses for the
$100/$105 put spread at various stock prices:

STOCK PRICE	SHORT $100 PUT	LONG $105 PUT	SPREAD VALUE	PRICE PAID	PROFIT/LOSS
$90	-$10	$15	$5	$2	$3
$95	-$5	$10	$5	$2	$3
$100	$0	$5	$5	$2	$3
$103	$0	$2	$2	$2	$0
$105	$0	$0	$0	$2	-$2
$110	$0	$0	$0	$2	-$2
$115	$0	$0	$0	$2	-$2

The profit and loss diagram below has a similar shape of the previous vertical call spread: Both have limited gains and losses. The difference is that the long put spread is *bearish*:

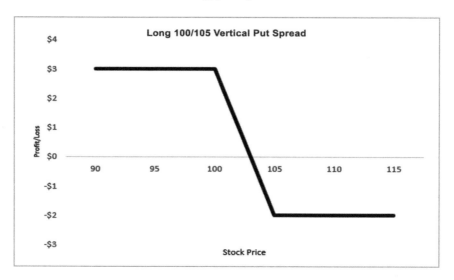

If you're ever looking to buy a call or put option but find the price is too high, you can always reduce the cost by selling another option against it. That's the reason for using the vertical spread strategy. For that benefit, you must sacrifice some potential gains. While no trader wants to sacrifice possible profits, if the initial long option is too pricey to take a position, you have no chance of any gains. Vertical spreads allow you to always participate for a small price, no matter how expensive the options may be. When unusual option activity heats up, many times the options become alarmingly expensive, and few traders take the trades. Vertical spreads change that, and that's why they're an essential tool for every option trader – especially when trading on unusual option activity.

THE SHORT PUT VERTICAL SPREAD

We just covered the long vertical put spread. For every long strategy, there's a short strategy. If you buy a vertical put spread, another trader must be the seller – the short vertical put spread.

Just as you can choose to take a long or short option position, you can choose to take the long or short side of a strategy. Depending on market conditions, which we'll talk about later in this chapter, you may want to sell a vertical spread rather than buy one. Short verticals often confuse new traders, but they're easier to understand if you always remember that the short position is the mirror image of the long position. Any gain on a long put spread will be a loss for the short put spread and vice versa.

How is the short put vertical spread created? It's built in the opposite way of the long spread. If the long put spread requires selling the $100 put and buying the $105 put, the short spread trader enters the opposite orders: Buy the $100 put and sell the $105 put. Because the more valuable option is sold, the trade results in a credit. The long put spread trader pays a debit, and the short put trader receives that cash as a credit. Short vertical spreads, whether calls or puts, are therefore also called *credit spreads*. Because opposite sides of the trade result in opposite outcomes, if the put spread buyer is bearish, the put spread seller must be bullish.

To understand the short put vertical spread, it helps to think about the rights and obligations with the individual positions. If you buy the $100 put, you have the right to sell shares for $100. If you sell the $105 put, you have the obligation to buy shares at $105. If you buy shares at $105 and sell them for $100, it creates a $5 loss. The short vertical spread trader therefore stands to lose the $5 difference in strikes. By now you should understand why. The long trader can earn the $5 difference, so the short trader might lose the $5 difference. Why would anyone choose to sell a vertical spread then?

Because you'll receive cash up front. Think of a short vertical spread like an insurance policy. You may pay a one-time premium for car insurance, and that's the most the insurance company can ever make. However, the company stands to lose more than the premium received. After all, it wouldn't make financial sense to pay a $1,000 premium if the company's policy limited the payout to something less than that. The only reason you're willing to spend that premium is because there's a chance the payoff to you could be greater.

That's how a short vertical spread works. You'll receive a one-time cash payment up front, and that's the maximum you could earn. In exchange for that credit, you may lose the difference in strikes. The only way the spread pays off the full credit is if the spread expires worthless, just like the auto insurance company needs the contract to expire without any damage to your car. If the policy expires worthless, the company earns the entire premium. For the short vertical put spread to expire worthless, you need the stock price to rise above the short strike, or $105 in this example. With the stock above $105, both puts expire worthless, and you earn the net credit received when you placed the trade. If the strategy pays off when the stock price rises, it's a *bullish* position.

In the previous example for the long put spread, the June $100 put was trading for $5 while the June $105 put was trading for $7. To enter a trade for the short put vertical spread, you'd buy the $100 put for $5 and sell the $105 put for $7 for a net credit of $2. The following table shows the value of the short $100/$105 put spread at various stock prices at expiration:

STOCK PRICE	LONG $100 PUT	SHORT $105 PUT	SPREAD VALUE	CREDIT RECEIVED	PROFIT/ LOSS
$90	$10	-$15	-$5	$2	-$3
$95	$5	-$10	-$5	$2	-$3
$100	$0	-$5	-$5	$2	-$3
$103	$0	-$2	-$2	$2	$0
$105	$0	$0	$0	$2	$2
$110	$0	$0	$0	$2	$2
$115	$0	$0	$0	$2	$2

If you compare the profits and losses in the table to those of the long vertical put, you'll find they're opposite. The gains to the buyer are the seller's losses and vice versa. However, the breakeven points for the long and short positions – regardless of the strategy – are always the same. If the buyer breaks even, the seller didn't make or lose money either. By using the values in the table, we get the following profit and loss diagram for the short $100/$105 vertical put spread:

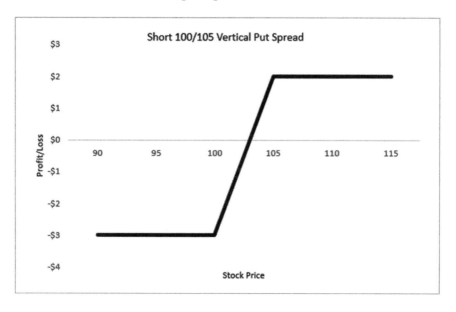

Interestingly, even though you're using put options, it results in a bullish position. You need the stock to rise to make a profit. It makes sense, however, if you remember that everything is opposite between the buyer and seller. If the put spread buyer is bearish, the put spread seller must be bullish. However, there's an even far more interesting result. You may have noticed that the profit and loss diagram for the short $100/$105 vertical put spread looks exactly like the long $100/$105 vertical call spread. It seems strange that you can create identical profit and loss diagrams by using calls or puts. For traders who aren't aware of that, you may be missing out on half of the valuable spread trades out there. If a strategy can be constructed with calls, an identical one can be constructed with puts. It's why we always teach our traders multiple ways to create the same strategy. To master vertical spreads, you must memorize a powerful principle:

Buying the call spread is identical to selling the corresponding put spread.

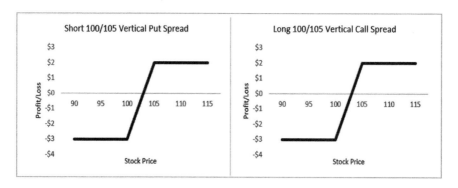

By corresponding, it means you're using the same expiration and strikes. As you'll find out shortly, the reverse is true too: Buying the put spread is identical to selling the corresponding call spread. They're just two different ways of accomplishing the same thing. The identical charts also highlight another important point. New traders often get fixed on choosing the credit trade because they feel a credit is better than a debit. And that would be true if you were receiving a credit for an asset. Remember, however, the only reason you're receiving the credit is that you're accepting an obligation, and you might end up losing the difference in strikes.

It shouldn't make a bit of difference if you pay $3 today but can earn $2 at expiration versus receiving $2 today and possibly losing $3 at expiration. Both choices result in a maximum loss of $3 and maximum gain of $2 over the identical range of stock prices and time. They're two different ways of saying the same thing, and that's why they produce the same charts. Again, we'll talk later in this chapter about why you may want to take one position over the other even though the profit and loss diagrams may look identical. For now, just understand that to enter a bullish vertical spread, you could either buy the call spread or sell the corresponding put spread.

SHORT VERTICAL CALL SPREADS

The first vertical spread we looked at was buying the $100/$105 call spread where you bought the $100 call and sold the $105 call. The only reason you could buy that spread is because another trader sold the spread. How did that trader create the position? It's constructed in the opposite way: Buy the $105 call and sell the $100 call. Because the lower-strike call has more value, the trade results in a credit – cash is received up front. But now you know that doesn't mean it's better. In exchange for that cash, you're accepting a potential *obligation* equal to the difference in strikes. By purchasing the $100/$105 call spread you could earn the difference in strikes, but if you sell the spread you could lose the difference in strikes.

Let's say you sold the June $100/$105 call spread. If the $100 call is trading for $8 while the $105 call is trading for $5, you'll receive a credit of $3, and that's your maximum gain. To collect that gain, however, you'll need the stock to fall at or below the short $100 call at expiration. With the stock below $100, both options expire worthless, and you'll earn the entire $3 credit. Because you need the stock to fall, it's a *bearish* strategy. However, if the stock price rises above $105, the spread is worth $5. Because you sold it to enter the spread, you must buy it back to close it. You'd pay the $5 price, which leaves you with a net $2 loss. Notice that your $3 maximum gain is exactly the maximum loss for the long $100/$105 call spread buyer, and your maximum $2 loss is exactly the maximum gain for the call spread buyer. Everything is opposite between the buyer and seller, but the breakeven points will always be the same:

STOCK PRICE	SHORT $100 CALL	LONG $105 CALL	SPREAD VALUE	CREDIT RECEIVED	PROFIT/ LOSS
$90	$0	$0	$0	$3	$3
$95	$0	$0	$0	$3	$3
$100	$0	$0	$0	$3	$3
$103	-$3	$0	-$3	$3	$0
$105	-$5	$0	-$5	$3	-$2
$110	-$10	$5	-$5	$3	-$2
$115	-$15	$10	-$5	$3	-$2

This diagram is the profit and loss diagram for the short $100/$105 vertical call spread sold for $3:

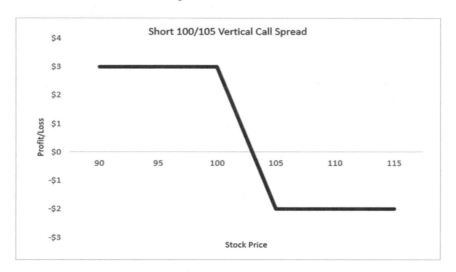

The chart shows the stock price must fall in order to reach maximum gain, which will be the $3 credit received. If the stock price rises above $105, you'll end up with the maximum $2 loss. The breakeven price is found by adding the credit to the short $100 call, which is $103. However, rather than memorizing formulas for the short spreads, once you know the breakeven point for the long call spread is $103, it must also be the same for the short call spread. The short call spread is *bearish*, and that usually takes new traders by surprise. After all, call options are bullish, so how can the resulting position be bearish? Remember, the long call spread is bullish, so the short call spread must have the opposite outlook.

As expected, the short $100/$105 call vertical spread produces exactly the same profit and loss diagram as the long $100/$105 put vertical spread:

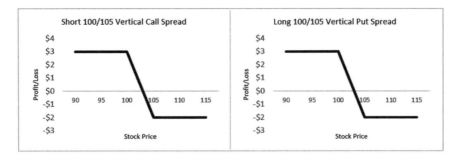

Once again, it's counterintuitive that you can create the identical profit and loss diagrams by using calls or puts. Make sure you remember the following principle:

Buying the put spread is identical to selling the corresponding call spread.

In the next section, you'll find out how to decide whether to use the debit or credit trade, but to make that decision easy, you must remember the two ways to construct them: Buying the put spread is identical to selling the corresponding call spread, and buying the call spread is identical to selling the corresponding put spread. Those are the keys.

YOU'RE NOT "GETTING PAID" TO USE CREDIT SPREADS

Traders often believe that credit spreads are better than debit spreads because they're "getting paid" to use the credit spread.

Remember, however, that credit spreads, whether using calls or puts, result in a liability equal to the difference in strikes. The broker is only concerned with maximum losses and will therefore hold a margin requirement equal to the difference in strikes. Therefore, all credit spreads are ultimately debit spreads. For instance, if you can buy the $100/$105 call spread for $3, you should theoretically be able to sell the $100/$105 put spread for $2. However, if you sell the put spread for $2, the broker will withhold a $5 margin requirement, which means your account is effectively debited $3 – exactly the same as the debit spread. Choose the credit spread over the debit spread if it results in better pricing or if it makes potential morphs easier. Don't use credit spread because you're trying to "earn income." All vertical spreads, long or short, result in debits to your account.

THE PRICING OF CALL AND PUT VERTICAL SPREADS

We just showed that buying the call spread is identical to selling the put spread and vice versa. Therefore, if you know the price of the long call spread, you can quickly figure out the credit you'd receive from selling the put spread. Because the long call spread and short put spread should result in the same profile, if the $100/$105 call spread is trading for $3, you know the $100/$105 put spread must be selling for $2. That's the only way the two spreads can create the same profit and loss profile. Both must result in a maximum loss of $3, and both must have a maximum gain of $2.

However, here's the catch. Those are the theoretical values. In the real world of trading, there are often small discrepancies in these prices, and that's one reason for deciding to take the long vertical spread or the short vertical spread.

For example, on July 27, 2018, Amazon.com closed at $1,817.27, up $9.27 after releasing earnings. The $1805/$1810 vertical call spread with 14 days to expiration was trading for $3.10, which means the most you could make would be $1.90. Theoretically, the same-strike put spread should be selling for $1.90. However, it was selling for $2.20 – an extra 30 cents. It doesn't sound like much, but it's an extra 16%. On 10 spreads, it's an extra $300. Rather than buying the call spread, if you sold the put spread, you'd receive a $2.20 credit, which means the most you could lose is $2.80. The short put spread has the potential to earn more money and lose less. The chart below compares the profits and losses for the $1805/$1810 long vertical call spread and the corresponding short put spread:

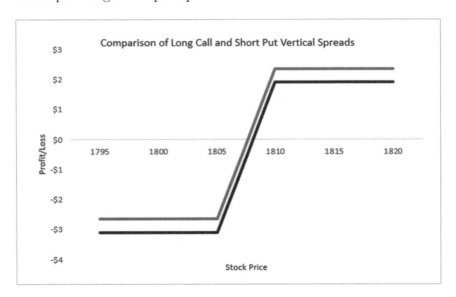

The black line is the long vertical call spread purchased for $3.10 while the gray line is the short vertical put spread sold for $2.20. It's easy to see that the short put spread stands to make more money and lose less, as its profit and loss curve sits higher at all stock prices compared to the call spread. Theoretically, we shouldn't see this type of discrepancy, as it should be corrected by a process called arbitrage, which results from a series of trades that result in a riskless profit. Here, traders would buy the cheaper spread and sell the more expensive spread, and in doing so, would increase the price of the put spread and reduce the price of the call spread until both produced the identical profits and losses. However, due to commissions and other trading costs, these small discrepancies often persist in vertical spreads. Strictly from a profit and loss standpoint, the short put spread is the better choice. Remember, options are tools and they're all about tradeoffs. Just because one spread may create a better profit and loss profile, it doesn't necessarily mean it's the one we're going to choose. We must also consider the potential for morphing.

MISSING PROFITS FOR THE MORPH

Depending on other factors, it may be better to sacrifice a little bit of profit in exchange for being able to alter this position should the stock break out. For example, perhaps Amazon is hitting a technical point of resistance, and we just don't think it's going to get much higher than $1,810. If that's our outlook, we'll probably sell the put spread and take the extra cash. But what if we're wrong?

New traders often think professional traders are never wrong. It's simply not true. What sets us apart is the way we set up our trades. We give ourselves more opportunities to escape from bad trades, manage risk, and end up with profits. We also allow for the profits to run by rolling up our strikes, and we minimize losses by keeping positions hedged. To master option trading, don't think you must win at every trade. That's an unrealistic expectation. Instead, learn to set up your trades in ways that give you alternate escape routes if things change – whether for better or worse. Our clients are very familiar with morphs, as they are a key to successful option trading. We spend entire classes on showing alternate morphs for different strategies in different conditions. While you're learning vertical spreads, don't just think about whether the long or short spread creates the best profile. Also consider if there's a strong possibility for the morph, and be sure to include that in your decision.

One thing we'll check is to see if Amazon may be at a point of technical resistance. What if the stock breaks through $1,810 and begins to run like lightning? If we feel it's a possibility, we may decide to buy the call spread even though it's not as attractive from a profit and loss standpoint. The reason is it's easier to alter this position into a long call position by simply buying back the short $1,810 strike. Doing so, we've changed our profit and loss diagram from a vertical spread to that of a long call, which means we now have unlimited potential for gains. In the business, placing a trade to change from one profit and loss diagram to another is called a *morph*.

Now think about what would happen had we sold the $1805/$1810 put spread and the stock broke out. There's not much we can do. If we buy back the short put, that leaves us with a long put, which is obviously the opposite direction of what we need. On the other hand, if we sold the long put, the short put can only make a limited amount of money if the stock rises, which defeats the purpose of the morph. If it breaks out, we want to increase the potential gains, not limit them. More importantly, at Market Rebellion™, we teach that retail traders should almost never hold naked short options. If you sell the long put, it would leave you with a naked put, which means you no longer have limited losses. They're virtually unlimited, at least all the way down to a stock price of zero. So, if we feel the stock may break out and we may end up morphing, we may choose to buy the call spread even though that trade by itself isn't as profitable as the short put spread. Whether you're bullish or bearish, vertical spreads make any option cheap and also allow for easy morphs should conditions change while you're in the position.

VERTICAL SPREADS MOVE SLOWLY

One of the drawbacks to vertical spreads is that their prices move slowly. The reason is that you're long one option and short another with strikes that are reasonably close to each other, so their behaviors will be nearly opposite. If your long call strike rises one dollar, the short call falls nearly one dollar, and the spread's overall value won't change much. You can also see why it happens by considering the deltas. If the $100 call has a delta of 60, and the $105 call has a delta of 58, the overall spread has two deltas, so it's behaving like two shares of stock. If you paid $3 for this spread and the stock rises one dollar, this spread will increase by only two cents to $3.02. While the slow crawl is a drawback if the stock price moves in your favor, it's a benefit if it moves against you, as vertical spread prices also fall slowly.

The previous profit and loss diagrams drawn for vertical spreads apply only at expiration, which means they're only good for the final seconds prior to expiration. If you have 30 days until expiration, the graph will look more like the gray line below:

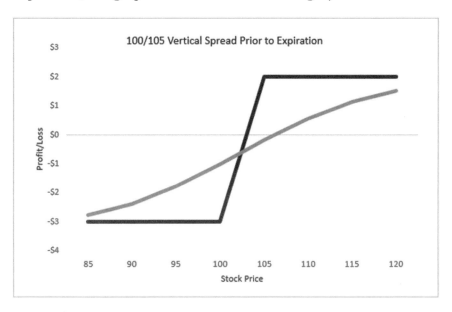

As expiration draws closer, the gray line will slowly move toward the black line. At expiration, it will fall right on the black line. With 30 days until expiration, however, the gray line is relatively flat, which shows why a vertical spread's price is slow to change. If that's true, you may be wondering why we'd consider them for unusual option activity.

Remember, for those trades, we're expecting large, aggressive moves in the stock. If the stock is currently $100 and pops to $115, this spread's value may rise from $3 to $4.70. It won't be worth the full $5 difference in strikes, unless you're close to expiration, but it'll still be a big money-making trade. Even though it's a limited profit trade, and even though you may not capture the full five-dollar value, paying $3 and selling for $4.70 beats missing the trade because you couldn't afford – or were too afraid – to buy the outright long calls.

WHICH STRIKES TO USE?

All option strategies are tradeoffs in risk and reward, so we can't say that one's better than another. By choosing different strikes, expiration dates, or strategies, you're just choosing different tools. Just as a carpenter can't say that a hammer is better than a screwdriver, an option trader can't say the July $100 call is better than the August $105 call. Each choice of strikes, expirations, or strategies will have crossover points in their profit and loss diagrams, so it's never a question of which is best. It's a question of which is best for you. In fact, Pete and I will often react to the same unusual option activity but take slightly different trades. That's not a disagreement on what's going to happen but a difference of opinion to what degree things will happen. We may both think a $100 stock may jump to $120, but if I want to be a little more conservative, I may choose the $110/$115 strikes. If Pete's a little more aggressive, he may buy the $115/$120 pair. We both have the same directional outlook, but we're just taking different degrees of risk.

The risk-reward tradeoff says that as you choose safer strikes, the cost of the spread will increase, and your rewards will decrease. On the other hand, if you pick strikes that are very risky – likely to expire worthless – the vertical spread will be cheap but possibly pay off a lot. The higher the risk, the higher the reward.

As a basic rule, if the stock price is halfway between the two strikes of your vertical spread, it will cost half the amount of the difference in strikes. For example, with the stock at $102.50, the $100/$105 call spread will trade for about $2.50 and make a maximum of $2.50. On the other hand, if you have a bullish vertical spread with strikes that are below the current stock price, the spread has a high probability of paying off – low risk – and will therefore not have much of a reward. For example, if you buy the $100/$105 vertical with the stock at $110, it may cost $4, which only leaves a one-dollar maximum gain. However, there's a high probability for that reward. On the other hand, if you bought the $100/$105 bull call spread with the stock at $95, you may only pay a dollar but have the potential to make $4 – but it's a low probability for a payoff.

In the chart below, we're comparing three vertical spreads with the stock at $102.50. The black line is the $100/$105 vertical priced at $2.50. The solid gray line is the $105/$110 vertical, so both strikes are OTM. It has a relatively small chance for making profits, so the market has bid the price down to only one dollar, which means the resulting maximum profit is $4. The dotted line is the $95/$100 vertical spread, so both strikes are ITM. It costs $4 and has a maximum gain of $1, but it represents a higher probability for success. By choosing different strikes, you can shift your profit and loss curve up or down and left to right to get different risk-reward profiles:

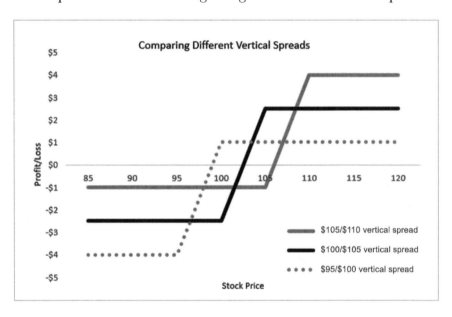

Notice how all three profit and loss diagrams have areas where the lines intersect, which shows that one isn't better than another. Pick any two diagrams to compare, and you'll see there are some stock prices where one performs better than the other – and some prices where it doesn't. If one spread was truly better than another, its profit and loss diagram would perform better across all stock prices.

Traders, however, often get the interpretations of these different vertical spread strike price selections backwards.

They'll notice the $105/$110 vertical has the lowest cost but also the highest reward and think it has low risk because the spread can only lose one dollar. And because it also has a higher maximum gain, it looks like it has low risk with a high possible payoff. What could be better than a low-risk trade that can make a fortune? The financial markets will never reward you for taking no risk. If there's a small price tag coupled with a big reward, it's for one reason: There's a high probability for failure. However, for unusual option activity, many times we'll use OTM vertical spreads. That's okay because we have good reasons for believing there will be fast, aggressive moves from the stock, so there's a relatively high chance they'll move ITM. And because they're relatively cheap, we can load up on the spread without spending too much money.

ANOTHER VIEW: DISCOUNTS AND PREMIUMS

We just showed that if the stock is $102.50, the $100/$105 call spread would trade for about $2.50. Notice that the long $100 call has $2.50 of intrinsic value – exactly the price of the spread. We could say the spread is trading for its intrinsic value. Now let's say the stock is trading for $110 so that both strikes are ITM. If we were at expiration, the spread would be worth $5. However, it won't be trading for $5 because we're not at expiration. Again, no trader will pay the maximum price for the spread, which leaves no room for profit. Even though the spread would be worth $5 at expiration, we'll see it trading at a discount today, perhaps $4. What if both strikes were OTM?

Let's say the stock is trading for $95. The $100/$105 call spread has no intrinsic value, which is to say it would be worthless if expiration was today. However, because time remains, it will trade for more than zero, let's say $1. Even though it has no intrinsic value, it's trading at a premium right now. Out-of-the-money vertical spreads therefore trade at premiums to their intrinsic value while ITM vertical spreads trade at discounts to their intrinsic value.

New traders often wonder why somebody would buy a vertical spread with both strikes ITM, as it seems the spread would trade at maximum value. That would be true if we were at expiration. Prior to expiration, the spread will trade at a discount to that maximum value. If you're using ITM vertical spreads, just be sure you're leaving enough room for profits. You don't want to pay $4.90 for a spread that can be worth $5, no matter how likely the chances are for success.

CHANGING GAMMA AND THETA

Choosing different strikes allows us to change the risk-reward profiles, but it also changes other characteristics that you must be aware of. If both options are OTM, you need the stock price to move in order to be profitable, and that means you have positive gamma. Your vertical spread will begin to quickly generate deltas if you're correct. The tradeoff is that you'll have negative theta, and the spread will lose money from the passage of time if you're wrong.

On the other hand, if both strikes are ITM, you don't need the stock price to move. You buy the spread at a discount, and strictly from the passage of time, the spread's value will increase, provided the stock price doesn't fall. For instance, in the above diagram, if you bought the $95/$100 vertical spread with the stock at $102.50, both strikes are ITM. You'll buy it at a discount, perhaps $4, but even if the stock price doesn't move, that spread will grow to a value of $5 at expiration. In other words, you'll have positive theta. In exchange, you won't have much gamma, and your spread's value just isn't going to move with changes in the underlying stock.

These are definitely advanced topics that we teach our traders, but the point to understand is that if you make changes to your strikes, you can greatly change the probability for success, but you can only do so by altering the rewards. Most traders, however, don't understand that choosing different strikes and using different strategies make big changes to the Greeks, and sometimes, those are the most important differences to consider.

WHICH EXPIRATIONS TO USE?

As a basic principle of finance, you should match your expirations, maturities, or time horizons to your needs. If you want to buy bonds for your kids' college in 10 years, buy 10-year bonds – not 30-year bonds. Buying different expirations exposes you to unnecessary price risk. The same philosophy holds with options. If you think the stock's price is going to have a moderate swing from $100 to $110 over the next month, you should choose one-month vertical spreads. Why not buy more – or less – time?

Remember, spread prices move slowly. Let's say you buy the 30-day $100/$110 vertical spread. If the stock's price is $110 or higher at expiration, the spread will be worth the $10 difference in strikes. However, if you bought a longer-dated one, say three months, that same spread will not be worth anywhere near $10. One of two things must happen: First, you'll either have to accept a smaller profit. Second, you can continue holding hoping that the stock price stays above $110 until expiration, but now you're faced with the risk that it may move lower. Hope is not a good strategy. The strategy ends up dictating when you can sell – but you want be the one making that decision.

On the other hand, if you bought less time, say a Weekly vertical spread, the stock's price may climb slowly during that week but the spread may still lose money. However, when you try to roll to the next week, you may find they're more expensive than they were last week. Not only did the first trade lose, but you had to pay more to get back in. You may end up with a double whammy loss.

We use the same idea for unusual option activity. If the activity occurs in a Weekly option, for example, it's expected that we'll see a big announcement during that week, so we'll buy the one-week vertical spread. However, we must choose from available expirations, and it's not always a perfect match. We may find there's a two-day and nine-day expiration available. For those times, we'll take the longer-dated one. We recommend to keep the expirations as short as possible because you want to see that vertical spread jump to its maximum value, or very close to it, when the news is released.

However, just as changing strikes will alter the risk-reward relationship, so will changing the expiration dates. If your strikes are ITM, shifting out to longer-dated options will reduce the spread's price. There's more time for the stock price to make the spread go OTM, so it becomes riskier and therefore the price drops. On the other hand, if you use OTM strikes, increasing the time to expiration will make the vertical spread more expensive because you're now giving the spread a better chance to become ITM.

STRANGE BID-ASK SPREADS

Every option has a bid and offer price, also called the asking price. The bids show the prices buyers are willing to pay, while the asking price shows the prices at which sellers are willing to sell. When you're dealing with vertical spreads, however, you're dealing with two options, so the vertical spread quotes are really made up of two individual option quotes. For example, assume we have the following two quotes for the $100 and $105 calls:

$100 CALL		$105 CALL	
BID	ASK	BID	ASK
$5.90	$6	$3	$3.20

How would the $100/$105 vertical spread be quoted? To buy
the $100/$105 vertical spread, you could buy the $100 call
for $6 and sell the $105 call for $3, so the asking price for the
vertical would be $3. On the other hand, if you wanted to sell
the $100/$105 vertical, you could currently sell the $100 call for
$5.90 and buy the $105 call for $3.20, so you'd receive $2.70. If
you're looking at vertical spread quotes, you'd therefore see the
$100/$105 vertical spread with a bid of $2.70 and asking price
of $3. Notice that the difference, or spread, is 30 cents, and it
will always equal the sum of the spread between two individual
option quotes. The $100 call has a 10-cent spread while the
$105 call has a 20-cent spread, so the $100/$105 vertical spread
will have a 30-cent spread. So, the first point to notice is that
because vertical spread quotes are generated from individual
strikes, the vertical spread quotes begin to get wide.

During periods of high volatility, individual spreads can get
exceptionally wide, so the vertical spread quotes can get, well,
really weird. In some cases, you may even see negative bids. It's
also not uncommon to see asking prices that are greater than the
difference in strikes, which means you'd be guaranteed to lose
money if you purchased for that price. For example, let's say the
stock is trading for $95 and the following quotes are available:

$100 CALL		$105 CALL	
BID	ASK	BID	ASK
$3.30	$5	$2	$3.50

These are OTM options, but priced for big stock price moves in
a short time. The $100/$105 vertical spread has a bid of -$0.20
and an asking price of $3. The reason for the negative bid is that
the bid on the $100 call slipped below the asking price of the
$105 call. A negative bid means that if you placed this order at
current market prices, you'd have to pay to close a long spread.
You're better off just letting it expire worthless. While you may
see negative bids, you'll never see negative offers, as that means

you'd receive money for a spread that should be a debit spread. That would be an arbitrage, and you'll never get the opportunity as a retail trader. Negative bids, however, are quite common, so you need to be aware that they can occur. How should you trade this vertical spread?

For vertical spreads, no matter what the quotes may be, you should generally place your trades as limit orders at the "mid" or "mark," which is just the halfway point between the bid and ask. Your broker's platform will show you these quotes as well. For the above quotes, the mark on the $100 call is $4.15 and for the $105 call is $2.75. If you were placing an order to buy or sell this spread, you should place your limit order at the difference of these, or $1.40. In most cases, it will fill quickly. When trading vertical spreads, try to avoid sending orders to buy or sell "at market" as the bid-ask spreads will eat you alive over time.

Vertical spreads are one of the most versatile of all option strategies. While they do limit your gains, they also greatly limit your maximum loss. Vertical spreads are relatively cheap and are generally priced less than the difference in strikes, which means you can spend very little money but still make excellent returns. For unusual option activity, the ideal trade is to take the outright long call or long put, but sometimes it's just not desirable because of the prices or the implied volatilities. For those times, we use vertical spreads. No matter how expensive the stock may be, no matter how high the implied volatility may be, and no matter how pricey the options may be, you can always make a vertical spread work. It's not magic. It's the versatility of vertical spreads.

VERTICAL SPREADS ARE ONE OF THE MOST VERSATILE OF ALL OPTION STRATEGIES.

Ch. 11 THE STOCK REPLACEMENT COVERED CALL

Up to this point, we've covered two basic strategies: long options and vertical spreads. For unusual option activity, most of the time we'll use short-term, out-of-the-money options, so the prices will be cheap. For these trades, it pays to just buy the call or put and have unlimited potential gains. Other times, you'll find that options are super expensive. Perhaps you're dealing with expensive stocks, say several hundred dollars or more, or when volatility is pushed to high levels. When option prices get to such prices that you're not comfortable paying the price, you can use vertical spreads. Remember, you can always make a vertical spread work no matter how high the stock's price or volatility may be.

However, there'll be times when option prices fall in between these two extremes. They're not so pricey that you're forced to use a vertical spread, but at the same time, they're not trading for the prices you'd like to see. It's hard to give examples of where these ranges are because prices are relative. One trader may be willing to pay $10 or $20 per contract to take an outright long call. For another, it's too much to pay. Keep in mind, we're not necessarily talking about the price in terms of volatility. Were just talking about the total dollars you must pay for the position. When prices are in this middle ground, you can turn to a third strategy, which is a *diagonal spread*.

Like its vertical spread cousin, diagonal spreads require that the trader buys an option and sells an option against it. With vertical spreads, we used different strikes with the same expiration. For diagonal spreads, we'll use different strikes and different expirations. To use the strategy for unusual option activity, we'll use a special combination of the diagonal spread, which we call the *stock replacement covered call*. Before we cover that, however, let's take a look at the basics of diagonal spreads.

DIAGONAL SPREADS: DIFFERENT STRIKES, DIFFERENT EXPIRATIONS

To construct a basic diagonal spread, you'll buy one strike at one expiration, but sell a different strike at a different expiration. For instance, buying the April $90 call and selling the January $105 call is a diagonal spread. Alternatively, you could switch the strikes and buy the April $105 call but sell the January $90 call. That's also a diagonal spread. Like its vertical spread cousin, the diagonal spread is named for the way the prices appear on the quote board, and they'll appear diagonally from each other:

STRIKES	JANUARY	APRIL
$90	10.22	11.15
$95	5.70	7.50
$100	2.35	4.65
$105	0.68	2.65

All option strategies have a long and a short side, which is usually determined by the trader who pays the debit. For example, if you buy a call, you're long the call. If you buy a vertical spread, you're long the vertical spread. However, diagonal spreads are different, and you can't determine the long position simply by which trader pays the debit for reasons you'll soon understand. Instead, diagonal spreads have a different definition. The long position is determined by the trader who buys the longer-dated option. Sometimes that will result in a debit, and other times it will be a credit, but it doesn't matter to the definition. If you buy the *longer-dated* option, it's a long diagonal spread. For example, if you buy the April $105 call and sell the January $90 call, it's a long diagonal spread, whether it resulted in a debit or credit.

Obviously, there are many combinations that can result, as you can switch to different expirations, different strikes, or both. If you buy the longer-dated option and a strike that's more ITM, it will result in a debit. Sometimes, however, diagonal spreads may be constructed by purchasing the longer-dated contract but selling the more valuable strike, which may result in a credit. For instance, buying the April $105 call and selling the January $90 call. Like all strategies, options are versatile, and there are many reasons why we may want to build a diagonal spread in different ways. For unusual option activity, however, we're going to use a special construction where the diagonal spread will behave more like another popular option strategy called the covered call, so we call it the *stock replacement covered call*.

THE STOCK REPLACEMENT COVERED CALL

To use this strategy, you'll buy a longer-dated option, but you'll also buy it ITM. In other words, you're buying a stock replacement option. However, because it's for short-term use, you don't need the deltas to necessarily be in the 80 to 85 range.

You'll probably buy in the 65-delta range for calls and 50-delta range for puts.

Next, you'll sell a shorter-dated option against it, which is usually an ATM or OTM strike. By selling a short-term call, it helps to offset some of your cost. Remember, however, that the true "cost" of an option is the extrinsic value, and because you're buying the call short term and ITM, there won't be much extrinsic value to offset.

For example, let's say you wanted to capitalize on some unusual option activity in a stock like Netflix (NFLX). We're choosing it because it's an expensive stock with fairly high volatility, which can make it a perfect candidate for this strategy. On August 20, 2018, the stock was trading for about $328 with implied volatility hovering just above 30%. It's the type of stock that will make most traders lean toward vertical spreads, but let's see how to make use of the stock replacement covered call.

Let's say the unusual option activity led us to believe an announcement was coming within the next two weeks. At that time, Netflix had 11-day and 18-day options, so you'd have to use the 18-day expiration. The $320 call was trading for $14.22 with a delta of 64, so it's a good choice for a short-term stock replacement strike. However, it's not in the single-digit prices you'll often see with short-term options. At the same time, it's not $60 or $70 prices you're likely to see for stocks like Amazon. It's somewhere in the middle, so this is a time you may choose a diagonal spread. The stock was trading for $327.73, and with the $320 call priced at $14.22, it had $7.73 of intrinsic value, which means the remaining $6.49 is extrinsic value. That's pretty close to half of the option's value, and it's the value that'll create the most problems. Your long option will lose that amount in the next 18 days from time decay, or theta. How can you reduce theta's effects?

This is where we may suggest selling a call against it to recoup some of the extrinsic value. The Weekly $335 call option with four trading days remaining was trading for $2.52. If you buy the $320 call for $14.22 and sell the $335 call for $2.52, your net debit is $11.70. The trade would look like this:

> Buy 18-day $320 call (-$14.22)
> Sell 4-day $335 call (+$2.52)
> _____
> Net debit $11.70

These trades result in the following profit and loss diagram:

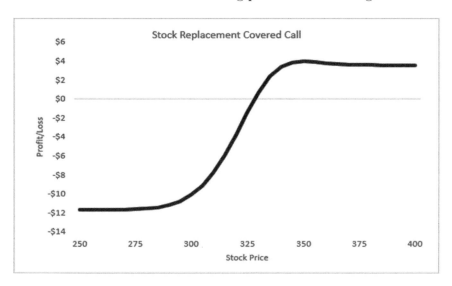

The chart loosely resembles a vertical spread because it has limited gains and limited losses. The reason you're not seeing the straight lines and sharp bends at the strike prices as with vertical spreads is because you're dealing with two different expirations, and the chart is drawn at expiration of the four-day contract. Remember, you'll only get those graphs at expiration, and because the chart only reflects one expiration, it's going to have curved lines. Before we get into the advantages of this strategy, let's answer some important questions first. Why did we suggest the four-day expiration to sell? And why the $335 strike?

SELL SHORT-TERM OPTIONS

Recall from Chapter Five that while longer-dated options are worth more in total, they're cheaper per unit of time. If you take the option's price divided by the number of days until expiration, you're actually earning more money – per unit of time – for shorter-dated options. As long as we're receiving enough of an option premium to put a dent in the extrinsic value – and cover commissions – we want to sell the shortest expiration possible. In this example, the long $320 call had $6.49 worth of extrinsic value, but you received $2.52 from the sale, which means 38% of the extrinsic value has been eliminated in a single trade. There's no reason to sell a longer-dated one. Second, by selling shorter-term options, there's less of a chance to get caught with the stock taking off to much higher prices. As you'll find out later in this chapter, even if that did happen, there are things we can do to still capture those profits. Still, there's no sense in locking yourself into the obligation to sell for any longer than you have to – especially with the potential for a big announcement coming soon. The idea is to select the shortest-term expiration that allows you to make a significant dent in the extrinsic value while also covering commissions.

WHY SELL THE $335 STRIKE?

In the previous profit and loss diagram, no matter how high the stock's price rises, you'll at least have a small profit. However, that's because of the way we constructed it. Depending on the strikes you choose, it may not work out that way. We paid $11.70 for the spread, but there was a $15 difference in strikes. If the stock makes a sudden, aggressive move and you don't want to make any of the adjustments we'll cover shortly, at least you have a profit to show for your efforts. But just selecting any strike to sell isn't necessarily going to ensure that, and it's a potential trap often overlooked by new traders. Some will set up diagonal spreads without accounting for the difference in strikes relative to the cost, and they may end up getting locked into a loss if the stock price shoots up quickly. For example, we could have chosen to sell the 4-day ATM strike of $327.50 for $5.45. We would receive more money, but our cost basis would be larger than the difference in strikes:

> Buy 18-day $320 call (-$14.22)
> Sell 4-day $327.50 call (+$5.45)
> Net debit $8.77

Notice that we've now paid $8.77 for a spread that can be worth a maximum of $7.50, the difference in the strike prices. If the stock price makes a sudden large move, this spread will be under water. Again, there are trades we can do to escape from this, but in the beginning, you may not have the confidence or knowledge to do it. While it's not a requirement, most professional traders will set up diagonal spreads so that the cost is less than the difference in strikes. You'll never have to worry about that potential problem with vertical spreads, but for diagonals, you do.

The idea is that you're going to continue to sell Weekly options against your long $320 call. If volatility remains the same, you should be able to collect about the same $2.50 for a strike that's seven points OTM. Each time you execute a sale, the proceeds further reduce the cost basis of your long $320 call. Currently, you paid a total of $11.70, but if you collect another $2.50 next week, it'll get reduced to $9.20. Each time the cost basis is reduced, it also gives you more flexibility to write lower-strike calls without the risk of the stock making a large upward move. Using this strategy provides some serious benefits: You can continue to collect premiums, continue to guarantee profits should the stock price rise, and continue to reduce the maximum loss. How do you roll to a new short call?

ROLLING OUT-OF-THE-MONEY CALLS

When you get close to expiration of the short-term call, the option will either be ITM or OTM. Let's start by assuming it's OTM, as it's the easiest to understand. First, you could decide to let it expire worthless and write a new call the following week when there's less time remaining. But as we covered in Chapter Five, there's always the possibility for the surprise assignment. If the stock price is close to the short strike, don't chance it. *When in doubt, close it out.* On the other hand, if you sell a new call on expiration Friday, you'll receive more money.

Let's say we're at expiration and the stock price is still trading near $328. Because the short $335 call is OTM, it's trading for only 10 cents. In this instance, you may decide to roll to the same strike. It's a judgment call. If you increase to a higher strike, you'll receive less money, but the option will also have a smaller chance of moving ITM. The decision often rests on what's happening technically with the stock, upcoming earnings, or other events that may affect your decision. Also, because the cost basis of the long call has been reduced to $11.70, you may not be as concerned about reducing it further, and may even decide to sell a higher strike. Each trader will come up with different decisions.

If you roll to the same strike, it's called *rolling out* since you're only rolling further out in time. You're not changing the strike price. Let's say you decide to roll to the 7-day $335 call trading for $3.10. Remember, the first call was sold on a Monday, which gave you four more days until expiration. By selling on Friday of the previous week, however, you'll have more time, so the option will trade at a higher price. Keep in mind, we are near the expiration so the 4-day option only has one day left. The trade would look like this:

> Buy 4-day $335 call (-$0.10)
> Sell 7-day $335 call (+$3.10)
> _____
> Net credit $3

This is called a *calendar spread*, *time spread*, or *horizontal spread*, so your broker's platform may label it in any of these ways. When the trade is executed, the purchase of the 4-day call was a closing transaction, so when the above order is executed, you'll just have the short 7-day $335 call against your stock replacement position. Now there's no way to be assigned on the expiring option – it's out of your account. By receiving $3, your cost basis is further reduced from $11.70 to $8.70.

Each week, continue doing the same thing. Just close the current short option and simultaneously sell a new contract. If the stock's price is too close to the strike, you can change to a higher strike. For instance, if the stock is trading for $332 at expiration, your short strike is only $3 OTM, so you may decide to sell the $340 strike. Now you're selling a different month and strike, so it's called *rolling up and out*, which is a short diagonal spread. Remember, it's what you're doing with the longer-term expiration that makes it long or short. If you're selling the *longer-term expiration*, it's a short diagonal spread. Again, we are near the expiration so the 4-day option only has one day left. The trade would look like this:

> Buy 4-day $335 call (-$0.10)
> Sell 7-day $340 call (+$2.60)
> _____
> Net credit $2.50

Each new credit continues to lower your cost basis. At any time, you could choose to quit writing calls – or possibly become more aggressive if the extrinsic values are going through the roof. It's important to remember that the idea of the strategy isn't to recoup 100% of your initial cost, or $11.70, in this example. If you happen to do that, great. Instead, your main goal is to reduce the majority of the extrinsic value. Are there exceptions?

Definitely. If earnings are being announced next week, it's probably best to not have a short call that will limit your profit potential. Remember, the long stock replacement call is already hedged – it's controlling shares of stock plus an attached insurance policy. The reason for selling calls against it isn't so much to provide added downside protection, but instead to reduce the cost of the extrinsic value. If earnings are being announced, rather than rolling to a new short call, you may want to roll up your stock replacement position to a higher strike to provide a little more downside protection.

Another reason for not rolling is if the stock has broken a long-term resistance. For example, let's say that for months, Netflix has always sold off when it traded at $335. Now that it's trading for $336, you might think it's going to continue to run on Monday morning, so you don't want short calls to limit those gains. If it turns out that it was a false breakout, you can always sell calls at that time. You'll get less money for them, but at least you know that the stock didn't continue its breakout on Monday. Whenever your short calls are OTM and about to expire, it's an easy trade. Either close it out and write new calls the following week or execute a simultaneous order to close the old ones and write the new ones on Friday.

ROLLING IN-THE-MONEY CALLS

Now that we've covered the easy condition, the short call closing OTM, let's talk about the more difficult one. If your short call isn't OTM at expiration, it's ITM. Unfortunately, this is a condition where many traders think the strategy has lost. If the short call is ITM, you'll have to spend money to buy it back, and possibly more than you sold it for, but that doesn't mean the overall strategy lost money. After all, it's a bullish strategy, and prices have risen. Things could be worse.

Let's say the short strike is only slightly in-the-money. You sold the $335 call, and the stock is trading at $338. Well, you sold it for about $2.50 and it's going to cost you $3 to buy it back. It wasn't the best outcome, but it's not that bad either. For those times, it's usually best to just fork over the cash and buy it back. The reason it's not a losing trade is because your long call gained that intrinsic value too. With the stock at $338, the $320 must be worth at least the $18 intrinsic value, plus any additional extrinsic value. Overall the position is profitable. What makes it less than ideal, however, is that you had to take cash from your money market and buy the call back. In this example, you lost $3 cash, but gained another $3 of intrinsic value, so it's not a losing position. It just shifted cash around in your account.

But now let's say the short call goes well ITM. Maybe the stock is trading for $350 and the short $335 call is trading for $15 at expiration. What do you do now?

First of all, understand that if you don't close it out, you'll be short 100 shares of the stock on Monday morning. Remember, option exercises are always for shares of stock. New traders often think they'll lose their long $320 call – not true. So, you'll definitely want to close out the position. However, it's going to cost $15. What if you don't want to spend the money? Worse yet, what if you don't have it? The answer is, you do.

With the stock at $350, you can roll up your long $320. With the stock at $350, your long $320 call must be worth at least the $30 of intrinsic value plus any extrinsic value. Also, your deltas are much higher.

You started with 65 deltas, but the stock price has risen and time has passed, so your deltas are pushing 85 or 90 by now. You can first roll up the long call to the new 65 delta strike and collect more than enough cash to buy back the short $335 call. The point is that once a short call goes ITM and you don't have the cash, it's not the worst thing to happen. It just requires that you first roll up your long call to generate the cash to buy back the short call.

One of the most fascinating things about option trading is that you'll have virtually unlimited choices to alter risk-reward profiles. In cases like these, one of our favorite strategies is to sell half the position and roll the other half. If we're holding 10 contracts, we may sell five and roll the other five up to the new 65 delta. Now we've recouped over 100% of our initial cost basis and can't lose on the trade. From there, we may just let the five calls stand alone. On the other hand, if we wish to continue selling calls, we may only do it against a portion, say two or three calls. That way, we always have some calls that can make an unlimited gain.

Diagonal spreads may seem complicated at first, as there are a lot of scenarios that can be painted. However, they all boil down to a simple concept: You're just selling a short-term call against your long stock replacement call option. Your main goal is to reduce that long call's extrinsic value. At a minimum, it's great if you sharply reduce or eliminate the long call's extrinsic value. Keeping that goal in mind, all you have to do is roll the option out at each short-term expiration. However, because we're teaching this for unusual option activity, it's best to not turn the strategy into a week-to-week selling strategy. Sell only long enough to recoup the extrinsic value, or at least a significant portion. From there, it's best to leave the long call alone to do what it was designed to do – capture unlimited gains from the anticipated big announcement.

Whether using straight calls or puts, vertical spreads, or diagonal spreads, option strategies provide known risk profiles to help you profit from unusual option activity.

Ch. 12 TRADER TALES OF THE "UNUSUAL" KIND

Mergers, acquisitions, upgrades, and downgrades occur quite often. And like clockwork, every three months, companies release earnings. Each of these events open the door for information to get leaked, and you can be sure someone will trade it. Seeing these trades isn't unique to Pete and me. Ask any floor trader, analyst, investment banker, or broker, and they've all seen it at some point. It's not only knowing how to spot it but how to determine if it's meaningful, and if so, how to *follow the smart money*.

We've spent years building our Market Rebellion™ team of experienced floor traders, brokers, and analysts, to educate retail investors so they can level the playing field. Let's check out some of the unusual tales from a few members of our experienced team. You'll see that unusual option activity isn't unusual at all. For Wall Street, it's business as usual.

TRADER TALES: RON IANIERI

My timing couldn't have been worse – but my experiences couldn't have been better. My first day at the Philadelphia Stock Exchange was October 19, 1987 – Black Monday – the day of the historic market crash when the S&P 500 lost nearly 30% of its value.

I didn't know anyone, which makes it nearly impossible to get on the trading floor. Of course, after that day, who'd want it? I started in Market Surveillance, which is an in-house regulatory department designed to investigate any abusive or manipulative practices to ensure orderly markets and instill public confidence.

As part of my duties, I would have to settle trade disputes, which arise when a trader and broker disagree on the transaction. For example, one person may have purchased 50 contracts, but insists it was supposed to be a sale. With the hectic floors, this sort of thing happens all the time, and someone must act as the judge to resolve disputes.

Other times, I just wrote reports and acted as a witness to what occurred. Any major disputes or trading violations – including suspected insider transactions – were immediately kicked upstairs to the investigators. The first step was to gather data and see if there was a viable case. If so, it would get sent to the SEC who handled it from there.

On one Friday afternoon, which happened to be option expiration, I was called to the Farmers Group crowd where I was told some unusual trading activity had occurred. With only 10 minutes left in the trading day, a customer placed an order to buy the $60 puts for the current month. That's right – it only had a 10-minute life. The stock was trading around $62.50, so it seemed highly unlikely the stock would drop by more than $2.50 to make the option go ITM. With my inexperience, I could only come to one conclusion about the trader – moron. Why would someone pay a nickel for puts that were $2.50 OTM that had, by now, less than five minutes before expiring?

It was unusual – highly unusual – as you wouldn't think anyone would throw good money on a contract they felt was going to expire worthless, but it sure seemed that someone had. The bell rang, and the puts looked like they expired worthless. It was now official. Moron, for sure.

That title, however, only lasted a few minutes.

Shortly after the close, a headline broke across our screens – and it was about Farmers Group. It turns out, B.A.T. Industries, a British conglomerate, was trying to buy Farmers. The market expected the deal to go through, but the California Insurance Commissioner just ruled it was blocked. The stock dropped to $56 in after-hours trading, and all of the OTM $60 puts we sold were no longer $2.50 OTM. They were now $4 ITM. Do the math to see how profitable insider trading can be: Every $5 spent on the puts instantly turned to $400. That means a $500 investment turned to $40,000 in minutes. Our traders took a huge loss in the after-hours market, but it was a big fat payday for the buyer. I reluctantly had to upgrade him from moron to millionaire.

The purchase was done by an insider who knew about the news prior to it being released to the public. Armed with inside information, he knew the stock was going to drop considerably on Monday morning, so it's not hard to put good money on OTM puts. Even with five minutes until expiration, they were a steal. Who would have known? Anyone with inside information.

A couple years later, and after a few appeals, he was finally ordered to pay restitution, plus a fine, and also earned a free stay at the "Graybar Hotel." But no amount of jail time would make up for the devastating losses that day. Some traders had to call it quits. I called it experience. But I'm still calling him a moron.

DRESSER INDUSTRIES MERGER

A few years later, after I had been hired away from Market Surveillance by one of the floor trading operations, and I got the position I was always after. I was now a specialist in charge of several different stocks. One of those names was an oil service stock called Dresser Industries (DI), but it normally didn't draw much interest. It was the bigger names like Schlumberger (SLB), Haliburton (HAL) and Black Hills Corporation (BHI) that had the high trading volumes. After a year as a specialist in Dresser, the largest orders I'd ever seen were for 100 contracts, and that was only on two occasions. Most of the order flow was the usual five-lot and 10-lot trades. For options, it never traded big volumes.

Well, one Wednesday afternoon around 3:45pm ET, a broker scurried into the crowd asking about the market and size of the $40 calls. Since the front month was expiring in two days and the stock was trading around $38, I assumed he wanted the quote for the next expiration month. But the broker said the order was for the current month – two days away. I quickly checked the open interest in the $40 strike and found there was no open interest, which meant this order was an opening transaction. I had flashbacks of Farmers Group.

I contacted Market Surveillance, as I sensed something fishy was going on. I only offered the minimum number of contracts and made the market as wide as rules allowed. Back then, options were quoted in fractions, so my first offer was at $0.38 of a dollar. The broker told me he was $0.38 bid for 500 contracts and wanted to know my next offer.

I made my next offer at $0.63 for 20 more contracts, the absolute minimum I could by exchange rules. The broker immediately bought. It seemed to be a ridiculous price to pay, but he then said he would pay up to $1.25 for 5,000 contracts. I had no interest, so I reversed the tables and said I would now pay one dollar for 500 contracts. Fortunately, I realized what was going on so I had my clerk continue buying shares of stock up to the closing bell. I didn't want to be short these calls without a hedge.

The next morning, the maniac trader seemed like a genius, capable of rivaling the greatest minds in history. He must have the world's only working crystal ball on his desk where most traders just have a calculator.

The company was merging with Halliburton in a $7.7 billion deal, valuing each Dresser share at $44. Fortunately, I learned from the Farmers' trade. Rather than taking large losses, by purchasing shares while selling the calls, I was able to make a lot of money from the overall transactions. The Dresser trade, however, taught me something important about making money: You don't need to know what's going on. You just need to follow someone who does.

TRADER TALES: STUART DORFMAN

The stock was Texas Eastern Petroleum. The day was was Monday, January 16, 1989. The trade was one that will live in my infamy forever.

On the previous Friday, January 13, the actively traded stock was priced about $30, and the floor traders were scrambling to handle the flood of orders coming into the crowd. Back then, we didn't have Weeklys, but the monthly contract was about to expire in five trading days.

Volatility had been high, which made it ripe for selling options, especially with such a short time until expiration. I was selling the $35 calls, and the normal protocol was to hedge the positions.

As a market maker, I'm more interested in collecting the option's extrinsic value, which must fall to zero at expiration. Once the calls are sold, all I need to do is wait for expiration, and I'll bank the profit.

Normally, I would keep the short position hedged, but with such a short time until expiration, I didn't see the need. It can be expensive, and who'd think a $30 stock would rise above $35 – a 16% gain – in just five trading days?

The $35 calls had been trading from anywhere between 50 cents and one dollar. It was quite a high premium with such a short time until expiration, so selling was the desired strategy. I ended up being naked about 300 contracts, or the equivalent of 30,000 shares. I arrived at work on Monday, January 16, and it was now painfully obvious why someone would want to buy the far-OTM $35 calls with only five days to go.

Coastal Corporation had announced it planned to launch a $2.6 billion offer for Texas Eastern, which would make it the nation's largest natural gas company.[93] That amounted to $42 per share.

That morning, the stock gapped up even higher, well above $44 – a 47% increase over Friday's closing price. My short OTM calls that were worth about 50 cents last week shot up to nearly $10 ITM. It was one of my worst trades, but one of my best lessons in risk management. Always remember that nobody is going to intentionally make a bad trade. It's real money they're using, so you must always ask why someone is willing to pay such a high premium for OTM strikes, especially when there's little time remaining. It appears to be a terrible trade, but there's a reason for it: They know something you don't. It's a lesson in unusual option activity that money can't buy. I paid $300,000 for it.

THE MACRO FALL OF MICRO WAREHOUSE

Micro Warehouse was a fun little trading stock. In 1987, it started as a small company in Connecticut, less than an hour from the financial epicenter – the Big Apple – but quickly became one of the best-known computer dealers in the U.S. It went public in 1992 and traded on the Nasdaq under the ticker MWHS.

It operated an online store of brand-name computers, software, and peripheral networking products to commercial and consumer users. Powered by a telemarketing sales force and color catalogs, it shipped to over 15 countries by 1995. The company was growing by leaps and bounds with worldwide sales pushing $3 billion, so why were the puts so expensive in late September 1996? The stock was trading over $32, and it was like any other trading day, small ups and downs, but well within expected ranges. We had the usual trades of 10 to 20 lots. But one floor broker strolls through the crowd and says he's interested in the $30 strikes. The stock was volatile, so options were always rich with extrinsic value. I was sure he wanted to sell, so I quoted him the prices – but he wanted to buy. Alarm bells were ringing in my head, as I still painfully recalled the Texas Eastern Petroleum trade. After all, at the time, Dell Computer was the 800-pound gorilla that could benefit from such a distribution network. But then he threw a curve ball.

He wanted to buy puts.

Not just a few, but 500 of the October $30 puts – over $2 OTM – with only three weeks until expiration. Well, a buyout would increase the stock's price, so selling puts isn't a danger. A disappointing earnings report came to mind, but the company's earnings weren't due until after expiration, so the coast was clear. At least, that's how it appeared.

Monday morning the following week, Micro Warehouse

announced it had accounting errors and would be forced
to restate earnings for 1994 and 1995 and possibly take an
$18-million charge. It's just fancy accounting language to say
the company lost millions of dollars in an unexplained overnight
fire. The shares plummeted 18%, falling $5.75 from $31.50 to
$25.75. Those 50-cent puts were trading for over $7, creating a
$350,000 loss.

The company only went from bad to worse. It was sold to
CDW Corporation, and less than three years later in 2003, it
filed for bankruptcy owing more than $30 million to creditors.
The moral of the story? Well, there's a few. First, no matter
how big and strong a company may have been in the past,
it doesn't guarantee that long put options aren't the right
choice. Second, know your risk, inside and out. Know the
effects of price and volatility changes on your options before
they happen. Afterwards is too late. If you can't live with the
risk, don't make the trade. Sometimes being proactive means
stepping away. You cannot effectively manage the risk if you
don't know what the risk is. And finally, when a few insiders
know information the rest of the market doesn't, they're
willing to pay premiums for OTM options. Any time you see
a large spike in volume or open interest on short-term, OTM
contracts, it may not be a dumb trade. It may be "smart"
people illegally going after easy money.

TRADER TALES: MIKE YAMAMOTO

While 2017 was one of its strongest years in recent memory for the broader market, Qualcomm's (QCOM) shares were conspicuously absent from the party. The chip maker gapped down sharply after quarterly results in January and remained at those lower levels for most of the year.

In the late summer of that year, option activity in QCOM reflected this malaise. Every week from August 1 to September 13, the stock saw significant downside option trades, the last of which was particularly bearish with large volume: With the stock at $50.82, 20,000 November $52.50 calls were sold for $1.38 above open interest of 2,169 contracts. On the opposite side of the board, 20,000 November $45 puts were bought for 48 cents against open interest of 1,312.

The session of September 14 was different, however. Just three days after QCOM had reached a 52-week low under $49, 14,400 December $57.50 calls were purchased for $0.51 to $0.61 above open interest of 1,600 contracts with shares at $51.02. It was the most bullish option trade QCOM had seen all year, which we announced to our subscribers on our Market Rebellion™ website.

Jon Najarian noticed the stark turn in sentiment. Qualcomm had been *"...a stock that hasn't done much for us, but I think it's about to,"* he said at that time on CNBC, based on that activity.

Then, on November 3, word began to leak that Broadcom (AVGO) might seek to buy Qualcomm in a hostile takeover attempt worth more than $100 billion. Those December $57.50 calls Jon had cited back in September traded up to $8.99, more than 17 times the original purchase price. The stock surged over 25% in the same time period, a huge move but one that was still dwarfed by that of its options.

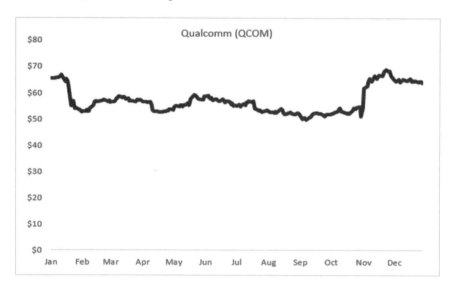

Broadcom finally made its official offer for Qualcomm on November 6, 2017.[94]

TRINITY INDUSTRIES

Trinity Industries (TRN) appeared to be heading for a banner year in 2014, as its stock shot to record highs into early autumn. But that all changed in October when a whistleblower won $682 million in a fraud case against the company involving the safety of highway guardrail parts that it manufactured.

Trinity's share price was cut from September 2014 to January 2015, and it plummeted from all-time highs above $50 to below $25.

TRN tried to rebound three months later, only to pull back into a downward trend that took it below $15 by March 2016. The stock worked back up to the high $20s by the end of that year but, while the rest of the market soared in 2017, TRN drifted sideways – until something curious happened, starting in the option market.

On Sept. 28, *Heat Seeker™* detected the purchase of 15,000 April $32 calls for $2.30 as part of a bullish roll with shares at $30.98. This was clearly a new position, as open interest in the strike was a mere 31 contracts before the activity appeared.

At that time, I noted in the Market Rebellion™ Unusual Option Activity live trading room that the trade was highly unusual. Trinity had not seen much option activity, and the 15,000 April calls were by far the largest volume in the name all year.

The next day, after the market ended its Friday session, the industrial manufacturer announced that a federal appellate court had ruled the company did not commit fraud as alleged in the 2014 case, overturning a lower-court decision.[95] As a result, those April $32 calls spiked to $5.70, more than doubling in value effectively overnight.

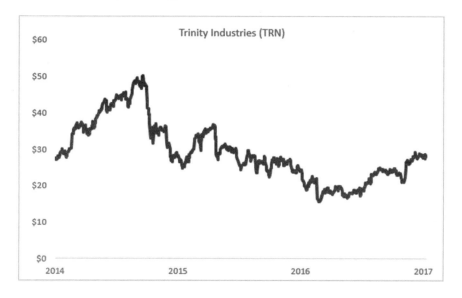

Jon had picked Trinity for his "final trade" on CNBC's *Halftime Report*™ [96] just hours after seeing the unusual option activity. [96] In updating that position the following Monday, he noted that the ruling from the 5th Circuit Court was *"...supposed to be sealed and not available to the rest of us—to anybody, no matter if you've got a fast news-reading algo or anything else, until that got released. But somehow, someone made a very prescient bet last week. These calls have done phenomenally for the people who bought them."*

SCIENTIFIC GAMES

The practice of "rolling" option positions is one that commands especially close attention by the Najarians. The reason, they say, is because it often indicates that the trader has been correct in his or her initial position and is showing a willingness to stay in the trade for more upside potential.

In the case of long calls, for example, the trader may be closing a winning position in one strike and opening a new position in another at a higher strike price and/or later expiration. And that was precisely what Pete saw in Scientific Games (SGMS) in early 2017, one of the first instances of unusual trading logged when our Unusual Option Activity service through Market Rebellion™ was just starting up.

Heat Seeker™ detected three large bullish trades in SGMS in four consecutive days in the last week of February that year:

- On Feb. 21, SGMS saw the purchase of 10,000 January 2019 $30 calls bought for $3.85 against no open interest, rolled from 10,000 January 2018 calls sold for $7.35 below open interest of 29,508 contracts. The stock was trading at $20.60 at that time.

- On Feb. 23, 19,000 October $22 calls were bought for $3.40 above open interest of 1 contract, rolled and increased in size from 12,500 April $16 calls sold for $5 and $5.10 below open interest of 12,924 contracts. Shares were $20.65 at that time.

- Then on Feb. 24, 5,000 January 2019 $22 calls were purchased in one print for $3.80 above open interest of 15 contracts. SGMS was trading for $20.10.

The stock surged as much as 10.3% the following week after earnings beat expectations on March 2. After that, SGMS began grinding higher for months, trading above $27 by mid-July.

Then on July 24, the company, which makes technology products used in gambling, rallied after second-quarter revenues surpassed expectations. Those January $22 calls tripled in value to $11.25, and the trader rolled those positions to 11,500 January $35 calls bought for $3.40 above open interest of 73 contracts with the stock trading at $33.55.

The trade was *"...very aggressive by somebody who was smart and right,"* Pete said on CNBC that day. *In emphasizing the significance of rolling, he added: "That particular trader wants to be involved for yet another run. I like to follow when they come after something that they've already had success with. When somebody's been right, I want to be with them."*

The next day, those January $35 calls traded as high as $7.60, more than doubling in value just 24 hours later. The stock was up 19.8% at the same time, an impressive move but nowhere near that of the options. Pete went on CNBC again to update the trade once more, saying, *"Something is going on there, and it's very positive. We even saw even more call rolling today, so people are expecting even more upside."*

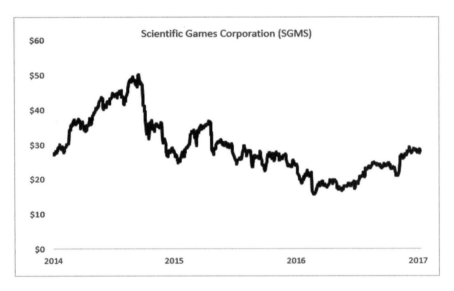

Scientific Games Corporation (SGMS)

TRADER TALES: GARY SMOLEN

When you're trading options, whether as a retail customer or as a market-maker, you often encounter unusual option activity. At times, prices may not move much, but you'll see unusually high volumes. Other times, prices will be way out of line. When you see it, it's not always clear why it's happening. But you always want to dig for the reason.

While trading as a market-maker on the floor of the Philadelphia Stock Exchange, I came across a situation involving unusual activity that seemed so unique that the details have stuck in my head to this day. The stock was Martin Marietta, and it was the Thursday right before September expiration. The stock was trading at $37, and there appeared to be something unusual about the September $40 call. This call, which appeared to be one day away from expiring worthless, was bidding one dollar, and no matter how many traded, the bid never disappeared. The message being "sent" was that the stock would be above $41 per share within one day, something that couldn't reasonably be assumed. Did it mean that someone knew something was going to happen, and when? Well, it came as no surprise when, that evening, the $46 per share merger bid for the company (by Lockheed Corporation) was announced. So, not only was Lockheed Martin (LMT) formed, but some people clearly trading on inside information also made a lot of money.

ALEX. BROWN BUYOUT

In 1996, the historic investment bank Alex. Brown had its best year, and with more stock offerings than any other investment bank, it also posted record profits. At the time, many bank consolidations had occurred, as banks were in heated competition to gain access to underwritings and other investment banking services. On Friday, April 4, 1997, a broker bought over 100 of the $60 calls. That wouldn't have been alarming, except for the fact that the stock was priced at $54 with two weeks until expiration. This made us suspicious. Trading began around 10 cents and throughout the day, worked its way up over 50 cents. Like most market makers, we'd hedge these short calls with long shares of stock, and it's a good thing we did, as our suspicions were confirmed.

On Monday, April 7, Banker's Trust announced it purchased Alex. Brown for $1.7 billion. It doesn't sound like much money by today's standards, but the news sent the shares soaring up $10, or 18%, to over $64 per share. The call options jumped to nearly $5, providing a healthy 10-fold return. Not bad for a couple days' worth of work. What makes it bad is that those profits were gained – stolen – from sellers who didn't have the same information. While working as a market maker, these types of stories happened all the time. If there was a buyout, merger, FDA announcement, or an exceptional earnings report on the horizon, the option activity would reveal it first. Anyone working in the pits shares similar stories.

THE FINAL WRAP

When Pete and I talk with our team, the topic often turns to the "war stories" from our trading days. As you've seen in this chapter, we've all shared similar experiences. We believe people will continue to trade on inside information. It's illegal. It's wrong. But it's probably not going away. You can't prevent it, but you can use publicly available information to legally profit from it.

As you've learned, there's a lot that goes on behind the scenes in the markets. The factors are complex, and there's a massive amount of new information circulating every day. It's far too much to keep track of, and frankly, much of it isn't available to most investors - including floor traders. But, you don't need to crack the code. You just need to know how to *follow the smart money* – and stay disciplined.

The *smart money* is key. However, like we said before, it's not just about knowing how to spot it, you need to know how to determine if it's meaningful. Even then, you're left with the daunting task of identifying the best way to trade on that information.

Every trader's situation is different, and therefore no two traders will, or even should, trade the information the same way. This is where many traders get lost, even after they understand how to *follow the smart money*. Spotting is one thing. Plotting is another.

To avoid that pitfall, it's imperative you get specific guidance on how the information applies to you – something that's impossible to deliver in a book. It requires discovery, back and forth communication, someone knowing your risk tolerances and objectives, and then showing you how to determine the best game plan. Like in a football game, there are many strategies in the playbook, but the coach directs the team to the play that may work best for that moment. Decades of experience goes into deciding the next few seconds.

The best way to make these decisions is by having guidance from a mentor.

Pete and I have had many mentors over the years – our parents, football coaches, other traders, financial experts – and more. Each has significantly shaped our success, not only personally, but also in our careers. We want to make a difference in people's lives just as our mentors have made in ours, but the two of us can't possibly provide one-on-one mentoring for all our followers.

To make such an impact, we've put together a team of experienced floor traders, brokers, and analysts to help us educate and mentor retail investors to level the playing field. They're highly trained, skilled, and most importantly, share our vision. As you know, the knowledge, experience, and character of a mentor makes all the difference.

We've created an opportunity for those who are serious to spend time working with our team. If you join our trading community, here's what you can expect:

- Interact with us and our team personally, as you learn how to take advantage of unusual option activity and follow the smart money

- Master the critical fundamentals every trader must know by watching dozens of hours of educational lessons that are available 24/7

- Learn advanced strategies from our collection of knowledge and experience in different specialties

- Work with a mentor, one-on-one, to learn how to apply the strategies to your specific needs

- Attend live, in-the-market webinars and Q&A sessions with our top trainers

- Receive real-time notifications of the most recent unusual option activity we've spotted so you can use your newly found skills and strategies to take advantage of it

We also offer special events where you can spend time personally with me and Pete, as well as our team, in a hands-on, live environment where we focus on the application of our strategies.

If you'd like to learn more about these opportunities, talk to somebody from our team about the details. They'll take the time understand your current situation and what you want to accomplish, and then help you determine if working with us is a good fit.

To set up a time to talk to our team, simply go to www.marketrebellion.com/smartmoney or call 1-866-982-4862. If you've found this book to be valuable, and your gut is telling you that you should act, listen to it. We've learned that when you listen to that voice, it's usually right. This isn't for everyone, and it may not be for you. We want to be sure it's a good fit, but it's impossible to know until we talk. So, if you're feeling any kind of nudge in that direction, reach out now while you're thinking about it. At least talk with us. There's no obligation. It's just a straightforward conversation. This call could completely change the way you trade and set you on an accelerated path to your financial objectives.

You may be wondering if what we offer will really be beneficial to you. Well, we've worked with people across the investing spectrum. If you're new to trading and are a little overwhelmed with all the information we've shared, our education and mentors can break it down for you and help you know how to get started. If you're an experienced trader, you may just need a little guidance to refine your approach, implement more discipline, create a solid plan, or just incorporate one little tweak that can significantly improve your odds.

Pete and I have shared information in this book that we've never shared before, and we go even deeper with our education. Our one-on-one mentoring is tailored to your specific needs.

GO TO WWW.MARKETREBELLION.COM/SMARTMONEY OR CALL 1-866-982-4862 TO SCHEDULE A TIME TO TALK TO OUR TEAM

We've packed this book with good, actionable content, and whether you decide to work with us further or not, we hope you've enjoyed it, and it's opened your eyes. We encourage you to re-read and study it, and more importantly, implement the concepts, so you can get the most out of it. Whether you're brand new to options or an experienced trader, we want nothing more than to help you learn what we've learned and be able to take action on it. No matter how successful you've been, *following the smart money* can make you better. As Coach Holtz once said, "If what you did yesterday seems big, you haven't done anything today."

Until later,

Get out there and trade smarter!

Jon & Pete Najarian

SOURCES

1. The Options Clearing Corporation https://www.theocc.com/.

2. Late Night Show, April 2012

3. Jonathan Stempel, Madoff victims' recovery tops $9.7 billion with new payout, Reuters, (February 2, 2017), https://www.reuters.com/article/us-madoff-payout/madoff-victims-recovery-tops-9-7-billion-with-new-payout-idUSKBN15H2EJ.

4. Elon Musk@Musk, Tweet, (Aug. 7, 2018), https://twitter.com/elonmusk/status/1026872652290379776.

5. Robert Ferris, Tesla shares surge 10% after Elon Musk shocks market with tweet about going private, CNBC, (August 7, 2018), https://www.msn.com/en-us/money/companies/tesla-shares-surge-10percent-after-elon-musk-shocks-market-with-tweet-about-going-private/ar-BBLCX4c.

6. Press Release, Securities and Exchange Commission, Elon Musk Charged With Securities Fraud for Misleading Tweets (Sep. 27, 2018), https://www.sec.gov/news/press-release/2018-219.

7. Press Release, Securities and Exchange Commission, Elon Musk Settles SEC Fraud Charges; Tesla Charged With and Resolves Securities Law Charge, (Sep. 29, 2018), https://www.sec.gov/news/press-release/2018-226.

8. "Whisper Number." Investopedia.com, 2018. Investopedia, (October 11, 2018). https://www.investopedia.com/terms/w/whispernumber.asp.

9. Francine McKenna, Study: Earnings surprises are bigger, thanks to growing use of non-GAAP metrics, Market Watch, (August 11, 2018), https://www.marketwatch.com/story/study-earnings-surprises-are-bigger-thanks-to-growing-use-of-non-gaap-metrics-2018-08-10.

10. Griffin, Paul A. & Lont, David H.. Evidence of a Positive Trend in Positive Quarterly Earnings Surprise over the Past Two Decades [PDF File]. Retrieved from http://aaahq.org/Portals/0/newsroom/8318EarningsSurpriseMS.pdf (last visited October 16, 2018).

11. Griffin, Paul A. & Lont, David H.. Evidence of a Positive Trend in Positive Quarterly Earnings Surprise over the Past Two Decades [PDF File]. Retrieved from http://aaahq.org/Portals/0/newsroom/8318EarningsSurpriseMS.pdf (last visited October 16, 2018).

12. Frank Armstrong III, The Real Problem With Facebook's Disaster IPO, Forbes Media, (June 18, 2012), https://www.forbes.com/sites/greatspeculations/2012/06/18/the-real-problem-with-facebooks-disaster-ipo/#4d8f5146668c.

13. Tomio Geron, Workday IPO Pops 72% On Open, Forbes Media, (October 12, 2012), https://www.forbes.com/sites/tomiogeron/2012/10/12/workday-ipo-pops-72-on-open/#599a827d95de.

14. Nathaniel Popper, Nasdaq Is Fined $10 Million Over Mishandled Facebook Public Offering, The New York Times, (May 29, 2013), https://dealbook.nytimes.com/2013/05/29/nasdaq-to-pay-10-million-fine-over-facebook-i-p-o/?mtrref=www.google.com.

15. Alistair Barr, Insight: Morgan Stanley cut Facebook estimates just before IPO, Reuters, (May 22, 2012), https://www.reuters.com/article/us-facebook-forecasts/insight-morgan-stanley-cut-facebook-estimates-just-before-ipo-idUSBRE84L06920120522.

16. Alistair Barr, Insight: Morgan Stanley cut Facebook estimates just before IPO, Reuters, (May 22, 2012), https://www.reuters.com/article/us-facebook-forecasts/insight-morgan-stanley-cut-facebook-estimates-just-before-ipo-idUSBRE84L06920120522.

17. Devindra Hardawar, Facebook shareholders sue company and its bankers over fishy IPO, Reuters, (May 23, 2012), https://www.reuters.com/article/idUS424631725620120523.

18. Devindra Hardawar, Facebook shareholders sue company and its bankers over fishy IPO, Reuters, (May 23, 2012), https://www.reuters.com/article/idUS424631725620120523.

19. Facebook, Inc. Form S-1 (May 15, 2012), https://www.sec.gov/Archives/edgar/data/1326801/000119312512235588/d287954ds1a.htm.

20. Facebook, Inc. Form S-1 (May 15, 2012), https://www.sec.gov/Archives/edgar/data/1326801/000119312512235588/d287954ds1a.htm.

21. Tim Worstall, Explaining Facebook's IPO: The Greenshoe, Forbes, (May 22, 2012), https://www.forbes.com/sites/timworstall/2012/05/22/explaining-facebooks-ipo-the-greenshoe/#49b5b0306c1c.

22. SEC of Sri Lanka Consultation Paper No. 10, Proposal to amend the SEC Act to introduce a range of administrative and civil enforcement powers to deal with capital market offenses (2012), pg. 21.

23. Steven Mufson, Crude Analysis, Washington Post Staff Writer, (May 27, 2008), www.washingtonpost.com/wp-dyn/content/article/2008/05/26/AR2008052601977_2.html?nav=rss_business.

24. Press Release, New York State Attorney General, New York A.G. Underwood Leads $100 Million 42-State Settlement With Citibank For Manipulating Interest Rate Benchmarks, (Jun. 15, 2018), https://ag.ny.gov/press-release/new-york-ag-underwood-leads-100-million-42-state-settlement-citibank-manipulating.

25. David Z. Morris, Citibank Fined $100 Million for Manipulating Key Global Interest Rate, Fortune, (June 16, 2018), http://fortune.com/2018/06/16/citibank-fined-libor-settlement/.

26. John Hielscher, Economy forecast to maintain robust growth through 2018, Herald Tribune, (June 25, 2018), https://www.heraldtribune.com/news/20180625/economy-forecast-to-maintain-robust-growth-through-2018.

27. Press Release, New York State Attorney General, New York A.G. Underwood Leads $100 Million 42-State Settlement With Citibank For Manipulating Interest Rate Benchmarks, (Jun. 15, 2018), https://ag.ny.gov/press-release/new-york-ag-underwood-leads-100-million-42-state-settlement-citibank-manipulating.

28. Sarah N. Lynch, UPDATE 1-Barclays reaches $100 mln U.S. Libor settlement -NY attorney general, Reuters, (August 8, 2016), https://www.reuters.com/article/barclays-libor-settlement-idUSL1N1AP11O.

29. Katharina Bart, Tom Miles, Aruna Viswanatha, UBS traders charged, bank fined $1.5 billion in Libor scandal, Reuters, (December 18, 2012), https://www.reuters.com/article/us-ubs-libor/ubs-traders-charged-bank-fined-1-5-billion-in-libor-scandal-idUSBRE8BI00020121219.

30. Jonathan Stempel, Deutsche Bank to pay $240 mln to end Libor rigging lawsuit in U.S., Reuters, (February 27, 2018), https://in.reuters.com/article/deutsche-bank-libor-settlement/deutsche-bank-to-pay-240-mln-to-end-libor-rigging-lawsuit-in-us-idINL2N1QH2HI.

31. Updated: Investing with Borrowed Funds: No "Margin" for Error, Finra, (January 18, 2018), http://www.finra.org/investors/alerts/investing-borrowed-funds-no-margin-error.

    a. Also FINRA rule 11820.

32. Forbes Financial Glossary Forbes Staff, Small Order Execution System (SOES), Forbes, (July 10, 2011), https://www.forbes.com/sites/forbesfinancialglossary/2011/07/10/small-order-execution-system-soes/#b6da76740b1e.

33. Nasdaq, Small Order Execution System (SOES) Definitions, pg. 30, 36, https://www.nasdaq.com/investing/glossary/s/small-order-execution-system (last visited October 16, 2018).

34. Harris, Jeffrey H. & Schultz, Paul H. (March 17, 1997; revised July 22, 1997). The trading profits of the SOES bandits [PDF file]. Retrieved from http://www.finance.martinsewell.com/day-trading/HarrisSchultz1998.pdf.

35. Scott Patterson, <u>Man Vs. Machine: How the Crash of '87 Gave Birth To High-Frequency Trading</u>, CNBC, (September 14, 2010) https://www.cnbc.com/id/39038914.

36. Golden Boy?; He's Dazzled Wall Street, but the Ghosts of His Company May Haunt His Future. The New York Times, David Barboza, 1998.

37. Secrets of the Soes Bandit: Harvey Houtkin Reveals Battle-Tested Electronic Trading Techniques (Aug. 27, 1998).

38. SEC v. Maschler, et al, Civil Action No. 03 CV 0264 (S.D.N.Y 2003).

39. Press Release, United States Securities and Exchange Commission, Litigation Release No. 17929 Securities and Exchange Commission v. Maschler, et al (Jan. 14, 2003).

40. Gretchen Morgenson, <u>Clues to a Hedge Fund's Collapse</u>, the New York Times, (September 17, 2005), https://www.nytimes.com/2005/09/17/business/clues-to-a-hedge-funds-collapse.html.

41. Martha Grabow, <u>Bayou ex-CFO sentenced to 20 years in prison</u>, Reuters, (January 29, 2008), https://www.reuters.com/article/us-bayou-marino/bayou-ex-cfo-sentenced-to-20-years-in-prison-idUSN2961367620080129.

42. Abha Bhattarai, <u>Fund Manager Turned Fugitive Is Sent to Prison</u>, The New York Times, (July 4, 2008), https://www.nytimes.com/2008/07/04/business/04bayou.html.

43. McNamara v. Bre-X Minerals Ltd., 197 F. Supp.2d 622 (E.D. Tex. 2001).

44. Photograph of Jack Welch, General Electric CEO, https://www.forbes.com/pictures/ehii45khf/jack-welch-at-general-electric-417-million/#7459022d53bd.

45. Lucinda Shen, <u>The Highest Paid CEO on the S&P 500 Made 2,000 Times the Average U.S. Worker in 2017</u>, Fortune, (May 9, 2018), http://fortune.com/2018/05/09/ceo-pay-wage-gap-best-paid-sp-500/.

46. <u>United ex-CEO Smisek got $36.8 million after his ouster</u>, Crain's Chicago Business, (May 2, 2016), https://www.chicagobusiness.com/article/20160502/NEWS10/160509996/united-ex-ceo-smisek-got-36-8-million-after-his-ouster.

47. Ahiza Garcia, <u>United's former CEO got $36.8 million after resigning because of federal probe</u>, CNN Business (Apr. 30, 2016), https://money.cnn.com/2016/04/30/news/companies/united-jeff-smisek-former-ceo/index.html.

48. Lucinda Shen, <u>Here's How Much Wells Fargo CEO John Stumpf Is Getting to Leave the Bank</u>, Fortune, (October 13, 2016), http://fortune.com/2016/10/13/wells-fargo-ceo-john-stumpfs-career-ends-with-133-million-payday/.

49. Press Release, Wells Fargo Reports Completion of Expanded Third-Party Review of Retail Banking Accounts, Paving Way to Complete Remediation Effort, Wells Fargo, (Aug. 31, 2017), https://newsroom.wf.com/press-release/wells-fargo-reports-completion-expanded-third-party-review-retail-banking-accounts.

50. Dan Caterinicchia and Anne D'Innocenzio, <u>Martha Stewart Settles SEC Charges</u>, The Washington Post, (August 7, 2006), http://www.washingtonpost.com/wp-dyn/content/article/2006/08/07/AR2006080700459.html.

51. Peter Lattman, <u>Galleon Chief Sentenced to 11-Year Term in Insider Case</u>, The New York Times, (October 13, 2011), https://dealbook.nytimes.com/2011/10/13/rajaratnam-is-sentenced-to-11-years/.

52. Michelle Williams, <u>SAC scandal's key players</u>, The Washington Post, (July 25, 2013), https://www.washingtonpost.com/apps/g/page/business/sac-scandals-key-players/337/.

53. Press Release, United States Department of Justice Southern District of New York, SAC Capital Portfolio Manager Mathew Martoma Sentenced In Manhattan Federal Court To Nine Years For Insider Trading, (Sep. 8, 2014), https://www.justice.gov/usao-sdny/pr/sac-capital-portfolio-manager-mathew-martoma-sentenced-manhattan-federal-court-nine.

54. U.S. Securities and Exchange Commission. (2013). The Making of a $275 Million Insider Trading Scheme [PDF file]. Retrieved from https://www.sec.gov/news/press/2013/2013-41-insider-trading.pdf.

55. Press Release, United States Securities and Exchange Commission, Steven A. Cohen Barred From Supervisory Hedge Fund Role, (Jan. 8, 2016), https://www.sec.gov/pressrelease/2016-3.html.

56. Bob Van Voris, SAC Capital to Pay $135 Million to End Last Insider Case, Bloomberg, (November 30, 2016), https://www.bloomberg.com/news/articles/2016-11-30/sac-capital-to-pay-135-million-to-end-last-insider-trading-case.

57. David Voreacos, Bob Van Voris, Patricia Hurtado, and Matt Robinson, Visium's Valvani Charged Over Drug Tips From Inside FDA, Bloomberg, (June 16, 2016), https://www.bloombergquint.com/business/visium-s-valvani-among-four-accused-of-criminal-securities-fraud.

58. Press Release, United States Securities and Exchange Commission, Hedge Fund Firm Charged for Asset Mismarking and Insider Trading, (May 8, 2018), https://www.sec.gov/news/press-release/2018-81.

59. Press Release, Hedge Fund Adviser Charged for Inadequate Controls to Prevent Insider Trading, U.S. Securities and Exchange Commission, (Aug. 21, 2017), https://www.sec.gov/news/press-release/2017-146.

60. Press Release, SEC Charges U.S. Congressman and Others With Insider Trading, U.S. Securities and Exchange Commission, (Aug. 8, 2018), https://www.sec.gov/news/press-release/2018-151.

61. Dan Mangan, GOP Rep. Chris Collins' son and son's fiancée bought drug company stock days before Collins warned about failed trial, the SEC alleges, CNBC, (August 10, 2018), https://www.cnbc.com/2018/08/09/rep-collins-son-and-sons-fiancee-bought-more-drug-company-stock.html.

62. Press Release, SEC Charges NFL Player and Former Investment Banker With Insider Trading, U.S. Securities and Exchange Commission, (Aug. 29, 2018), https://www.sec.gov/news/press-release/2018-170.

63. Press Release, Securities Fraud Charges Announced Today Against Former Junior Analyst for Major Investment Bank and Current NFL Player, The United States Department of Justice, U.S. Attorney's Office, Eastern District of Pennsylvania, (Aug. 29, 2018), https://www.justice.gov/usao-edpa/pr/securities-fraud-charges-announced-today-against-former-junior-analyst-major-investment.

64. Kendricks, Mychal. (August 29, 2018). Statement of Mychal Kendricks [PDF file]. Retrieved from http://www.investmentnews.com/assets/docs/CI116800829.PDF.

65. Insider Trading, U.S. Securities and Exchange Commission, https://www.investor.gov/additional-resources/general-resources/glossary/insider-trading.

66. Press Release, United States District of Pennsylvania, Securities Fraud Charges Announced Today Against Former Junior Analyst for Major Investment Bank and Current NFL Player, (Aug. 29, 2018), https://www.justice.gov/usao-edpa/pr/securities-fraud-charges-announced-today-against-former-junior-analyst-major-investment.

67. Therapeuticsmd, Inc., 2013 10K filing, Exhibit 14.02, 2013 Insider Trader Policy, https://www.sec.gov/Archives/edgar/data/25743/000138713113000737/ex14_02.htm.

68. Securities & Exchange Commission v. Sargent, 229 F.3d 68 (1st Cir. 2000) (holding tip to dentist with a long standing relationship met personal benefit requirement); see also Securities & Exchange Commission v. Maxwell Technologies, Inc., 341 F. Supp. 2d 941 (S.D. Ohio 2004) (finding a tip to barber with limited relationship did not meet the personal benefit requirement).

69. Press Release, Office of the Press Secretary, FACT SHEET: The STOCK Act: Bans Members of Congress from Insider Trading, The White House, (Apr. 4, 2012), https://obamawhitehouse.archives.gov/the-press-office/2012/04/04/fact-sheet-stock-act-bans-members-congress-insider-trading.

70. Press Release, Office of the Press Secretary, Statement by the Press Secretary on S. 716, The White House, (Apr. 15, 2013), https://obamawhitehouse.archives.gov/the-press-office/2013/04/15/statement-press-secretary-s-716.

71. Tamara Keith, How Congress Quietly Overhauled Its Insider-Trading Law, Political News from NPR, (April 16, 2013), https://www.npr.org/sections/itsallpolitics/2013/04/16/177496734/how-congress-quietly-overhauled-its-insider-trading-law.

72. Jennifer Hansler and Tami Luhby, Trump admin temporarily halting some payments under Obamacare program, CNN, (July 7, 2018), reprinted at https://fox2now.com/2018/07/07/trump-admin-temporarily-halting-some-payments-under-obamacare-program/.

73. What We Do, U.S. Securities and Exchange Commission, (June 10, 2013), https://www.sec.gov/Article/whatwedo.html.

74. Melissa Allison, U.S. Chastises Exchanges, Chicago Tribune, (September 12, 2000), http://www.chicagotribune.com/news/ct-xpm-2000-09-12-0009120419-story.html.

75. Certain Activities of Options Exchanges, File No. 3-10282 (Securities & Exchange Commission September 11, 2000) (final admin. review) https://www.sec.gov/litigation/admin/34-43268.htm.

76. Bryan Burrough, Bringing Down Bear Stearns, Vanity Fair, Aug. 2008, at 1. https://www.vanityfair.com/news/2008/08/bear_stearns200808-2.

77. Bailout increases by $800 billion, The Washington Times (November 26, 2008), https://www.washingtontimes.com/news/2008/nov/26/bailout-increases-by-800-billion/.

78. Hilary Lewis, Who Bought $1.7 Million "Lottery Ticket" On Bear Stearns Collapse?, Business Insider (August 11, 2008), https://www.businessinsider.com/2008/8/who-bought-1-7-million-lottery-ticket-on-bear-stearns-collapse-.

79. Eric Salzman, Foul Play in the Bear Stearns Murder? Someone Call Frank Drebbin!, Monkey Business Blog, (August 11, 2008), http://www.monkeybusinessblog.com/mbb_weblog/bear_stearns/.

80. Doris Frankel, Bear Sterns Unusual Option Bets Gets Payoff:, Bloomberg (August 11, 2008), https://www.reuters.com/article/us-bear-puts-trade/bear-stearns-unusual-option-bets-gets-payoff-bloomberg-idUSN1147350220080811.

81. Hilary Lewis, Who Bought $1.7 Million "Lottery Ticket" On Bear Stearns Collapse?, Business Insider (August 11, 2008), https://www.businessinsider.com/2008/8/who-bought-1-7-million-lottery-ticket-on-bear-stearns-collapse-.

82. Tom Taulli, Juno Therapeutics Inc (JUNO): 3 Reasons to Be Bullish, Yahoo Finance, (September 27, 2017), https://finance.yahoo.com/news/juno-therapeutics-inc-juno-3-105457613.html.

83. Video, Bulls charge into Hanesbrands & this airline. Plus, a trade update on a stock that's soared, CNBC (Jan. 22, 2018), https://www.cnbc.com/video/2018/01/22/unusual-options-activity-hanesbrands-delta-juno-therapeutics-celgene.html.

84. Blackstone to Buy Hilton Hotels for $26 billion in Cash, New York Times, (July 4, 2007), https://www.nytimes.com/2007/07/04/business/worldbusiness/04iht-hilton.1.6482269.html.

85. Dealbook, Before Hilton Deal, a Spike and a Good Call, The New York Times, (July 5, 2007), https://dealbook.nytimes.com/2007/07/05/before-hilton-deal-a-spike-and-a-good-call/?.

86. Video, Bulls charge into Hanesbrands & this airline. Plus, a trade update on a stock that's soared, CNBC (Jan. 22, 2018), https://www.cnbc.com/video/2018/01/22/unusual-options-activity-hanesbrands-delta-juno-therapeutics-celgene.html.

87. Maggie McGrath, <u>Fast Food Mash-Up: Arby's Buying Buffalo Wild Wings In $2.9 Billion Deal</u>, Forbes, (November 28, 2017), https://www.forbes.com/sites/maggiemcgrath/2017/11/28/fast-food-mash-up-arbys-buying-buffalo-wild-wings-in-2-9-billion-deal/#6509bd616003.

88. Uday Sampath and Sai Sachin Ravikumar, <u>Wendy's sells stake in Arby's owner for $450 million</u>, Reuters, (August 16, 2018), https://www.reuters.com/article/us-wendy-divestiture/wendys-sells-stake-in-arbys-owner-for-450-million-idUSKBN1L11M3.

89. Robert Manor and Melissa Allison, <u>Terrorist trade probe widens</u>, Chicago Tribune, (September 19, 2001), http://www.chicagotribune.com/business/chi-0109190296sep19-story.html.

90. Hilary Lewis, <u>Who Bought $1.7 Million "Lottery Ticket" On Bear Sterns Collapse?</u>, Business Insider (August 11, 2008), https://www.businessinsider.com/2008/8/who-bought-1-7-million-lottery-ticket-on-bear-stearns-collapse-.

91. Matthew Herper, <u>Geron Investors: Cancer Vaccine Not Enough</u>, Forbes (September 6, 2000), https://www.forbes.com/2000/09/06/mu5.html#3d8bcfa32cf0.

92. <u>EntreMed Stock Skyrockets</u>, CNN Money, (May 4, 1998), https://money.cnn.com/1998/05/04/companies/entremed/.

93. Associated Press, <u>Coastal Bids to Become Biggest Gas Firm With Offer for Texas Eastern</u>, Los Angeles Times, (January 17, 1989), http://articles.latimes.com/1989-01-17/business/fi-613_1_texas-eastern-corp.

94. Greg Roumeliotis and Diane Bartz, <u>Broadcom unveils $121 billion 'best and final' offer for Qualcomm</u>, Reuters, (February 5, 2018), https://www.reuters.com/article/us-qualcomm-m-a-broadcom/broadcom-unveils-121-billion-best-and-final-offer-for-qualcomm-idUSKBN1FP1KX.

95. <u>Trinity Industries, Inc. Wins at Fifth Circuit Court of Appeals</u>, Business Wire, (October 2, 2017), https://www.businesswire.com/news/home/20171002005768/en/Trinity-Industries-Wins-Circuit-Court-Appeals.

96. Video, This stock is up 14% since Jon saw unusual activity on Thursday, CNBC (Oct. 2, 2017), https://www.cnbc.com/video/2017/10/02/this-stock-is-up-14-percent-since-jon-saw-unusual-activity-on-thursday.html.